D0592707

SOCIAL SECURITY AND THE MIDDLE-CLASS SQUEEZE

SOCIAL SECURITY AND THE MIDDLE-CLASS SQUEEZE

Fact and Fiction about America's Entitlement Programs

Leonard J. Santow
and
Mark E. Santow

Foreword by Henry Kaufman

Westport, Connecticut
London

WIDENER UNIVERSITY
WOLFGRAM
LIBRARY
CHESTER, PA

DISCARDED

WIDENER UNIVERSITY

Library of Congress Cataloging-in-Publication Data

Santow, Leonard Jay.
    Social security and the middle-class squeeze : fact and fiction about
America's entitlement programs / Leonard J. Santow and Mark E. Santow
        p.   cm.
    Includes bibliographical references and index.
    ISBN 0-275-98881-3 (alk. paper)
        1. Social security—United States.   2. Medicare.   3. Medicaid.
4. Entitlement spending—United States.   5. Middle class—United
States—Economic conditions.   I. Santow, Mark E., 1967–   II. Title.
    HD7125.S26 2005
        368.4'3'00973—dc22   2005017485

British Library Cataloguing in Publication Data is available.

Copyright © 2005 by Leonard J. Santow and Mark E. Santow

All rights reserved. No portion of this book may be
reproduced, by any process or technique, without the
express written consent of the publisher.

Library of Congress Catalog Card Number: 2005017485
ISBN: 0-275-98881-3

First published in 2005

Praeger Publishers, 88 Post Road West, Westport, CT 06881
An imprint of Greenwood Publishing Group, Inc.
www.praeger.com

Printed in the United States of America

∞™

The paper used in this book complies with the
Permanent Paper Standard issued by the National
Information Standards Organization (Z39.48-1984).

10 9 8 7 6 5 4 3 2 1

Skepticism, contrary to widespread error, makes everything possible again: ethics, morality, knowledge, faith, society, and criticism, but differently—a few sizes smaller, more tentative, more revisable and more capable of learning and thus more curious, more open to the unexpected.

—Ulrich Beck, *Democracy without Enemies* (1998)

Better the occasional faults of a Government that lives in a spirit of charity, than the consistent omissions of a Government frozen in the ice of its own indifference.

—Franklin Roosevelt, speech at Philadelphia's Franklin Field (1936)

CONTENTS

————◅«(◐)»▻————

FOREWORD

I have known Leonard Santow for most of my professional career. We first met in the early 1960s when he joined a prominent Wall Street government securities firm after serving as an economist at the Federal Reserve Bank of Dallas.

Our friendship has endured for many years; and I, therefore, do not write about this book from a distant perspective. For more than forty years, Len has been a member of a "Foursome" luncheon group that meets every few months. Len, Albert Wojnilower, and I have been members of this group from the start. Paul Volcker was also part of the original group. As Paul's responsibilities changed, others took his place—Guy Noyes, Rimmer de Vries, Charles Sanford, and, recently, Martin Leibowitz.

The "Foursome" Luncheon never has had an agenda. The discussions are far-ranging. When the subject of fiscal policy comes up, we always listen carefully to Len's views and analysis. On this subject, Len is what I would call an economist's economist. The federal budget is highly complex. It isn't just a matter of receipts and expenditures. There are many line items as well as off-budget activities. Many have seasonal, cyclical, and nonrepetitive characteristics. Len tracks the many budget activities of our government on a daily basis, and his projections have been vastly more accurate than those provided by our government. These projections include several important components. One is the financing needs of the U.S. government. This is not just a matter of taking the difference between expenditures and revenues.

Len speaks in terms of net new cash needs requirements and how these credit demands are to be met—through the issuance of bills, notes, and bonds. Moreover, one of the key features of the federal budget is the flow of funds into and out of the Social Security programs and the expenditures for medical assistance for individuals. Here Len's knowledge is incisive and multidimensional.

It is not surprising that this book contributes so much to the unraveling of the issues and solutions to the Social Security and medical assistance programs. In addition to Len's expertise, this book is enhanced by its co-author, Mark Santow, Len's son, who is an American historian. He brings to this book not only a historical perspective, but also humanism. The combination of Leonard, the economic conservative, and Mark, the social liberal, works exceedingly well. Every effort is made to preserve objectivity. The treatment of the problems pertaining to Social Security and the medical assistance programs by the two authors has a comprehensiveness that very much reflects the talent of each.

In shaping their analysis, the Santows make a number of key observations. First, that Social Security is a pay-as-you-go system when the funds needed to meet benefit payments can come from employer-employee tax payments, other taxes, or from borrowing. They conclude that Social Security is neither an immediate problem, nor will it be one in the foreseeable future. Second, their analysis concludes that the Medicare and Medicaid funding problem is quite severe, particularly in view of the sharply rising costs of these programs. Third, they strongly advocate that these programs should be addressed by Congress as one package because, as they say, "they are related both from an economic and social perspective." This is because the beneficiaries of these programs are often the same.

While this logic is quite persuasive, the political reality may not make such an approach very likely. It can be argued that if the long-term funding of Social Security cannot be remediated by our elected officials, how can they ever get their arms around the funding of Medicare and Medicaid? Ultimately the remediation of these funding problems, which are far more severe than the problems of funding of Social Security, may have to come from rapid strides in medical technology, from new drugs, and from improvements in the efficiency of medical services. While the authors are right in their recommendation to have Congress look at all these programs simultaneously, the political will to do so will not come soon to the fore.

One of the many interesting chapters in this book deals with "Misconceptions and Myths about Social Security." For example, Social Security is not a savings program. It is more analogous to an insurance benefit. Surplus funds, also, do not sit in the U.S. Treasury. They are used to finance other activities of the government. And, as often is forgotten, Social Security is designed to repay a higher portion of benefits for lower-income earners. The authors remind us that Social Security was designed as an important support for the elderly in the low-income category and not as a major benefit for all. Equally telling is their analysis of why privatization of part of Social Security is not a panacea. Proponents of privatization should reflect on the twenty-four questions raised by the authors that should be answered if this program is to be successful. Particularly vexing is the question of whether or not in periods of recession and stock market debacles the government will help bail out people who made bad investment decisions.

Finally, the authors make a series of well-founded recommendations with respect to Social Security, Medicare, and Medicaid, which are very thorny and highly charged political issues. Len and his son have gone a long way in this book to diffuse them.

Henry Kaufman

ACKNOWLEDGMENTS

Nicholas Philipson, for his suggestions that broadened our horizons and induced us to discuss topics that initially were not covered.

William Griggs, for his suggestions on topics that needed reworking, rethinking, and reorganizing.

Joan Byrne, for her suggestions that made the book more readable for Americans seeking the facts and not political hype.

Henry Kaufman and Albert Wojnilower. For their incisive comments on what we achieved by writing this book, and where we may have fallen short.

Maya, Shana and Sharon, for putting up with our endless late night phone calls, revision, and baseball chatter.

Chapter 1

A Practitioner and a Historian Combine Ideas

I t is unusual that a book would have coauthors with the same last name. This is because it is a father-and-son duo. The father, Leonard, is an economist whose primary expertise is fiscal and monetary policy, while the son Mark is a professor of twentieth-century American history. Leonard is an economic conservative while Mark is a liberal.

Yet, strange as it may seem, these two approaches can meld quite well in the real world. You can have new and innovative programs as long as you finance them in a proper and conservative way. In this book, Leonard concentrates his efforts on specific Social Security, Medicare, and Medicaid recommendations, while Mark takes a more far-reaching view of economic and social needs and how they might be met. This combination of backgrounds makes this book an unusual endeavor, and we hope one with a positive outcome. It is Mark's task to determine the most pressing social and economic problems, especially for the middle class, and address how these problems can be alleviated. It is Leonard's task to design a system that pays for these programs in an equitable and logical manner, one that does not put any additional financial pressures on those who are already having trouble making ends meet.

The Recommendations

Mark, the historian, discusses what is needed to renew the "promise of American life." Reminding us of the important historical role of our government in fostering the growth of the middle class and encouraging widespread opportunity, he calls on us to once again see politics as a means for achieving common goals. Social Security, Medicare, and Medicaid are all part of the larger structure of opportunity that has shaped the lives of American families for generations. They must be seen in this larger context if reforms are to avoid unintended and undesirable consequences. What will make us effectively free and secure in the twenty-first century? Where do entitlement programs fit (if at all) in the answer? Insufficient wages and rising costs over the past couple of decades have caused American families to feel increasingly insecure economically. Opportunity and social mobility are not what they once were.

To address this, we emphasized the need for new approaches in several areas, with Leonard designing the financial side of the recommendations. The areas that we concentrated on were:

✓ Universal preschool education funded by estate taxes.

✓ Automatic cost-of-living adjustments (COLA) for minimum-wage earners.

✓ Alternative minimum tax eliminated for middle-income earners and reduced for the wealthy.

✓ Rethinking and making changes in sunset tax provisions.

✓ New tax computation approach that means simplification and savings.

✓ Inducements for the private sector to provide health care coverage.

✓ Additional age alternatives when individuals can start taking Social Security.

✓ Payroll taxes unlimited on income, but no taxes paid on an initial part of income.

✓ A new COLA approach for Social Security with minimum annual increases.

These proposals are an attempt to put many people in a financial position where they can better cope with their daily and long-term financial pressures. They are also an attempt to reduce the number of people who have been left behind, and to improve the chances for those striving to move ahead.

Yet this is only part of our objective in writing this book. There is a need for greater fiscal responsibility on the part of government when it comes to Social Security, Medicare, and Medicaid. If the government falls short here, it will adversely impact the financial position of all Americans and offset what we are trying to achieve by our previous recommendations.

Our primary recommendation with respect to Social Security, Medicare, and Medicaid is to look at them as a package. Addressing Social Security by itself is not sufficient, especially since Social Security has no near-term funding problems, while that is not the case for Medicare and Medicaid. Our idea is to put all three programs under one financing umbrella and use payroll taxes to finance all three programs on a pay-as-you-go basis. This approach would help put all three programs on a sounder financial footing. In doing this, our recommendations must take into consideration the financial pain when additional monies are raised, especially with respect to the poor and the middle class.

With the programs on a pay-as-you-go basis, the payroll taxes that come in during a year will pay the benefits for those three programs during that year. Who pays and how much would be weighed against who receives and how much. It would be an approach similar to previous Gramm-Rudman legislation, where increases in spending were paid for by either tax revenue increases or a cutback in spending. Incidentally, when using a pay-as-you-go approach, there is no need to have a trust fund, and definitely no need to have the current rogue trust funds that exist for Social Security and Medicare. Pay-as-you-go is a sound, conservative financing approach. In contrast, partial or full privatization of Social Security is neither conservative nor is it fiscally sound. Therefore, privatization is both unnecessary and counterproductive.

If the government wants to induce private savings, it should enhance benefits in the private sector for such programs as Keoghs, IRAs, 401(k)s, and educational savings funds. There is plenty of room to expand all of these programs, and especially the Roth IRA approach. Encouragement of Upromise, Universal 401(k)'s, and stakeholder programs should also be considered.

Educating the Reader

In writing this book, we also had other objectives in mind. These include familiarizing the reader with Social Security, Medicare, and Medicaid. Considering the importance of these programs and their impact on people's lives, it is surprising how little is known about them. Many misconceptions exist, and this book makes an attempt to set the record straight. How the programs actually work is detailed. In this regard, the overstated financial difficulties of Social Security are explained, as are the understated financial problems of Medicare and Medicaid. The data presented will show the degree of the overall problem. Recommendations are also made to improve the analysis and reporting procedures for the programs. What must be kept in mind is that the recommendations in this book should not be viewed as an end-all. Therefore, we challenge others to devise techniques that achieve a great deal of public good in a cost-efficient way. The focus needs to be on specifics, not generalities; on actions, not platitudes.

While we believe that proposals to privatize Social Security are irresponsible and based on faulty data, they have one critical (potential) virtue: They may force us to reconsider what freedom means in the twenty-first century and what role our government can and should play in protecting and extending it. We hear a lot of talk today about self-reliance and personal responsibility. It is appropriate to emphasize such things. We value them. But it is not all we value, and some of that sense of self-reliance is a seductive illusion. As legal scholar Joseph Singer has argued, we can reflect values of empathy and solidarity politically and economically while still protecting individual liberty and allowing for economic growth. Freedom doesn't require us to subject everyone to what Roberto Unger has called "the savagery of impatient money." These things are not incompatible, but our political discourse today is decidedly off kilter. It doesn't reflect the balance between the things that most Americans desire, that our past reflects, and that most of our faith traditions demand. We do not have to have a society that "radiates indifference," in order to have growth and productivity.[1] (See Notes section following Appendix II.)

Based on the last two presidential elections, it is easy to believe the American people are deeply polarized, separated into two ideologically coherent and incompatible camps bent on total victory. Given these divisions, meaningful public action on serious problems seems impossible. This view strikes us as being greatly overdrawn. While one can make the case that our political elites in Washington *are* polarized, the American people are more easily found in the messy, pragmatic middle—where they have always been. Over the past decade an interesting way of thinking has emerged in some quarters, offering the notion of a politics of the "radical middle." Articulated most persuasively by Michael Lind and Mark Satin, this politics seeks to go beyond the 'left' and the 'right' by drawing on the best of both of them. What would a radical politics of the middle concern itself with? Recall that the word "radical" finds its origins in the word "root"—meaning that to be *radical* is to *get to the root of things*. The primary concern of such a politics would be to work through and improve our basic institutions of representative democracy and capitalism in order to provide a fair start in life for all citizens. Rather than being divisive and self-interested, a politics of the radical middle would seek a higher common ground. Taking a future-oriented approach, it would utilize the best insights from all perspectives to grapple with big, long-term challenges. It would embody, Satin argues, "idealism without illusions."

While we do not fall into any particular philosophical or political camp, this captures some of what we are after here: getting to the root of things, and seeking a higher common ground.[2]

Two Guiding Ideas

Our discussion in the rest of this book will be guided by a number of ideas and principles, but two in particular come to mind. At first glance, one of them is narrowly economic, and the other moral and political—but in reality they are quite similar. The first is the rather basic notion that if we are to create or sustain government programs, we must be realistic and honest about how they will be paid for. And if we cannot come up with fair and reasonable ways to pay for them, then we may have to do without. In a representative democracy, what our government does, in the end, is reflected in our willingness to keep our promises to one another. One might refer to this as a traditionally "conservative" concept, but one finds little of it in Washington today, on either side of the political spectrum. We prefer to describe it, actually, as moderate and restrained. It is an optimism tempered by humility; or, if you prefer, "pessimism of the intellect, optimism of the will." Call it "pay as you go," call it "Gramm-Rudman." In reality, it is little more than the kind of shared discipline exercised by American families every day.

The second principle is a more philosophical one. In his seminal 1973 work A Theory of Justice, Harvard philosopher John Rawls sought a definition of justice that would hold a middle position between socialism and free market libertarianism—one that would maximize what John Dewey once referred to as "effective freedom." Economic and social inequalities are an inevitable consequence of liberty, luck, and history, Rawls conceded. But while some inequalities are justified, others are clearly not. How can we determine which ones are and which ones are not? Given the growing inequalities of American life in recent decades, this is a fundamental question.

To sort this out, Rawls articulated something he called "the difference principle." The gist of it was this: Social and economic inequalities must satisfy two conditions if they are to be considered just. These inequalities must emerge under conditions of fair equality of opportunity; and they must be to the greatest benefit of the least advantaged members of society. In other words, inequalities are tolerable (even desired, if productive) in a free and just society, only if they lift up our citizenry from the bottom, in absolute terms. Inequalities can make the rich richer, as long as they also increase the effective freedom of those at the bottom. Rawls envisioned a kind of "thought experiment" to explain these arguments. He asked readers to imagine themselves being in an "original position" trying to agree on a scheme for a just society. To make our deliberations fair and equal, Rawls stipulated that they take place behind a "veil of ignorance." No one would know what position they would occupy in the society we chose—what their natural talents, social background, wealth, or beliefs would be. Under these conditions, he argued, a rational person would choose the society that would make his worst possible life as good as possible. In other words, he would choose to maximize his minimum well-being—by opting for a society that embodied the difference principle.

Gravitating toward the Middle

We are not philosophers, and we didn't write this book as some sort of blueprint for a just society. We seek to honor the spirit of this idea rather than use it as some kind of iron rule. Since this book—like all of our public policies generally—is the result of deliberation between people who don't always agree, our arguments gravitate toward the middle. One consequence, perhaps, is that the book is virtually guaranteed to bother people from all parts of the political spectrum. But the difference principle seems to us to be a useful, commonsense, pragmatic rule of thumb to shoot for when evaluating or proposing social and economic policies. Will a particular proposal enhance or preserve equality of opportunity? Will it, if enacted, lift up our citizenry from the bottom—even as it enriches those at the top? As we will argue in the following pages, we believe that (partial or full) privatization of Social Security fails this test. Social Security, whatever its flaws, passes it; indeed, more than almost any other American undertaking, it embodies it.

And we also believe that our country is drifting from the root principles and social arrangements implied by the difference principle. Polling indicates that most Americans are well aware of this and are in despair of having any remedy emerge from our present set of political institutions and ideas. As a result, we believe that a renewed public philosophy, which takes seriously both our freedoms and our common obligations, needs to be articulated. It will need to be liberal and conservative, pragmatic and idealistic, radical and conservative; it may give rise to a politics of the "radical middle." One can see some of its manifestations in American public discourse already. Some of what we present here will anger liberals. Some will bother conservatives. Yet, the American people should have nothing to fear from the truth.

It is in this spirit that we offer the analysis and proposals contained in this book. We don't propose to solve all of the problems discussed here. Before we change old programs or create new ones, we need to read, think, and speak to one another. We need, in other words, a measure of democratic deliberation. Ideology and warnings of impending doom have made this kind of talk elusive in recent years. This is our humble attempt to further that enterprise. We believe it is of some significance that this book brings together not just two people with very different political and professional viewpoints, but two people from different generations as well. With one of us facing retirement and the other facing parenthood and the early stages of a professional career, we believe that we are well placed to offer some thoughts on how to fulfill our obligations to one another. We all do the same, after all, every day—at our kitchen tables, at holiday gatherings, at houses of worship, and in what we say to our spouses and our kids.

We encountered a number of obstacles in writing this book. Aside from the inherent difficulties of having two people with very different political views collaborate on a discussion of issues of profound political import, we quickly began to see that an examination of Social Security, Medicare, and Medicaid led us into other issues and debates that we had not anticipated. One result is that we examine some topics that deserve much more attention than we give them. We wanted breadth, but also brevity and readability. We decided that our first priority was to explain major economic and social problems that face society, and to present specific recommendations as to how these problems could be alleviated. If public discourse shifts somewhat in this direction as a result of our effort, we will be more than satisfied.

Chapter 2

GOVERNMENT AND THE PROMISE OF AMERICAN LIFE

B ack in 2001, then–treasury secretary Paul O'Neill told the *Financial Times* that he questioned whether government should provide Social Security, Medicare, or any social insurance. "Able-bodied adults should save enough on a regular basis so that they can provide for their own retirement and, for that matter, health and medical needs," he argued. While this statement is rather naïve as a description of social and economic reality, it does raise an important question: Why should there be any social insurance at all? Full-throated public defenses of these programs are hardly in short supply—they don't refer to Social Security as the "third rail" of American politics for nothing—but the careful observer of American politics rarely encounters a thoughtful answer to the above question.

The idea of social insurance was easily understood by the Depression, World War II, and Cold War generation that created it. As Robert Reich once described it, social insurance "was a natural impulse, a first cousin to patriotism." That sense of commonality, of social solidarity, sounds and feels rather foreign to us today. Literally foreign, in a sense—like something one sees in Sweden or France, or the former Soviet Union, not in the individualistic, freedom-loving United States. The 9/11 terrorist attacks perhaps opened a window for its renewal, but to date, that opportunity has not been taken advantage of by either party. The gradual drift of American society into separate worlds of privilege and resignation in recent decades has weakened our sense of commitment to one another, of sharing a common journey, a common destiny.[1]

Three ideas make up the foundation of the comments in this and the following chapter:

1. How we talk (and don't talk) about government in the United States today hinders our ability to discuss large common problems and come up with fair and efficient solutions that acknowledge and justly distribute costs. We must attempt to recover and renew the public philosophy that formed the creation of social insurance in the first place—a philosophy of patriotic and enlightened self-interest, a "New Nationalism."

2. While it is important and responsible to focus on what's wrong with government programs, it is also important to remember what they often do well. I will briefly discuss what Social Security, Medicare, and Medicaid do well, and then offer a not-so-gentle reminder of the critical role of government historically in enabling the promise of American life.

3. Today we face a "middle-class squeeze," due to rising costs in child-rearing, health insurance, housing, and education. Our economy is not producing enough social mobility and opportunity; it is producing too much economic insecurity and inequality. Aside from its occasional appearance in election-year boilerplate, there has been little public discussion of this. As we consider ways to modernize Social Security, Medicare, and Medicaid for the long haul, we also need to discuss ways to renew our common commitment to widespread opportunity and shared prosperity.

Talking about Government

In his 1909 work *The Promise of American Life,* Herbert Croly reflected on the meaning of the "American Dream." Inspired by the recent example of Theodore Roosevelt's presidency, Croly articulated a vision of public purpose and government action that became the basis of modern American liberalism. The promise of America, he argued, "consisted largely in the opportunity which it offered of economic independence and prosperity" for an ever-growing number. Worried that the capacity of government had not kept up with recent dramatic changes (the growth of cities, massive immigration, the rapid growth of large corporations, and the shift of the American workforce into wage labor and industry and away from the era of the "yeoman" farmer), Croly called for a "new nationalism" that would renew that promise in a new era.

Most famously, Croly called for the use of "Hamiltonian means for Jeffersonian ends." While today this may read like a historian's inside joke, the meaning is actually quite clear: Croly believed that the power of the state can and should be used to further individual liberty and independence. The nineteenth-century philosophy of self-sufficient individualism was having trouble fitting into the reality of the nation's modern, bureaucratic, and corporate economy and society, in which most citizens worked for wages—and thus, for someone else.

If the individual autonomy that is needed for democratic citizenship to work were to be preserved in a new era, the state would have to play a key role. This was not a philosophy of altruism, though it certainly did comfort the afflicted (and, on occasion, afflict the comfortable). It was a philosophy of patriotic enlightened self-interest. It sought to use the power of the democratic state to aid capitalism (rather than just capitalists); it assumed that democracy and capitalism together would create a virtuous circle of freedom, opportunity, and progress only if access to important social goods was broadly distributed. Students find it hard to understand why the American people actually voted for the sixteenth Amendment in 1913, allowing for a federal income tax. The growing power of this public philosophy, deeply rooted in the bedrock of American ideals, explains a great deal of it.

As historian Eric Foner and others have argued, this new public philosophy didn't involve a rebalancing of freedom and equality so much as a redefinition of the former. John Dewey, the philosophical father of modern American liberalism, argued that in this new era we needed to differentiate what he called "effective freedom" from the more "highly formal and limited concept of liberty" as a pre-existing condition of autonomous individuals that "needed to be protected from outside restraint." Effective freedom involved more than just freedom from overt coercion. It meant the "effective power to do things," and thus was a function of the "distribution of powers that exists at a given time." It also meant, in the words of E. J. Dionne of the *Washington Post*, "being given the means to overcome various external forces that impinge on freedom of choice and self-sufficiency." It meant, Dionne concluded, "being free to set one's course." In the new America of the twentieth century, this "effective freedom" could be found only in cooperation with others, through the instrument of liberal democratic government.[2]

Franklin Roosevelt articulated the outer limits of effective freedom in his 1944 State of the Union address, in which he called for a "second Bill of Rights." The speech, presented while the American people were at war and worried about an uncertain future at home and abroad, is well worth re-reading today. His concern was freedom, not equality. The experience of Depression, the ideas of the New Deal, and the disaster of World War II convinced Roosevelt that Americans needed to update their traditional notions of liberty for a new time. Beginning with his justly famous "Four

Freedoms" speech in 1941, Roosevelt had come to believe that the nation's commitment to defending freedom around the world had to be rooted in an understanding of the "things worth fighting for." According to legal scholar Cass Sunstein, the external threat of fascism and totalitarianism "deepened the need for a fresh understanding of America's defining commitments," one that would have an appeal around the world as an example of "what free societies and decent governments offer their people."[3] The potential parallels with the post-9/11 world are hard to miss.

In particular, Roosevelt believed that threats to security from abroad must force a rethinking and strengthening of security at home. "The ... supreme objective for the future," Roosevelt argued, "can be summed up in one word: Security." For Roosevelt, this meant not only physical security; it also meant "economic security, social security, moral security—in a family of Nations." While these things may seem unrelated to us today, for the "greatest generation," freedom from want and freedom from fascism were all part of the same language of solidarity and patriotism. This generation was well aware of human vulnerability to catastrophic events beyond their control, as was Roosevelt personally. As he put it, "we have been compelled to learn how interdependent upon each other are all groups and sections of the population of America." This interdependence—and the very recent example of fascism in Europe—convinced Roosevelt that "true individual freedom cannot exist without economic security and independence," because "necessitous men are not free men." "In our day," he argued, certain "economic truths have become accepted as self-evident," in effect creating a "second Bill of Rights under which a new basis of security and prosperity can be established for all." "Security" in this sense committed the government to providing equal opportunity so citizens could receive a good education, find a useful and well-paid job, own a decent home, have adequate medical care, and get protection from the economic fears of old age, sickness, accident, and unemployment.

What did Roosevelt mean by the statement "necessitous men are not free men"? As early as his 1932 campaign speech to the Commonwealth Club, he insisted that modern economic conditions—specifically the rise of corporations and the Depression itself—required a redefinition of liberty and the rights needed to protect it. In a modern economy dominated by "the often intangible forces of giant industry," Roosevelt argued on the third anniversary of the signing of the Social Security Act, a person's "individual strength and wits" cannot guarantee security or freedom anymore. More than anything else, Roosevelt argued, Americans want "work, with all the moral and spiritual values that go with it; and with work, a reasonable measure of security" for them and their families. Modern freedom required having an opportunity to make a decent living—not just enough to live by, but also "something to live for," in Roosevelt's words.

The imbalance of economic power in American society, Roosevelt insisted, had led a growing number of citizens to believe that liberty was no longer real. Government must do more than just protect the right to vote; it must also "protect the citizen in his right to work and his right to live . . . freedom is no half-and-half affair." This would not deny individual responsibility; rather, it would define it in a way that seemed reasonable and fair to people in the real world. Freedom from desperate conditions— security—was thus an essential supplement to political freedom. This was an old idea, deeply rooted in the nation's founding. It was based on the old republican notion of freedom as "self-government," as articulated by Paine, Jefferson, and many others. The needy lack the independence and security to be self-governing, and thus they are not free citizens. Roosevelt's innovation was to connect this idea of freedom to the powerful concept of "security." It became the centerpiece of a powerful public philosophy that dominated American politics for most of the next half century. While often honored in the breach, it defined postwar liberalism until very recently.[4]

Roosevelt, of course, wasn't proposing an actual change to the Bill of Rights. Rather, what he was doing was offering a concrete account of the nation's changing understanding of "what citizens were entitled to expect." The public, Roosevelt argued, had come to see a new set of principles or rights as being "self-evident." His goal was to make them manifest, and offer the nation a more formal commitment to them. According to Sunstein, the speech was an attempt to both recognize and redefine the nation's "constitutive commitments." Some rights and commitments are embedded directly in constitutions and founding documents, or are encompassed by them. Others, however, are widely accepted by the public, and cannot be eliminated without a big change in social understanding. These commitments, according to Sunstein, help to create or constitute a society's basic values. Violations of them do not constitute a breach of law, but rather of trust.

The Social Security program is a good example of such a public promise. While the courts have never recognized a person's "right" to receive Social Security benefits, the nation's commitment to the program has been so widely accepted over the past half century that in practice it has gained "near-constitutional sturdiness," according to Columbia law professor Louis Henkin. While public officials often disagree—as they do presently—over how best to respect this commitment, it is "widely agreed that the nation is committed to the Social Security system in some form that fundamentally protects the economic expectations of its beneficiaries."[5] The present debate over Social Security, we argue, presents American citizens and their elected representatives with an opportunity to once again make manifest our constitutive commitments. And to renew and perhaps remake them.

This perspective, this "public philosophy," guided the ideas and actions of reformers in general through much of the postwar period. Indeed, throughout the developed West (and Japan) in the decades after World War II, the notion of a "social contract" that democratized wealth and opportunity became widespread, contributing to economic expansion and the growth of a stable and prosperous middle class. Welfare states were established, embodying a generation's hopes for universal economic security and protection from the worst of life's hazards.

The U.S. and the nations of Western Europe organized their programs differently, and they still do. In Europe, the emphasis has been on institutionalizing social protection, generally through government-run programs. The American approach differs in four important respects: It is more decentralized, it is a much more balanced mixture of public and private, it doesn't provide universal health care as a right, and most of its benefits are tied to employment rather than citizenship.[6] The focus has been on facilitating access to the market. Underneath these substantial differences, however, lay a common assumption: that restoring and strengthening democracy in the wake of fascism (and in the face of the communist threat) required proactive policies that promoted social advancement and solidarity.[7]

The G.I. Bill, passed a few months after Roosevelt's address, typified this use of Hamiltonian means to achieve Jeffersonian ends, helping to spark a massive expansion of home ownership and college attendance.[8] Economic, tax, and social policy, investments in infrastructure (highways, education, and especially housing), and the growth in collective bargaining were primary factors that helped to broadly distribute the nation's unprecedented prosperity. This in turn provided widespread access to property ownership, education, and mass consumption.[9] For the first time in its history, the United States became a middle-class nation. Social Security, Medicare, and Medicaid were largely products of this philosophy. The atrophy of this philosophy in recent decades has contributed to our inability to honestly discuss and solve our problems today. There was nothing inevitable—or permanent— about the democratization of property and opportunity that characterized the first three post–World War II decades. It may not survive the deep economic and social transitions that are under way presently if we do not take affirmative steps to revive and revise it.

Government Should Listen To Ideas—Not Sell Them

In the spirit of a renewed philosophy of public responsibility, we offer a concrete set of proposals we hope will be objectively evaluated by the American people and by public officials. We believe it is not unreasonable to recognize that shared benefits must also involve shared burdens. To paraphrase Oliver Wendell Holmes, taxes are the price we pay for a civilized society. Belief in the public good and in the efficacy of government has in recent decades been increasingly displaced by a belief in the marketplace (or a particularly ideological interpretation of it). This has led some Americans to assume that government is by nature incapable of fairly and efficiently serving the commonweal. They point to the growing cost of entitlement programs, and their answer is often to privatize, or abolish, not to improve or revitalize.

In a sense, this attitude toward government has become a self-fulfilling prophecy; the worse the funding crisis appears to be, the more that radical "solutions" get a serious hearing. As more extreme views take center stage, those who oppose them give in to the temptation to defend the status quo and deny the need for a more open, honest, and shared accounting of needs and costs. There is little talk of what we believe should be the bottom line: How can we ensure both a dignified retirement for the elderly and equal opportunity for future generations, and do so in a way that is affordable, fair, and sustainable?

A decade of ideologically motivated and empirically questionable doomsday language with regard to Social Security in particular—coming largely from self proclaimed conservatives—has had a powerful effect on how these issues are viewed by many young Americans. Repeated and often irresponsible talk of unavoidable "crisis" has shifted the frame of the debate away from trying to solve our common long-term problems in a manner consistent with our values and institutions, toward a series of "reforms" that could weaken the promise of American life for coming generations. Many of our politicians—in both parties—seem unable to deal with the Social Security issue objectively because their views are dominated by ideological considerations. The 2000 and 2004 elections taught us that Americans see a crisis of "values" in our society. Honest and realistic political leadership constitutes one of those values that the American people see in crisis.

Part of why an honest and open public discussion of the issues under consideration has been so elusive in recent years is that the balance of public discourse has been tipped too far in the direction of reward without sacrifice, of rights without responsibilities, of the present over the future, and of individual self-interest over civic obligation and the common good. The calculus is simple: If we desire to maintain social programs—or create new ones—we must find a just, efficient, and politically palatable means for funding them. The issues discussed in this book present daunting tasks for both our political leadership and American families. But they also present both major political parties with an opportunity that hasn't come along since Franklin Roosevelt's day: to define a new social contract between the American people and its government, and in that contract, for the government to renew its commitment to the American people.

What Our Government Does and Has Done Well

The constant back-and-forth volleys in our political discourse about "big" versus "small" government shed a lot of heat and very little light. Both parties, if you go back in American history far enough, can make some legitimate claims to both positions. Today, however, the size of government changes little (other than growing larger) with a change in party dominance. The size of government isn't really the issue. In a modern society, government seems to grow with the economy and the population. This doesn't mean, of course, that there are not legitimate questions about whether some functions are better (or more legitimately) performed by the public or private sector.

Clearly, for reasons of both equity and efficiency, some functions belong in the public sphere. Social insurance is one of them. Government is more effective at dealing with the basic social risks that capitalism invariably produces than the market is. Social Security is the best example. Arguments to the contrary are based on ideology, not fact. Yet it is incumbent upon government to run its programs properly, and on a cost-effective basis. Since the 1960s, opposition to big government—at least rhetorically—has moved increasingly to the center of American politics. Building on the campaign of Barry Goldwater in 1964, what was once a rather extreme position within the Republican Party has now become more commonplace. The electoral success of the Republicans in the past two decades has moved this position to the political center. Even Democrat Bill Clinton declared the "era of big government" to be over.

Worried about voter backlash against any effort to raise money through taxes, well-meaning politicians of both parties try to put off the day when taxes will need to be raised to meet outsized budget deficits. Some even avoid grappling with large and expensive issues in the first place. Decades of constant argument about the inability of government to deal with important issues has created a kind of self-fulfilling prophecy: Other than in foreign affairs, the federal government hasn't grappled in a serious way with fundamental long-term issues faced by Americans since the early 1970s. Seeing this unwillingness of government to grapple with serious problems has caused many Americans to become disillusioned with their politicians.

Historian Robert Dallek cites a comment someone made to Eleanor Roosevelt shortly after her husband's death: "I miss the way your husband used to speak to me about my government." Government, even metaphorically, is not the enemy; it is, after all, "our" government. A politics that dissolves the personal connection between citizen and government in favor of an adversarial one threatens to undermine our capacity for discussing and meeting common needs. Like an autoimmune disease, as Deborah Tannen has recently argued, an unreflective hostility to government threatens to turn the protective forces of the body politic against the body itself.[10] As Franklin Roosevelt eloquently put it in 1936, "Better the occasional faults of a Government that lives in a spirit of charity than the consistent omissions of a Government frozen in the ice of its own indifference."[11]

Our History Suggests That Our Government Can Do Better

Many Americans have forgotten the critical role that our government has played in the past in providing opportunity, stabilizing the middle class, and ensuring that as capitalism changes, it remains compatible with liberty and democracy. The deeply ideological variant of market fundamentalism that has so dominated public discourse in recent decades is ahistorical. While clearly markets are an essential component of progress, efficiency, and liberty, we all too easily forget that markets are above all political creations based on political choices.

The great wealth of the United States is based in part on the social and legal framework created by its citizens, through the instrument of government: stable currency, the patent system, enforceable contracts, open courts, property law and ownership records, protection against crime and external threats, infrastructure, and public education have all shaped the direction and success of our political economy. Free markets and property rights rest on government and a set of enforceable legal rules that determine who can do what. The real questions, thus, are the pragmatic ones. What form of government action best promotes human interests? Freedom? Opportunity? One doesn't have to believe that the choices we have made in the past were perfect in order to recognize the critical point: We can choose. We can make those choices consciously, or we can allow the chaos of events to make them for us. "To govern," John Kennedy once said, "is to choose."[12]

Since the founding of the nation, the U.S. government has taken steps to ensure a broad distribution of property ownership and the tools of democratic citizenship. As Michael Lind pointed out recently, our government has played a critical role in the creation, maintenance, and re-creation of the nation's successive middle classes. Using "Hamiltonian means to Jeffersonian ends" has a long history that predates Herbert Croly. As early as the 1780s the U.S. government guaranteed that all federal lands would be broken up into fee simple properties in order to avoid European-style feudalism. Through purchase, annexation, and conquest, the American government ensured over the next century that such properties were plentiful.

Public schools—referred to, importantly, as "common schools"—were created around the nation during the antebellum period. During the Civil War, the Homestead Act provided 160 acres of free public land to settlers willing to live on it and improve it for at least five years. "Land grant" public universities ensured access to education and technical knowledge for ordinary citizens. Economic development was furthered through the subsidizing of railroads, while the Army Corps of Engineers built much of the infrastructure in the Western states. Tariffs protected American industry, and the wages of the skilled workers who made it flourish. Immigration laws shaped wages and the labor supply.[13]

To counteract the Great Depression, New Deal programs were instituted. The by-product of these programs was to help create the largest and most inclusive middle class in our history, in effect giving birth to the United States as a middle-class nation. The G.I. Bill helped veterans go to college and trade school, and offered subsidies for affordable housing, which encouraged them to start families earlier. In the postwar period, spending on public education, from kindergarten through graduate school, increased exponentially. The tax code encouraged and rewarded home ownership (and thus, the construction industry). Millions of American families, as a result, acquired wealth through the equity in their homes, allowing them to pass on their economic gains to their children.

New Deal–era legislation encouraged collective bargaining while the tax code gave employers incentives to provide pensions, allowing blue-collar workers to be members of the middle class for the first time. American trade and foreign policy ensured a growing world market for our goods. Social Security was extended to cover more of the elderly in the postwar decades, freeing young people from having to support their parents. Government itself, at all levels, increasingly provided middle-class employment.

The system as a whole was stabilized by the regulation of banking, securities underwriting, accounting, electric power, civil aviation, telephones, broadcasting, and labor relations. The courts, which initially provided a powerful obstacle to the New Deal, came to recognize both the importance of individual and civil rights, and the right of the people to legislate for the common good through their elected representatives. This new public philosophy, of a property-owning democracy, embedded itself into the very structure of the law and the state. This aided the American people in building a society of shared prosperity that did indeed seem to lift all boats.

Social Security, Medicare, and Medicaid have been, and continue to be, a critical component of this social contract. Social insurance has benefited all of us, as Jacob Hacker points out, by helping people to deal with the inevitable risks of modern capitalism "without draconian restraints on the free play of the competitive market."[14] Whatever their flaws and limitations, all three programs have dramatically improved the health and well-being of millions of Americans, particularly the elderly. Social Security in particular is one of the greatest successes of the American state, on a par with the creation of land grant public universities, the G.I. Bill, the expansion of home ownership since World War II, and victory in World War II and the Cold War. The elderly were once the poorest age group of Americans; today their poverty rates are comparable to the rest of the population. This shift in living standards was primarily a function of government, and this should be kept in mind when considering legislation that would radically alter Social Security.

The Record of Social Security

Public servants should stand on their record, and so should Social Security. With all of the crisis talk about the program, it is important to realize its accomplishments, and its critical importance:

✓ *It has substantially reduced poverty among the elderly. In 1959 (before Medicare, Medicaid, and the indexing of Social Security to inflation), more than 35 percent of the elderly lived in poverty. Today, 10 percent do. Almost half of today's elderly would live in poverty without these programs.*

✓ *Despite recent fears, Social Security remains the most popular and universally used program in American history. One-quarter of people sixty-five years old and older depend on it for at least 90 percent of their income; 60 percent count on it for at least half.*

✓ *Social Security is very efficient: Administrative costs are 1 percent of benefits, versus 12 to 14 percent for private insurance.*

✓ *Social Security retirement benefits are portable. This helps keep our labor market fluid and the U.S. economically competitive.*

✓ *Social Security benefits are risk-free and inflation-proof. As people live longer, this fact becomes more and more important for keeping the elderly out of poverty.*

✓ *Social Security is especially valuable for women, low-income workers, and minorities. The benefits are progressive, meaning that low-wage workers have a greater percentage of their wages replaced by Social Security than high-income earners do. Because they are guaranteed a minimum benefit for life, this gives workers at the bottom end of the income scale (who generally don't have accumulated wealth or private pensions) a chance at a decent retirement. Because it is indexed for inflation, it protects women, who live longer.*

✓ *Social Security provides disability and life insurance coverage without regard to the health of the individual. It has protected millions of children against impoverishment when a wage-earning parent died or became disabled, improving their chances of gaining an education and leading a productive life. It provides about $12 trillion in life insurance, more than that provided by the entire life insurance industry.*

✓ *In addition to the concrete benefits Social Security distributes to over 47 million Americans each month, the program also provides a critical non-monetary benefit: those who have contributed throughout their working lives know that regardless of the ups and downs of their careers, the market, and their health, a guaranteed pension awaits them.*

The Social Security program is not without problems, although some of them have been eliminated or isolated over the decades. While the distribution of benefits is progressive, the payroll tax is overly regressive. Social Security by itself cannot come close to meeting all the financial needs of the elderly. This is because the elderly are subject to heavy medical expenses and frequently need emergency services that can wipe out their life savings in a matter of months, or even weeks. Even Social Security plus pension income, plus investment income, plus savings, plus private insurance can be insufficient to meet financial needs, especially of the emergency variety. This is why Medicare and Medicaid were created, and why they have been aggressively expanded despite inadequate funding.

The Record of Medicare and Medicaid

Medicare and Medicaid have never enjoyed the broad political support that Social Security has. While both health programs have directly led to substantial gains in the health and well-being of the elderly and the poor over the past four decades, most observers recognize that the complex hybrid of public and private that Medicare and Medicaid represent has created substantial inefficiencies, gaps, and costs. Indeed, while the financial crisis of Social Security has been grossly exaggerated, the financial problems of Medicare and Medicaid have been very much understated. Yet, having said all of this, Medicare and Medicaid have had a distinguished record and many accomplishments:

✓ *Medicare quickly resulted in a large increase in the use of medical care by the elderly. In the program's first three years, 100,000 participants entered hospitals each week. Before Medicare, only one-half of persons sixty-five and older had health insurance. Today, nearly all elderly Americans are covered. Since its inception, more than 93 million elderly and disabled Americans have been provided with affordable health care coverage.*

✓ *The proportion of Americans using the services of a doctor grew significantly and rapidly. From 1963 to 1970, the proportion increased from 68 to 76 percent, while the percentage of Americans that had never been to the doctor fell from 20 to 8 percent. The poor began to go to the doctor at the same rates as everyone else, clearly indicating the success of Medicaid in particular.*

✓ *Life expectancy at age sixty-five has increased since 1960: For women it has grown from 15.8 years to 19.2, and for men it has increased from 12.8 to 16 years*

✓ *Much like Social Security, both programs have helped alleviate the burden on young families of caring for their elderly relatives, making it easier for them to purchase a home, start a business, stay out of debt, and provide opportunities for their children.*

✓ *Medicaid led to immediate improvements in prenatal care and infant mortality. Prenatal visits by poor women rose dramatically from 1965 to 1972, while infant mortality among African-Americans fell by half. The difference in life expectancy between whites and blacks shrank from eight to five years. While these dramatic improvements are not entirely attributable to Medicaid and Medicare, the timing of the changes indicates an important connection.*

✓ *Medicare has established strong federal quality standards for hospitals, nursing homes, and home health care agencies, which benefits all Americans.*

✓ *Both programs have become critically important for the health and welfare of Americans of all ages. Medicare and Medicaid serve approximately one-quarter of the American population. Medicare covers almost one-half of nursing home costs. One-third of all births are covered by Medicaid. The program also covers immunizations and other preventive and screening services for children, reducing the incidence of hospitalization and saving the nation billions of dollars.*[15]

✓ *Medicare holds down costs better than the private sector does, paying doctors and hospitals less per service. Its costs have grown more slowly than private health plans over the last 30 years. Medicaid payments are also well below private levels, and it negotiates very low prices on prescription drugs.*

Social Security, Medicare, and Medicaid have helped millions of American families live their lives with some degree of effective freedom. To argue, as some do today, that government can only be an obstacle to freedom, growth, and well-being is ideology, not fact. If government—particularly at the federal level—has failed to adequately respond in scale or scope to the dramatic changes experienced by American families and the economy in the past three decades, the reason is not some inherent failure in government itself. The culprits are a failure of leadership, a population that did not demand better from its public servants, a population that did not get involved in the most important issues of the day, an excessive amount of attention devoted to the "right" approach to government, and a failure to realize that solving the basic problems of the American people are what really counts. It is little wonder that under these circumstances there has been a declining sense of national purpose.

Why Is a Crisis Necessary for the Government to Act on Serious Problems?

Over the course of the twentieth century, American social provisions (with a few notable exceptions) have tended to focus largely on crisis management. This has become increasingly true since the 1960s. This short-term approach invariably costs all of us—in terms of money, human suffering, productivity, and respect for the legitimacy and efficacy of our common institutions. As historian Michael Katz has pointed out, as a nation we have too often focused on the size of welfare rolls rather than the sources of poverty among single mothers; on the need for homeless shelters, not the crisis in affordable housing; and on the cost of medical care, and not its capture by the marketplace in recent decades. Health care remains more of an earned privilege than a human right. We do not provide family or child allowances. We continue to permit unseemly high rates of child poverty and spend far less than is necessary on job training and low and moderate-income housing. The private patch in the American social provision system has not kept up with the financial needs of many Americans, and wage increases for the poor and many in the middle class have not been able to fill the void.

Social Security, Medicare, and Medicaid will become even more critical for the standard of living of elderly Americans in the coming decades. We hope to initiate a real discussion of the specific means by which we can ensure that these programs deliver adequate benefits at a reasonable and acceptable cost. It is imperative that we put these programs on a sound financial footing, and it is also critical that we seek to build on their successes. The obstacles are not just economic or social—they are political, and this is in terms of both will and vision.

More needs to be done to renew our common commitments. It is time to do so, and the increasing urgency of the issues discussed in this book provides us with an opportunity to consider how this can be done. Our most important common enterprises face a crisis of legitimacy. Certainly this "crisis" includes Social Security, Medicare, and Medicaid—but it also involves welfare, public schooling, corporate governance, upward mobility, our role in the world, and even our electoral and political process.

In the wake of 9/11 we should be able to find the means to reestablish a faith in our collective capacity to redeem our fundamental ideals. By demonstrating the fact of human vulnerability and interdependence, World War II pushed the "greatest generation" to renew and expand America's defining commitments. For the first time in more than fifty years, Americans find themselves in another crisis position, although with considerably different circumstances. Like fascism, the threat of world terrorism now distills things down to the essentials: What do we stand for? What makes us free? What makes us secure? In order to aggressively pursue the answers to these questions, we must first be willing to discuss the issues in a civil and logical way, without cant or ideology.

Chapter 3

THE MIDDLE CLASS AND THE AMERICAN DREAM

M any analysts (and people in the Bush reelection campaign) were struck by the apparent anomaly between the strong GDP numbers in 2004 and the negative perceptions of American voters as reflected in opinion polls. In March 2004, according to political scientist Jacob Hacker, roughly half of the Americans polled agreed that the nation "no longer has the same economic security it has had in the past," despite low unemployment and inflation.[1] Who was right, the economists or the American public?

The answer is that GDP growth is not an adequate measurement of individual well-being. Bigger increases in GDP are better than smaller increases when it comes to economic well-being, but big GDP advances may not percolate down to the average individual. For example, in 2003 real GDP grew by 4.4 percent, in 2004 it advanced by 3.9 percent, and in 2005 it is likely to grow by about 3.5 percent. These are solid advances, but this good showing seems to have done little to improve the financial position and alleviate the economic concerns of the middle class. Many of the traditional statistics that we use to measure the progress of the economy tell us little about the state of American families.

In particular, they tell us little about change over time. American families are filled with a great deal of anxiety about the economy in general, but their anxiety derives primarily from their own place in it—and their growing sense of slippage and insecurity. This perception is not a case of 'awareness lag,' economic illiteracy, or a manifestation of a more general post–9/11 fear for the future. It is to be taken seriously. It is backed up by increasingly convincing data. When considered in conjunction with the issues raised by Social Security, Medicare, and Medicaid, this anxiety calls on us to reconsider our public commitments not just to the elderly, but also to the maintenance of the opportunity structure itself. Croly's 'promise' is in some danger now. As we reconsider the nature of our shared commitments, we would do well to talk honestly and without ideology about how to renew that promise for the 21st century.

In this chapter we will lay out in some detail the state of the American dream today. It will confirm two things: first, that American families are finding themselves being increasingly squeezed economically, and second, that rising economic anxiety is a serious problem, rooted in very real changes in the labor market and the economy, and powerfully connected to the future of Social Security and other programs. As we argue elsewhere in this book, any attempt to reform or improve our entitlement programs must take into account the larger picture of how to best enhance the opportunity for economic improvement for the majority of Americans.

The problems encountered by Social Security, Medicare, Medicaid, and the financial squeeze on the poor and middle class offer the American people the opportunity to rewrite our social contract with ourselves. To do this in the most just, efficient, and nonpartisan manner, we need to examine what has worked in the past, what in recent years has gone wrong, and what we need to do to get things right.

The Middle-Class "Squeeze" and the Promise of American Life

A new phrase entered American politics in 2004—the "middle-class squeeze." Most clearly articulated by Elizabeth Warren and Amelia Warren Tyagi in their book *The Two-Income Trap: Why Middle-Class Mothers and Fathers Are Going Broke,* the "squeeze" refers to two simultaneous phenomena that have emerged in the past three decades:

1. *The stagnation of household income, despite an increase in two-income families and in average hours worked per week.*
2. *The increase in costs for goods and services essential for attaining, maintaining, and passing on middle-class status (housing, transportation, health insurance, child care, education, and taxes).*

Income stagnation is well known and widely accepted among academics, if not in the general public. After rising quickly and in lockstep with productivity growth in much of the postwar era, real median family income growth began to markedly decelerate three decades ago. Since 1973 the purchasing power of many American families has shown little improvement. Hourly wages of the bottom 60 percent have not kept up with inflation. From 1970 through 1997, the average income of the bottom 99 percent of Americans declined or stayed flat. Wages jumped in the late nineties, so that if one looks at the 1970 through 2000 period, average income for that same group grew 8.3 percent—the equivalent of $90 a year before taxes, or a five-cent-an-hour raise. Most of that 8.3 percent increase came between 1970 and 1973, and between 1998 and 2000.[2] The trend of stagnation has now reemerged, except for the very top of the income scale. In the last three months of 2004, real wages endured their steepest decline since 1991. According to David Wessel of the *Wall Street Journal*, hourly wages for private sector workers in 2005 continue to lag behind prices, productivity, and corporate profits.[3]

As most American families probably know, work itself has changed, too. Workdays for many are longer, the unemployed are finding it increasingly difficult to get back into the labor market, and elderly Americans are returning to paid labor in record numbers to make up for retirement and health care shortfalls. The typical American family spends twenty-two more hours per week at work than in 1969, with little to show for it economically.

Almost half of the workforce nationwide doesn't have paid sick days. American workers put in three full–time weeks more per year than their British counterparts, and nine weeks more than the French and the Germans.[4] For families headed by workers without a college degree, real income has actually declined. While unemployment remains low, the effects of job loss on work hours, pay, and prospects for reemployment have gotten much worse in the past two decades. While this has been especially true for less skilled men, it is getting harder and harder for all jobless Americans, regardless of education, to get back into the workforce.[5] When they do finally return to work, most employees with at least some college education report earning lower wages in their new jobs—30% less, on average.[6]

The average length of unemployment is higher now than at any time other than the early 1980s. Since the 2001 recession, about one-fifth of the unemployed have been out of work for more than six months. Even though the overall unemployment rate has fallen since December 2003, when it was 6.0 percent, much of the improvement has been through the hiring of part-time workers and temporary consultants.

According to Nicholas Ricardi of the *Los Angeles Times,* the number of long-term unemployed who are college graduates has nearly tripled since the bursting of the tech bubble in 2000. Almost 20 percent of the long-term jobless are college graduates. If a degree-holder loses a job, that worker is now more likely than a high school dropout to be chronically unemployed. The problems of long-term unemployment "are even more pronounced for older workers, for whom retirement issues loom large," according to Riccardi. The number of long-term unemployed who were forty-five or older doubled from 2000 to 2003.[7]

Four out of five Americans were making less in real terms, or were no better off in 2000 than in 1970. Real income growth was stagnant not just for the poor and the working class, but in many cases for the middle and upper-middle classes as well. This stagnation—and the economic insecurity that comes with it—is spreading up the socioeconomic ladder, affecting more and more individuals and families generally thought of as being middle class. Americans are accustomed to thinking of the poor as somehow qualitatively different from the rest of us. But increasingly, according to Peter Gosselin of the *Los Angeles Times*, they are "experiencing an extreme version of the economic turbulence that is rocking families across the income spectrum."[8] Our social policies have yet to catch up to these changes, leaving families increasingly on their own. Americans have coped with stagnant wages over the past three decades by working more hours, going into debt, and sending married mothers into the paid workforce in large numbers. But this has imposed new costs, too: day care, extra cars, more meals eaten out, less time with children, and more stress. As Jacob Hacker puts it, "We live in a twenty-first-century economy dominated by two-earner families, yet, social protections for working Americans have changed remarkably little since the mid-twentieth century—and when they have changed, they have usually been cut, not expanded."[9]

With little fear of significant legal sanctions, American businesses in all sectors strongly and actively resist unionization. According to Christopher Swann of *Financial Times*, globalization, de-industrialization, and the decline of unions has led to a long-term shift in the balance of power between workers and employers. In the last business cycle, companies captured almost one-third of economic gains from productivity; in the previous seven cycles, workers had reaped nearly 75 percent of the benefit from increasing efficiencies. Rising productivity no longer translates into higher wages for American workers.[10]

In this "brave new world of work and family," according to Hacker, "even stable full-time employment of household heads is not a guarantee of economic security."[11] Global wage competition, the decline of manufacturing, the weakening of labor unions, and the shift into retail and service-sector employment have all played a role. The result has been a large increase in inequalities of both income and wealth in recent decades. Government tax policies have not helped matters, in many cases accelerating the trend of income inequality.

The second development—the increase in costs for essential goods and services—is very well known to millions of families around the country, but it has generated surprisingly little public debate and discussion given its importance (and the fact that its victims tend to vote). The cost of education, child care, health insurance, and housing have risen more rapidly than income in the past thirty years, eating up gains from having two parents in the workforce. This "squeeze" on middle-class households has accelerated recently.[12] Child care costs in some cases have swelled to as much as 40 percent of middle-class family income. More than 40 percent of the newly uninsured in 2003 were middle-class. In 2001, 3.2 million households earning between $17,500 and $50,000 (a category made up disproportionately of young adults) spent more than half of their incomes on housing. Almost one in four American households spent more than 30 percent (the top amount generally considered affordable) in 2002.[13]

This year, more families are likely to file for bankruptcy than for divorce. There has been a 33 percent increase in families filing for bankruptcy since 2000. The overwhelming majority of them, by any measure, are solidly middle-class. Even though married couples today earn 75 percent more than they did thirty years ago, and spend 20 to 25 percent less on food, clothing, and housing, they still experience a rate of bankruptcy nearly six times higher than in 1970. In 2003 the average bankruptcy filer was 38 years old, and more likely to be college-educated than the average American.[14] Women are the largest single group of bankruptcy filers; their numbers have increased eightfold since 1981. Half of all bankruptcy filers cite health problems, childbirth, a death in the family, or substantial medical bills as the prime reasons for filing. In the 1960s these were minor reasons. Something has clearly changed.[15]

According to Warren and Tyagi, for every family declaring bankruptcy, seven more have debt loads suggesting they should. While rates of home ownership have reached historic highs, home foreclosures have more than tripled in less than twenty-five years. The average age of the first-time homebuyer has jumped almost ten years in the last three decades. Homeowners have less equity on average today than at any point over the past fifty years. Why? Rising fixed costs and stagnant wages have forced many families to take out home equity loans to cover day-to-day expenses and pay off debts.[16] From 1983 to 1998 the share of households with zero or negative net worth increased from 15.5 percent to 18 percent. The share of households with zero or negative financial net worth (excluding home ownership) was 26 percent in the late 1990s. Poor stock market performance, especially in the high-tech area, home equity loans, and credit card debt have worsened this situation.[17]

Bankruptcies, home foreclosures, and credit card debt are all more common in families with children. Average household debt today is a whopping $17,283, nearly 40 percent of average family income. More than half of that debt is owed to credit card companies. Credit card debt among Americans under the age of thirty-five increased 55 percent between 1992 and 2001. In the last twenty-five years non-mortgage debt has risen from 15 percent to almost 24 percent of after-tax income for American families. Overall household debt (including mortgages) has climbed from 62 percent to almost 120 percent. While the democratization of credit in the last decade may be a positive thing, for a growing number of American families "borrowing has become for this generation what unemployment compensation, the G.I. Bill, and government-guaranteed mortgages were for a previous one—a way to tide over one's family during bad times and reach for a better life."[18] If interest rates go up, which is likely with the recent firming of monetary policy, millions of Americans that had considered themselves solidly middle-class will face the abyss. Growing budget deficits, the weak dollar, and the proposed borrowing to pay for Social Security privatization all add to the concerns of middle-class people.[19]

Let's make this more concrete. The average homeowner in the state of Pennsylvania has one of the highest credit scores in the nation, saves more than the average American, and is less likely to be unemployed or divorced. Nonetheless, according to the *Washington Post,* much of the state is facing a foreclosure epidemic. It is hitting low-income and minority homeowners— and their communities—especially hard. In 2000, the Philadelphia sheriff auctioned off 300 to 400 foreclosed properties a month; in 2005, the number has tripled. Foreclosures, especially in poor and working-class areas, can set off a rapid downward spiral for entire neighborhoods. But this epidemic is not unique to urban areas in the state, or around the nation. Suburban Montgomery County, north of Philadelphia, has seen a 14.6 percent increase in foreclosures since 2000. The only reason suburban foreclosures at present haven't had the same kind of contagion effect is that the homes are easily resold. But if the housing bubble bursts or interest rates go up, all bets are off.[20]

Foreclosure rates rose in 47 states in March 2005. With mortgage bankers and brokers (especially sub-prime lenders) coming up with ever-riskier ways for Americans with poor credit to buy homes, this trend may prefigure a national crisis. Interest-only and adjustable-rate mortgages account for 63 percent of all new mortgages. In the past fifteen years mortgage and home-equity borrowing has risen from 35.1 percent of home values to 43.9 percent, leaving families more vulnerable to unexpected economic jolts. More than 8 percent of homeowners now spend at least half their income on their mortgage. According to Julie Williams, acting U.S. Comptroller of the Currency, "if we are not careful, the American dream can quickly turn into the American nightmare."[21]

Congress has now passed legislation with the rather Orwellian title of "the Bankruptcy Abuse Prevention and Consumer Protection Act." The legislation, rejected a number of times by Congress since the late 1990s despite the best efforts of credit card companies, makes it much harder for families to file for Chapter 7 bankruptcy. Chapter 7 allows debtors to erase their obligations after forfeiting a state-determined percentage of their remaining assets. Bankruptcy courts previously had broad discretion to decide who can file for it, or for Chapter 13, which has much less generous terms. The legislation will replace judicial discretion with a means test on household income, based on the assertion of credit card companies that most filers are just profligates who live beyond their means. This, of course, is somewhat disingenuous, given the marketing strategies of these companies, and the fact that their profits have soared (by 163 percent since 1997) despite a 17 percent increase in bankruptcy filings in the same period.

Recent studies cited in the *Washington Post* indicate that half of all Chapter 7 filers do so in the wake of major medical expenses. At the same time, according to the *Post,* the legislation does nothing to institute real consumer protection—such as closing loopholes that allow wealthy debtors to shift assets and firms like Enron to enter bankruptcy to avoid paying legal claims, worker wages, and health insurance. Those same workers will now have a hard time getting the same relief. This is precisely the wrong way to deal with the growing squeeze on American families.[22]

As a result of inadequate wages and rising costs, profound changes in the relationship between life stages, family formation, and economic independence are taking place. While discussions of Social Security and Medicare in particular have focused a great deal of attention on the size and life cycle of the "baby-boomer generation," there are worrisome developments coming down the pike for succeeding generations. Since these are the workers and taxpayers who will be paying, this contraction of opportunity is a vital and often neglected component of the debate about our entitlement programs. Young adults today are increasingly unable to save for retirement, pass on middle-class status to their children, or help care for their elders. This doesn't have implications just for a few families "left behind." It has serious potential consequences for maintaining the viability of our way of life well into the future. If we intend to have a serious discussion about reshaping these programs, we should be guided by the facts and by a broad long-term view, not by ideology.

Comparisons with Earlier Times

In the years after World War II, Americans typically assumed the full responsibilities of adulthood (defined as leaving home, finishing school, achieving economic independence, marrying, and parenting) by their late teens or early twenties. This is no longer the case. Increasingly, for all but the wealthiest young adults, adulthood no longer begins when adolescence ends. The transition to adulthood now takes longer than it has at any time in our history. In the year 2000, just 46 percent of women and 31 percent of men aged thirty had completed the five transitions listed above. In 1960, 77 percent of women and 65 percent of men had done so. According to sociologist Frank Furstenberg, we are seeing the emergence of a new phase of life in the United States: early adulthood. Many readers (including my coauthor) are well aware of this, if only through direct personal experience.[23]

Young adults are increasingly stuck in a labor market that is substantially different from the one their parents entered. Contingent (temporary or part-time) work is disproportionately concentrated among younger workers. Nearly 40 percent of them have a bachelor's degree or higher. Most of these jobs do not offer health insurance, or when they do, young workers already overburdened by other costs often refuse it. Nearly half of full-time workers between nineteen and twenty-nine years of age lack job-based health benefits, while one-third of those between the ages of twenty-five and thirty-four lack any health insurance whatsoever.[24] Seventy-five million Americans—one-third of the entire non-elderly population—found themselves uninsured at some point during a two-year period.[25]

Corporations are no longer the agents of successful social mobility they once were for so many. At least up through the 1960s, American corporations created elaborate internal hierarchies that provided an expanding number of decent jobs with good pay, benefits, security, and upward mobility. Beginning in the 1970s, however, competitive pressures have encouraged companies to shift some risks to employees—by reducing layers, contracting out activities, shifting to part-time work, and eliminating defined-benefit pensions and health benefits. It has become increasingly difficult for young adults today "to start at the bottom and rise up the company hierarchy by dint of hard work and self-improvement." Beginning in the 1990s, this insecurity began to extend into the upper middle class. While the economy in the aggregate may have gained from these changes, they have shifted the risks of our newly flexible post-industrial economy increasingly onto workers. Stable employment, widely available and affordable health insurance, guaranteed pensions, short unemployment spells, long-lasting unemployment benefits, and well-funded job training programs used to enable working families to ride out the ups and downs of the market economy. But things have changed. In the late 1980s the Conference Board, a business research group, found that 56 percent of major corporations surveyed agreed, "employees who are loyal to the company and further its business goals deserve an assurance of continued employment." A decade later, just 6 percent of those polled concurred with the same statement.[26] Twenty-five years ago, middle-aged men could expect to be with same employer for eleven years. Today, the average is a little more than seven. In the post-war decades, large firms tended to provide employment security; indeed, many of them saw it as their patriotic duty. But the average size of a workplace shrank 18 percent nationally from the late 1970s to 2004, leading to increasing job insecurity, weakened unions, and stagnant wages.[27]

The shifting of risk in the private sector has coincided with a scaling back of economic protections for working families in the public sector as well in the past thirty years. Over much of the 20th century government added to these protections with each generation, expanding the circle of public risk-management programs to include almost all citizens. In the mid-seventies, for example, workers could collect up to 15 months of unemployment benefits. Today, despite a 50 percent rise in the average length of unemployment since the 1970s (to twenty weeks), benefits are only available for six months. Unemployment compensation became taxable in the mid-eighties, while tightened state eligibility restrictions greatly reduced the fraction of the workforce entitled to it. Of the eight million unemployed workers in September 2004, less than three million were collecting benefits.

The minimum wage was once government's primary way to ensure that work paid, but today it is only one-third of average hourly earnings—its lowest level in fifty years. Federal job training funds have been drastically reduced as well, while welfare reform has forced millions of poor women into an already overcrowded low-wage labor market. University of Pennsylvania economist Peter Cappelli sums up these changes well: "for almost a century, business and government worked in tandem to expand the economic protections afforded working Americans through social insurance programs and career employment. In the last 25 years, we've stripped most of these away." The end result, according to Cappelli: "You're on your own."[28]

As a result it has become increasingly difficult for young adults without a college or advanced degree to find steady work that pays a family-raising wage. Economists Timothy Smeeding and Katherine Ross Phillips found that in the mid-1990s, just 70 percent of American men ages twenty-four to twenty-eight earned enough to support themselves, while fewer than half earned enough to support a family of three. At the same time, the costs historically associated with the transition to adulthood, as discussed above, have rapidly increased.[29]

To enter or remain in the middle class, it has become imperative to make a commitment to education that spans at least one's early twenties, postponing marriage and child-rearing and piling up substantial debt while accumulating little or no wealth. Public tuition costs have increased 47 percent since 1993–94. In the 1990s, college costs increased at public and private colleges by an average of 38 percent. Average annual tuition at public four-year universities increased from approximately 4 percent of a middle-class family's income in 1980 to more than 12 percent in 2002. For low-income students, it increased from 13 percent to 26 percent over the same period. The fiscal crisis facing state governments will translate into more tuition increases in the coming years. Private school tuition has increased even more rapidly. Middle-class families now face the same educational burden that poor families did a generation ago.[30]

At the same time, federal aid has increasingly shifted from grants to loans. In 1980 just over half of federal aid to college students and their families came from grants; in 2000, grants made up only 41 percent. One critical result is that young adults are carrying far more debt well into their twenties and thirties than previous generations. The changes have been stark, and rapid: In 1992, 42 percent of students borrowed money for college. In 2000, almost two-thirds did so. According to Tamara Draut and Javier Silva, the average college senior graduated with $18,900 in student loan debt in 2002. The burden is disproportionately heavy on minority students. According to the Drum Major Institute, 55 percent of black student borrowers graduated with "unmanageable debt, meaning that their monthly repayments were more than 8 percent of their monthly income." The debt burden for graduate students is much higher.[31]

Debt, of course, is not necessarily a bad thing—it is what makes modern capitalism run, in a sense. Ideally, it allows young adults to build credit ratings and learn financial responsibility. Investing in education increases their human capital, thus enabling them to pay the debt off quickly and benefit in the long term. The problem, however, is that for a growing number of young adults, the debt burden has become so onerous that it is affecting their life choices in a negative way. Nearly 40 percent of twenty-five to thirty-four-year-olds recently reported delaying the purchase of a home due to debt, while over 20 percent reported that debt burdens caused them to postpone having children. Financial burdens prevent many students from finishing school, leaving them without the long-term income benefits of a degree, but with all the costs.

Combined with the fact that young adults have higher unemployment and underemployment rates, earn lower entry-level wages, and often don't receive health benefits from their employers, the cost of education isn't just weakening equality of opportunity in the United States; it is, quite simply, eliminating it for millions of young adults from working and middle-class backgrounds. The effect is particularly stark on young black adults, who suffer higher unemployment, lower wages, and generally far more limited family assets to fall back on.[32] As Draut and Silva conclude, the "ability for young adults to build wealth and accumulate assets is greatly undermined by debt burdens that stymie their economic advancement now and well into their adult lives."[33]

A college education wasn't necessary for middle-class status, economic independence, or the ability to financially support a family in 1960. Today, however, it is absolutely essential, yet increasingly out of reach. Twenty million low-wage workers are struggling with a high school diploma or less. The growing cost of college and housing today, according to Furstenberg, "forces many youth into a state of semi-autonomy," reversing decades-old generational trends. Parents are providing financial assistance to their young adult children more than ever before. Forty percent of people in their late twenties still receive aid from their parents, according to Robert Schoeni and Karen Ross. This is putting a growing strain on the mothers and fathers of young adults, cutting into their standards of living and their ability to prepare for retirement and the growing costs of health associated with aging. While inheritances from parents will help some young adults, one of the consequences of increasing longevity is that heirs increasingly receive these assets later in life—past the time period in which major life choices are made about marriage, family, and career.[34]

All of this occurs just as many young families are taking on the growing costs of child-rearing. The cost of providing essential education for American children, once borne by taxpayers generally, has been increasingly left to individual families. The growing importance of college has reverberated downward, causing a kind of credentialing "arms race" at lower levels of our educational system. For middle-class families, ensuring a good education for their children often means buying an expensive home in the shrinking number of suburban districts that have high-quality schools. This has created a bidding war for homes in these areas, and since the early 1970s, the amount families have borrowed on the average mortgage has increased by 69 percent (adjusted for inflation), while average incomes have stagnated. Because college has become so critical for achieving middle-class status and a decent standard of living, parents make the necessary sacrifices.

For almost all middle-class parents, this sacrifice now includes paying for preschool. The educational and child development literature has made it

clear to parents that quality preschooling has become an absolute pre-
requisite for elementary school. Nearly two-thirds of four-year-olds now
attend, compared with 4 percent in the mid-sixties.[35] Nearly half of working
families with children under thirteen have child-care expenses. Yet child-care
costs have been rising much faster than both income and inflation. While
the consumer price index increased 29 percent in the 1990s, fees charged
by child-care centers and nursery schools shot up by 56 percent.[36] In 2000,
according to the Children's Defense Fund, the average yearly cost of child
care for a four-year-old in a city was more than the average annual cost of
public college tuition in all but one state. Less than 40 percent of families
eligible for federal child-care subsidies actually receive them.[37]

As Warren and Tyagi point out, the effective definition of a basic education has expanded to include at least six additional years (four of college,
two of preschool), most of which is paid for by parents. Many American
families are literally bankrupting themselves in order to give their children a
shot at a decent life. Relative to the two generations that preceded them, they
are being forced to do more with less—and to do so very much alone. Com-
pleting the steps necessary for supporting a family has become increasingly
difficult and time-consuming. For young people from poor and working-
class backgrounds, it has become all but impossible. All of this has come at a
time of inadequate government support, putting heavy demands on families
and allowing inequalities of birth to shape destinies to a far greater extent
than in the past. In the long run this is not tenable, for families, for our
economy, or for our social cohesion and stability.

While popular discussions of these issues are often framed in terms of a
kind of generational "warfare," the squeeze on young adults and parents
puts a crimp in the economic well-being of several generations at the same
time—and on our ability to pay for our common needs. Young adults today
may be the least equipped generation in the past half century to participate
in the care and security of their elders, both within their own families and
in terms of the nation as a whole. It is a cruel irony indeed that while young
Americans seem to support some form of Social Security privatization more
than any other age group, they are likely to be the ones to primarily pay the
piper if the new system and their investments go terribly wrong. They will
see an increase in economic risk upon retirement and face the burden of
supporting their parents if their investments underperform.

It is unfortunate that too much of the discussion of Social Security,
Medicare, and Medicaid gets lost in the details of tax rates, benefit levels, and
economic projections. If we do not look to equality of opportunity at the
earlier stages of adulthood, no amount of adjusting the current programs will
sustain our common promises.

A Watered-Down American Dream?

Americans like to think of our nation as being uniquely open and meritocratic. In contrast to the hidebound and sclerotic feudal societies of Europe, America was founded as a "city on a hill" where all could rise and fall by their own efforts. Inequality in "old Europe" limited freedom, because social mobility did not exist, and economic privilege and political power were closely wedded. But in the U.S., inequality was seen as a justifiable price to be paid for economic dynamism, because upward mobility and opportunity were available to all. Our economic and social policies still seem to be based on the perception of unlimited opportunity, and voters continue to elect politicians who oppose using government as a tool to restrain growing inequalities of wealth and life chances. The problem is that those perceptions no longer fit the reality.

The ability of American society to generate equality of opportunity has always been more limited than is popularly believed, but we made remarkable progress in the first three decades after World War II. Despite the economic prosperity of the 1990s, that progress since 1975 has been decisively reversed. In 1988 only 26 percent of those surveyed judged the U.S. to be a "have/have-not" society; by 2001 that number had increased to 44 percent.[38] We are seeing the bottom rungs of the ladders of opportunity being knocked out. American families are well aware of this, and frustration grows at the inability of our political leadership to take it seriously.

The perceptions reflected in the poll numbers above are backed up by the data. Income and wealth inequalities have risen to levels not seen since the Gilded Age, without a compensatory increase in social mobility. If anything, where and to whom one is born matters more today in the United States than it has in more than a century. In 1979 the average income of the top 1 percent of earners was 133 times that of the bottom 20 percent; by 2000 the income of the top 1 percent had risen to 189 times that of the bottom fifth. That same top 1 percent now earns more income than the bottom 100 million of their fellow Americans. The Congressional Budget Office estimates that the after-tax income of the top 1 percent of American households grew by 111 percent from 1979 to 2002, while those families in the middle-fifth grew by an average of 15 percent—just 0.6 percent a year. In 2002, the top 1 percent received 11.4 percent of the nation's after-tax income, up sharply from 7.5 percent in 1979.[39]

Thirty years ago the average real annual compensation of the top one hundred chief executives was thirty-nine times the pay of the average worker. Today, it is over one thousand times the pay of the average worker. In 2001 the top 1 percent of households held 33.4 percent of all net worth—the highest since before the Great Depression. A mere 5 percent owns more than two-thirds of America's financial assets.

Wealth ownership has become, in a word, *extremely* concentrated—more than is generally understood. According to Nobel Prize–winning economist Lester Thurow, "No country not experiencing a revolution or a military defeat with a subsequent occupation has probably ever had as rapid or as widespread an increase in inequality as has occurred in the United States in the past two decades."[40]

Social mobility for the majority of the population is at best stagnant and may very well be declining. According to the Economic Policy Institute, in the 1990s, 36 percent of those who started in the second poorest quintile of the population stayed put, compared with 28 percent in the 1970s and 32 percent in the 1980s. Earl Wysong compared the incomes of 2,749 father-and-son pairs from 1979 to 1998, and found that nearly 70 percent of the sons in 1998 had remained either at the same level or were doing worse than their fathers had in 1979. Gary Solon and Miles Corak have found that the correlation between the incomes of fathers and sons is higher in the U.S. than in most other wealthy industrialized nations. Bhashkar Mazumder, a Federal Reserve Bank of Chicago economist, recently looked at data for thousands of men born between 1963 and 1968 to see what they were earning when they reached their late 20s or 30s. Only 14 percent of the men born to fathers on the bottom 10 percent of the wage ladder made it to the top 30 percent. Only 17 percent of the men born to fathers on the top 10 percent fell to the bottom 30 percent. As Mazumder puts it, "the apple falls even closer to the tree than we thought.[41]

Just over half of students from families in the top income quartile earn college degrees, compared with 22 percent of those in the middle half, and only 7 percent in the lowest quartile.[42] Three-quarters of the students at the country's top 146 colleges come from the richest socioeconomic fourth, compared with just 3 percent who come from the poorest fourth. A student at one of these universities is twenty-five times more likely to run into a rich student than into a poor one.[43]

We have been here before, of course: during Herbert Croly's day. Some may look back fondly to the McKinley administration, but it was precisely during that period—the "gilded age"—when inequality threatened to unravel the very legitimacy of American economic and political institutions. It was in response to the calcifying of class inequalities in the late nineteenth century that a coalition of philanthropists, reforms and activists emerged. Worried that a class-based society would ruin the character of the nation, these "progressives" sought to use government to expand opportunity, democratize power, and institute meritocracy. As Croly put it, "A democracy, not less than a monarchy or an aristocracy, must recognize political, economic and social distinctions, but it must also withdraw its consent whenever these discriminations show any tendency to excessive endurance."

We may be facing a similar reckoning today. Inequality—of wealth and income, but also of life chances—can threaten our prosperity and our system of government if it goes too far. Even now, as Robert Putnam points out, "a sense is abroad in the land that our national experiment in self-government is faltering."[44] Thomas Jefferson held that only under conditions of widespread small-scale individual property ownership could a people "safely and advantageously reserve to themselves a wholesome control over their public affairs."[45]

While one could argue that young people from minority and working-class families have always faced the prospect of trying to run up a down escalator, the situation has worsened in recent decades: The escalator is moving faster, and too many people are walking in the other direction. Changes in the labor market and in the cost of schooling, health insurance, housing, and child-rearing are both squeezing the middle class *and* restricting access to the social mobility that has characterized the American dream since the nation's founding. The "middle-class squeeze" isn't putting pressure just on household budgets; it is narrowing the middle class itself, pushing families downward while restricting upward movement. Issues of justice aside, this doesn't bode well for national prosperity or social and political stability.

Do We Have a Tax Burden Problem?

The story of taxation in recent decades is both an example and cause of this growing inequality. Taking the federal, state, and local levels together, the burden of taxation has increasingly shifted down the socioeconomic scale in recent decades, falling increasingly on middle-class and working-class Americans. This is mainly because government at all levels has become increasingly dependent on regressive taxes. The rate at which state and local government levied sales, property, and income taxes all rose over the past three decades, eating primarily into the incomes of middle-class and working-class families.

In the early 1980s, and again in the last few years, the federal tax system became more regressive, with increases in the payroll tax and sharp declines in taxes on the wealthy. In 2001, according to the Federal Bureau of Labor Statistics, taxes at all levels consumed 19 percent of the income of the highest fifth, while the rate was 18 percent for the bottom fifth. This was before the tax cuts of the Bush administration, and increases in taxes by states and localities to make up for funding shortfalls (and unfunded mandates) in health care and education. In 2004, the overall share of federal, state, and local taxes that high-income households paid was only a bit larger (less than 2 percent) than their share of national income. Only the federal income tax keeps the system even mildly progressive.[46] These changes have made the overall tax burden more regressive, and this is not by accident. The Bush administration would like to see that trend continue, and that is why many in the administration prefer consumption taxes rather than income taxes.[47]

Actually, this is not a new story. Taxation at the federal level has become less progressive since the early 1980s. While one can make a convincing case that the top tax rates on income were way too high and needed to be reduced, this is not the entire picture. Payroll taxes are a regressive tax, at least in the way they are structured today. The tax rate is the same for low and middle-income people, and above a certain income level ($90,000 in 2005), there are no payroll taxes to be paid (except for Medicare). Thus, whether intended or not, the payroll tax has proven to be a vehicle by which more of our fiscal burdens have been shifted from the wealthy to the middle class.[48]

As a matter of fact, many American households now pay more in payroll taxes than they do in income taxes. And payroll taxes, of course, do not apply to capital income—rent, dividends, interest, and so on—which is heavily concentrated at the top of the income scale. Payroll taxes amounted to only 5 percent of federal revenues in 1950. Today they are 29 percent of such revenues. Thus, middle-class anger at their growing tax burdens is well founded.[49] In 2000, almost 61 percent of federal tax revenue came from progressive sources (personal and corporate income taxes). By 2003, only 52.4 percent did. A similar shift has occurred at the state and local level, with increases in property taxes and sales taxes squeezing millions of American families.[50] In 2005, according to the Congressional Budget Office, federal revenues fell to 16.8 percent of GDP, the lowest average in four decades. The growing deficit is thus no surprise.[51]

Risk and Insecurity

The anxiety of so many working families is in part related to the income squeeze, high costs, and tax burdens discussed above, but it has a deeper root: More and more families are confronting the risk of large drops in living standards caused by loss of income or catastrophic expense. Static measures like poverty, inequality, median wages, and unemployment rates don't really capture it. Economic insecurity has risen in the past two decades, both in degree and in the number of American families experiencing it. Partially or fully privatizing Social Security threatens to make this insecurity worse. Recent reforms of the bankruptcy laws will do the same.

It is these anxieties that help fuel the debate about Social Security and health care reform, at least at the grassroots level. It remains to be seen whether politicians of either party understand its origins and its depth, and whether they can find the language and the policy proposals to tap into it in a positive way. It constituted the "white noise" of the 2004 presidential campaign, a kind of free-floating and widespread anxiety that both campaigns sought to explain (or perhaps more accurately, exploit).

Clearly the inability of the Kerry campaign to speak to these issues—seemingly tailor-made for the Democrats—crippled his candidacy. It is surely one of the great ironies of American history that it is precisely this anxiety (especially among the young) that President Bush and other advocates of partial privatization of Social Security have attempted to fan, by constantly talking about the "crisis" of the program.

Of course, as the Bush administration has recently admitted, partial privatization will do nothing to address the fiscal shortfall of Social Security. But after more than a decade of hearing politicians from both sides of the aisle describe Social Security as on the road to being irredeemably broken has had a powerful effect on the nature of people's anxiety. At least among younger adults, it has become a political force in favor of "reform," largely because no alternative scenarios seem to be presenting themselves. We hope to take several important steps toward doing so in the next chapter of this book.

Using data from the Panel Study of Income Dynamics, a forty-year project that tracks the same families from year to year, Jacob Hacker discovered that family incomes rise and fall a lot more than we think. Income instability, according to Hacker, is now five times as great as in the early 1970s. "In area after area," Hacker writes, "there is evidence of a vast shift in the economic security of most Americans." Researchers for the *Los Angeles Times* looked at the same data, and confirmed Hacker's findings. In the early 1970s, inflation-adjusted incomes of most families in the bottom fifth (under $23,000 a year) bounced up and down no more than 25 percent a year; by 2000, this income volatility had doubled. Put another way, over twenty million working poor families face the very real possibility of seeing their income halved in any given year.[52]

What about middle class families? Though families in the economic middle did face some income instability in the 1970s as well—as much as 16 percent a year—they ended the year an average of 2 percent ahead. This trend has been decisively reversed in the past 25 years; those in the middle fifth, interestingly, now encounter the same level of economic insecurity the poor did thirty years ago. Even as economic volatility increased for middle-class families, average family income fell. In the aggregate, the bottom 60 percent of the American class structure has encountered more risk for less reward in the past generation. Little improvement is in sight.[53] Most of the reasons are clear and have already been discussed: stagnant wages, changes in the nature of work and the labor market, and rising costs of housing, health care, child-rearing, and education.

But Hacker's longitudinal data indicate another key finding: There hasn't been just an increase in economic risk for families. There has been a *transfer* of risk, from corporations, mediate institutions (like unions and pension funds), and the government onto families and individuals. Social policies—both public and private—cover a declining portion of the risks faced by many citizens. The shifting of risk has been a democratic phenomenon, touching families almost all the way up the earnings structure. This is taking place at a time of large-scale economic transformation and social dislocation, precisely when both justice and efficiency may require movement in the other direction. Given this shift, it is hard to imagine a policy idea more ill advised and badly timed than any degree of privatization of Social Security.

Our largest social programs, both private and public, have focused primarily on risk protection. Retirement pensions, health insurance, unemployment compensation, survivors' benefits, and even such things as child care and worker retraining serve an insurance purpose, because they help "cushion families against the income shock of major life events."[54] They also *socialize* or pool risk, by spreading threats to income across citizens of varied circumstances.

Whatever its flaws and gaps, this is the genius of Social Security. But the recent trend is toward what Hacker calls "risk privatization." The result is that "many of the most potent threats to income are increasingly faced by families and individuals on their own, rather than by collective intermediaries." While some so-called conservatives and libertarians may argue that this constitutes an expansion of individual freedom, it is a funny kind of freedom indeed.

The American approach to retirement security has three legs, although many people do not have access to all three. Social Security is one part of a larger system of mostly private saving, insurance, and investment that would allow seniors to live out their lives in dignity. It was to serve as a "safety net," a bottom-line guarantee against disaster. And it has done so, quite successfully, and will continue to do so if we don't choose to shred the net.

The other two legs of our retirement system are traditional employer-provided pensions, and private (often tax-subsidized) savings. The United

States has always been comparatively miserly in its social protections and benefits relative to the rest of the industrialized world, in part because we have generally tied programs to employment status rather than citizenship. But millions of Americans have until recently been able to rely on what is essentially a "private" welfare state, which has provided health insurance and retirement pensions through employment. This sector is not small—it constitutes more than one-third of all U.S. social spending. But the distribution and character of these private benefits, according to Hacker, has changed dramatically in recent decades. Rates of coverage have fallen sharply for lower-income workers while benefit plans provide increasingly insecure income guarantees.

Private health insurance coverage fell in the past two decades from its peak of more than 80 percent of Americans to less than 70 percent. The share of workers who received health insurance from their employers fell from 66 percent to 54 percent from 1979 to 1998, while employees have been forced to pay a larger share of the cost of coverage. The trend has continued in recent years. A growing number of employers now self-insure, leading to a general decline in risk-pooling. Public programs have not filled the gap adequately.[55]

Similar shifts can be found in retirement security. As economic change weakened the stable employment climate of the 1950s and 1960s, employers shifted away from defined-benefit pensions that offered a fixed payment for retirees toward more risky defined-contribution plans like 401(k)s. In 1975 just under 40 percent of private sector workers had some form of defined-benefit pension. By 2003, only 20 percent did.

Government played a critical role in this shift. Beginning in the Reagan Administration, the Federal Government began to use tax breaks and subsidies to encourage a shift from defined-benefit to defined-contribution pensions in the private sector. The idea, according to Karen Ferguson, director of the Pension Rights Center, was to "relieve the employers of this burden and empower individuals." The new pensions were portable, and in theory available to everyone. Personal savings, it was believed, would be increased. Some free-market conservatives also hoped that encouraging an expansion of the private sector system would lessen public support for (and need of) Social Security—and of course, the political party with which it is generally identified.

By most measures, this shift has been a failure. This is of critical importance, given the strong preference of Republicans in Washington for partially privatizing Social Security. The policy shift in the early 1980s has certainly lightened the burdens of corporate employers—that part was a success. When economist Teresa Ghildarducci looked at 700 companies over nearly two decades, she found that their annual pension contributions dropped by one-third when they shifted from defined-benefit to defined-contribution pensions. And many of the defined-benefit pension plans that remain have been under-funded or even (in a growing number of well-publicized cases) abandoned altogether. But individuals have hardly been empowered by the transition, and personal savings have completely collapsed.[56]

In the 1980s, contributions to IRAs, 401(k)s and Keogh plans rose dramatically, encouraged by federal tax breaks and subsidies. The percentage of Americans who have one of these accounts has gone up from 5.8 percent in 1975 to 40 percent in 2003. This was not an even trade for most American workers, however. Most people have very little money in these accounts. Among older workers today (aged 55 to 64), the median value of their savings in 401(k)'s is $27,000, enough for an annuity of $398 a month. And this is despite the fact that they've been investing during the strong bull market of the past two decades. The income provided by all pensions (defined-benefit and defined-contribution) is low as well: The median income for those who received them in 2000 was $7,800. Just over half of those sixty-five and older had no pension income at all.[57]

And pension protection overall is shrinking. In the private sector twenty years ago, 51 percent of employers participated in pension plans of some kind. Today 46 percent of them do so. The value of all pension wealth for those in the middle of the income spectrum and below has fallen 17 percent in those two decades. Pensions have become less valuable, and fewer families have them.[58]

The private savings rate, as is well known, has fallen 80 percent in the past 25 years. President Bush's notion of an "ownership society" draws its intellectual and political appeal from the widely perceived need to increase savings. Yet, elderly Americans generally have very little in the way of savings to draw upon, which is why so many of them desperately need a functioning Social Security system that provides adequate benefits. On average, those over the age of sixty-five in 2003 drew upon assets (savings in all forms, and home equity) for an income of $310 a month.

Yet, the "average" doesn't give us a very accurate picture of the elderly population, however, since it includes the wealthiest senior citizens. The median was just $160 a month (half of all seniors received less, in other words).[59] The precarious economic condition of millions of aging Americans is demonstrated most clearly by a rather startling recent development: Half of all the new jobs created in the U.S. in the last year were taken by people over age fifty-five. The reasons are twofold, according to Dean Baker of the Center for Economic and Policy Research: The falling value of retirees'

401(k) accounts, and rising health care costs. The number of Americans over fifty-five in the paid labor force has grown 35 percent since February 1999. Clearly, the last thing that American seniors need—now and in the future— is more risk through privatizing.[60] As Thomas Frank wrote in 2002, the goal of Social Security is not to furnish citizens with a shot at dynamic net worth. Its purpose is to minimize "the catastrophic possibilities that are unavoidable in a free-market system."[61]

The funding crisis in the defined-benefit private pension system is adding even more risk to the lives of American families. It should also raise red flags about partial privatization of Social Security. According to Wayne State University law professor Ellen Dannin, "the crisis in private retirement plans can be viewed as a laboratory experiment of what we can expect from a privatized Social Security system." The Pension Benefit Guaranty Corpo- ration (PBGC) is a quasi-government agency created to insure private re- tirement funds, much like the FDIC insures bank accounts. Employers pay premiums for each pension plan participant, with rates set by Congress. In 2001, the PBGC had a surplus of $11 billion; today, it has a deficit of $23.3 billion and growing. Each time a company defaults on its pensions and PBGC picks up the tab, the capacity of PBGC to insure other private pension plans is weakened. The crisis is rooted in the financial weakness of com- panies that promised their workers guaranteed retirement benefits, but failed to fund them. According to the General Accounting Office, the degree of under-funding in the private pension system has "dramatically increased, and additional severe losses may be on the horizon." Just over 80 percent of the Fortune 100 companies have defined benefit plans, and even these large firms are under-funding them by $79 billion. Why are so many pensions under-funded? Because most companies assumed they could fund them through stock market investments and high interest rates. The lessons for Social Security reform are hard to miss.[62]

The original title of the Social Security Act of 1935, tellingly, was the Economic Security Act. As Michele Landis Dauber has argued recently, while Roosevelt used the analogy of individual retirement savings accounts to justify the payroll tax to the public, he often described his Social Security program as a kind of disaster relief program designed to protect people from the "hazards and vicissitudes" of old age. New Dealers frequently drew comparisons be- tween fires, floods, hurricanes, and "economic earthquakes" that could strike without warning and wipe out savings, leaving the elderly unable to fend for themselves and younger children unable to pick up the slack.

Roosevelt even went so far as to make speeches in support of the pro- gram against the backdrop of disaster sites. John Winant, chair of the Social

Security Board in 1936, argued that by enacting the SSA, the nation had rejected "the assumption that blind economic forces will forever take their cyclical toll of human misery." By spreading risk, *New Yorker* magazine wrote in 1936, the program would "wipe out the long, insistent dread of eventual poverty" for millions of Americans. That dread has not disappeared; the road to privatization would expose millions of Americans to precisely the risk that Social Security "draws its support from guarding against."[63]

A Fork in the Road

A growing number of Americans no longer fully share in the benefits of our free enterprise system. Where, and to whom one is born, has become more important for determining opportunities and life chances than at any time in modern American history. Children who grow up in privilege begin their lives with overwhelming advantages. Some of the advantages are measurable, like inherited wealth. Others are more difficult to quantify, like social connections, cultural capital, an educational head start, physical health, and a general sense of efficacy and self-confidence that the American system will work for you.

Over the past three decades we have done very little to enhance real opportunity and security for the vast and aspiring middle class. As a result, many of them have become understandably skeptical that government can do anything positive. This skepticism has inflicted itself on both political parties, but it may be hurting the Democrats more since for decades they built their appeal on serving the poor and the middle class. This anxiety and anger can easily metastasize into something much larger and uglier, and that is not in the interest of any American.

There is a very old tradition of political thought in American life—as old as the nation itself—generally referred to by historians as "republicanism." Thomas Paine and others posited that freedom is heavily dependent upon broad ownership of property, a sense of national community and the common good, and the practice of citizenship and its virtues. Property ownership promotes freedom by giving individuals the resources they need to live a fully human life on their own terms. The modern idea of property ownership promises some measure of security: that if we work hard, we will reap what we have sown. Abraham Lincoln, William Jennings Bryan, Theodore Roosevelt, John Dewey, Franklin Roosevelt, and Martin Luther King Jr. all made similar arguments in the years since. In the post–World War II period, this nation came as close as any in human history to making this a reality.

Pursuing this common enterprise, in part through the instrumentality of government, helped make this happen. It wasn't inevitable. And it will not be permanent or long-lasting if we do not choose to honor, reform, and extend this legacy.

Chapter 4

EXPLAINING AND ANALYZING ARE NOT ENOUGH

A number of things should be clear: First, the lack of wage growth in the past three decades is having profound effects on living standards and opportunity across generations, with no end in sight. Second, market institutions and the array of social programs provided by our government are trying to play catch-up and are not fully succeeding. Third, there are many people who view government as a necessary evil and fail to realize its potential for doing good. Finally, the already unacceptably large budget deficit puts a crimp in the ability of the government to successfully deal with domestic social and economic problems.

A Time for Bipartisan Action

If the promise of American life is to be renewed for present and future generations of young people, it will require a new commitment to a public philosophy of shared prosperity. We must decide what we believe we owe one another and what we are willing to pay to guarantee it. It is a question of political will and a measure of our commitment to a shared future. Back in the 1930s, social insurance was seen as being a critical component of a system of basic economic security that was essential to making capitalism and democracy work. While much about our society and our economy have changed since the Depression, the existence and distribution of risk and insecurity for the most part has not. Risk is endemic in modern capitalist societies; it is what gives them their dynamism, and their productivity.

At the same time, if there is too much risk and insecurity—or if it is unjustly distributed—it can threaten the legitimacy of the values and institutions that support both capitalism and democracy. We will not grow ourselves out of many of our economic and social problems. We also will not "tax cut" our way out of many of our problems. We need to remove our ideological and partisan blinders. Once we do this, a very different set of options and possibilities presents itself.

Our approach in this book is to come up with specific recommendations that transcend sectors of the economy and sectors of the social and economic spectrum. We have no grand plan, but rather are trying to attack various problems that need to be attacked. We cannot exactly measure what our recommendation will achieve since an improvement in one area will lead to improvements in other areas. There would be benefits from synergism.

What we strongly believe is that if many of our recommendations are adopted, they will have a major positive impact on the economic and social fabric of the country. Moreover, they may even help dissolve some of the viciousness, anger, retribution, and division that have infected our country, and our people. You have heard of road rage; many are currently afflicted with political rage. When you have political rage, you are not in a state of mind to solve anything.

To show what can be done by various pieces of legislation, look at the results of programs such as the expansion of the Earned Income Tax Credit (EITC), the passage of welfare reforms that shifted money into child care and job retraining, and the enactment of family leave legislation. Results have been achieved even though the programs were limited in scope and not generously funded.[1]

With this background in mind, we offer a series of ideas and recommendations that—if liberals and conservatives, Democrats and Republicans, are able to keep an open mind—could achieve bipartisan support.

Universal Preschool and a Reformed Estate Tax

Universal preschool is a long-overdue extension of the commitments to one another and to our children implied by public schooling. New Jersey and other states are already experimenting with various forms of this.[2] It is probably best organized and run at the state level, where constitutional responsibility for public education lies in most cases anyway. Because quality preschool is so critical both for working parents and for the future academic performance of children, it is essential that funding be adequate and equitable.[3]

Presently, children receive or don't receive preschooling based on the ability of their parents to pay. As three decades of research into the Head Start program tells us, preschooling is absolutely essential for early childhood learning and social and cognitive development.[4] The present setup builds unequal life chances into our educational system from the very beginning. This is not only unjust; it is an inefficient distribution of national resources.

Much like other kinds of social spending (for education at other levels, for public infrastructure, for health), it is an investment that can help pay for itself in the long run. A study commissioned by Congress on the fiftieth anniversary of the G.I. Bill discovered, not surprisingly, that this program paid for itself—and then some. Universal public preschool will have long-term positive effects economically, increasing the likelihood that children of all backgrounds will grow up to be healthy, educated, and productive citizens. At the same time, it will free up thousands of dollars of their parents' money, which can be used for any number of productive purposes: paying off debt, buying a home, starting a business, saving for retirement, saving for college, and so on. Such a program would have the benefit of creating jobs since there will be a need to hire new teachers and build and equip physical facilities.

A universal preschool program that meets its objectives needs to be properly funded. We propose dedicating all federal estate tax revenues to a universal preschool program. These funds would be given to state governments, which in turn would determine, along with local instrumentalities, how the funds would be distributed within their states.

Some background is necessary here with respect to what has happened to estate tax laws. For years, marginal estate tax rates were very high, with the top rate being 55 percent. When the highest marginal income tax rate was 70 percent, the highest marginal estate tax rate was 55 percent. When the highest income tax rate was cut, and is now roughly half of what it was before, no change was made in the highest marginal estate tax rate. This made little sense from an equity point of view, or from the point of view of inducing private savings. Thus, something had to be done.

Unfortunately, what was done was to reduce estate tax rates on a temporary basis, but then because of a sunset provision, the rate would snap back to 55 percent, unless something is done to change the law. Of course, something will be done to change the law because going back to 55 percent is not an acceptable option for either party. That battle has yet to be fought. Therefore, our proposal takes advantage of the current state of limbo of estate taxes by coming in with a compromise that seems reasonable.

Our proposal is that the first $2 million of an estate should be tax-exempt, then from $2 million to $5 million the rate would be 10 percent, from $5 million to $10 million the rate would be 20 percent, and over $10 million the rate would be 30 percent. These rates are hardly confiscatory, especially when compared with what they were in the past, and could help many small businesspeople who have worked hard to accumulate assets and live the American dream. An estate tax reformed in this way would affect few families: in 2000 only 9,548 taxable estates were $2.5 million or more in size. This approach would raise roughly $1 billion per month for preschool education. In addition, states could also use their own estate and gift taxes to help finance preschool programs.

The political appeal of dedicating a reformed estate tax to preschool education should be obvious. Originally put in place in the Progressive Era, the estate tax was designed in part to preserve opportunity and the creativity and fairness of the free enterprise system. In today's America, where early education is critically important for determining the future of individuals and society, this original purpose would be reinvigorated. Some of our wealthiest citizens, like Warren Buffett, George Soros, and Microsoft's Bill Gates, have made precisely this argument. The estate tax has always been considered by its critics an attempt to soak the rich and equalize incomes. Not so in this case. The attempt here is to have the generation that has passed on do something worthwhile for a new generation coming on.

Payment of the estate tax "represents a suitable act of recognition by the wealthy of the role played by fellow Americans in creating the conditions for the very system necessary for their own success."[5] Particularly if it is dedicated to universal preschooling, a reformed estate tax would go a long way toward maintaining those conditions, and even expanding and improving them. It would constitute a kind of social inheritance. Moreover, it will significantly help alleviate many caught in the middle-class squeeze and renew our commitment to equal opportunity and social mobility.

Annual Cost-of-Living Adjustments for Minimum Wage Earners

The increase in the percentage of Americans that can be described as "working poor" has been noted by a number of writers recently.[6] By one estimate, more than 9 million work and live in poverty, while 30 million can be described as "low-wage." A critical component of our postwar social contract is fraying: the notion that work should pay.

Nearly half of those earning the minimum wage work full-time; another third work between twenty and thirty-four hours a week. These numbers have been growing. Many support families. It is no longer accurate to think of minimum-wage jobs as being filled predominantly by teenagers, mothers trying to get out of the house, or those who want to earn some extra spending money. Seventy-two percent of those earning the minimum wage are adults. More than 10 percent of workers aged twenty-five to thirty-four—folks in the process of trying to marry, have children, and purchase a home—make under eight dollars an hour.[7]

Jobs at the lower end of the wage scale are growing in number very quickly, and an increasing number of children are being raised in families headed by one or two minimum-wage earners—many of them cobbling together more than one job, since so many employers that pay minimum wage hire only part-time workers. A full-time year-round minimum-wage worker will earn between $10,000 and $15,000 a year—lower than the federal poverty level. This remains true even if one includes income derived from the Earned Income Tax Credit (EITC).

Very few of these workers receive work-related benefits, and most are one financial or medical emergency away from desperate poverty. Indeed, most low-wage workers are disconnected from the social services designed to keep them in the workforce, like job training, food stamps, and child-care subsidies. Only 41 percent of eligible adults collect food stamps; an even smaller fraction receive child-care subsidies. Only half of adults eligible for Medicaid actually receive it.

Many of the working poor never qualify for unemployment insurance, which was designed for an economy of full-time, full-year factory workers. Today, in an economy where temporary and part-time work is common, our state-federal system covers less than 40 percent of the unemployed.[8] Over the next decade a growing number of Americans will find themselves in this part of the labor market. Their children, and thus a large portion of the next generation—tomorrow's workers, taxpayers, and voters—will suffer the consequences.

Social Security recipients receive an annual cost-of-living adjustment, so why shouldn't those who are minimum-wage earners? Polls and referenda indicate that the American people strongly support an increase in the minimum wage. Florida voters in 2004 voted for a statewide minimum wage increase; 82 percent of Americans in a March 2005 poll taken by the Pew Research Center saw an increase in the federal minimum wage as an "important priority."[9] It is not only a matter of fairness, but it is also a matter of survival. The real value of the minimum wage has been declining for three decades. Since 1979 it has lost more than one-quarter of its purchasing power. The minimum wage is 33 percent of the average hourly wage today, the lowest level since 1949. Up through the 1970s the minimum wage was high enough to lift a family of three up to the federal poverty level. It no longer is. The increase of 1997—which lifted the wages of 9 percent of the workforce—has been completely erased by inflation. By the end of 2005, the minimum will have remained at the same level for nine years, equaling the longest stretch without an increase in American history.

An annual cost-of-living adjustment would prevent the need for occasional legislative increases in the minimum wage while increasing the likelihood of making welfare reform a success. In other words, set the minimum wage at a proper amount, and then have a cost-of-living adjustment every year. The minimum wage raises the wages of low-income workers in general, not just those below the official poverty line. Many families move in and out of poverty, and near-poor families are also beneficiaries of minimum wage increases. A cost-of-living adjustment will allow for improved planning by employers, will minimize negative employment effects, and will stimulate consumer demand. It would be a positive step, helping to keep people off welfare and limit their debt burdens.[10]

Changing the Alternative Minimum Tax (AMT)

For those unfamiliar with it, the primary purpose of the AMT is to prevent high-income individuals from using such things as exemptions, deductions, credits, and preferential tax rates to reduce their overall tax burden to negligible or nonexistent levels. It was created in 1969, at the very end of the Johnson administration, after Treasury Secretary Joseph Barr reported to Congress that a small number of wealthy households were using loopholes in the income tax system to avoid making any payments whatsoever. In response to an angry public outcry, the incoming Nixon administration adopted the first version of the AMT. It has been changed subsequently, with today's system basically in place in 1982.

The AMT operates alongside the regular income tax, though it has its own rates and rules on what is deductible. In computing the AMT, limits and exclusions are placed on tax-reduction items such as long-term capital gains, tax-exempt interest, tax shelters, medical expenses, itemized deductions, credits, interest on second mortgages, incentive stock options, state and local taxes, exemptions, and even in some cases standard deductions. It is often referred to as the "stealth tax," according to David Johnston, because of how it "sneaks up on people."

Most people are unaware of its existence (until it hits them); computer software that prepares tax returns generally calculates income and deductions under both systems, and the taxpayers owe whichever is higher. The AMT's first effect is to reduce the value of their exemptions and deductions, leaving more and more of their income taxable. While there are only two rates in the AMT, 26 percent and 28 percent, as people phase into this penalty system, their marginal rates can go as high as 35 percent.[11]

Frankly, there is nothing wrong with the concept. However, the AMT has been carried too far with respect to upper-income individuals and should not be paid at all by middle-income individuals. The AMT has been creeping down the income scale for years: in 1995, about 414,000 taxpayers paid it. The Treasury Department estimates that by 2010 about 17.9 million families will pay it, including almost the entire upper middle class (in this case, those making between $100,000 and $500,000 a year). Nearly three-quarters of those making between $75,000 and $100,000 will pay it; according to the Brookings-Urban Institute, 97 percent of families with two children in this income group will be paying it. This is the middle-class personified: It is a police officer married to a middle school guidance counselor; a teacher married to a social worker.

Research indicates that the decision to shift a taxpayer from the regular rate computation system to the higher-rate AMT system is heavily influenced by that person's family status, with married parents getting hit the hardest. By 2010 almost 85 percent of all taxpayers with two or more children will be forced into the AMT-rate approach. Former Reagan and Clinton administration economist Len Burman describes this shift well: "What was a class tax is becoming a mass tax."[12]

Recent tax cuts have made the AMT problem worse. To hold the cost of the first set of cuts to $1.3 trillion over the first ten years, according to Johnston, "someone had to lose out." Instead of reducing the top rate to 36 percent (rather than 35 percent) or revising the AMT to exempt those making less than $500,000, "the Administration relied on the stealth approach of letting the alternative tax silently take back from those making less than $500,000 a year some or all what they were told to expect." This design meant that those making between $75,000 and $500,000 "would subsidize the tax cuts for those in the million-dollar-and-up income class."

According to Jerry Tempalski, an economist in the Treasury Department's Office of Tax Analysis, one of the effects of the recent tax cuts will be to start sweeping large numbers of these families into the AMT beginning in 2005. In effect, according to Johnston, "it is a subsidy of the super rich paid for by the middle class and the upper middle class."[13] In April 2005, there was a surge in individual income tax payments. It was spearheaded by AMT payments, and it will be the primary factor that will reduce the budget deficit from $413 billion in fiscal year 2004 to between $320 billion and $330 billion in fiscal year 2005. While reducing an excessive budget deficit is worthwhile reducing it on the backs of successful middle-class Americans is questionable at best.

The original justification for this law was not to soak middle-income taxpayers. It was designed to apply only to the very rich who were trying to get around paying their fair share of taxes. If the AMT was not meant for middle-income individuals, then it seems logical that it should be easy to change the law. Not so. The amount of tax revenues raised from the AMT is huge and growing, and with the government running a large budget deficit, it is not being aggressive in rectifying the injustice. As a matter of fact, the government does not reveal how much money is raised by the AMT, and how much comes from the middle class. According to the Tax Policy Center, in 2008 the federal government will have become so dependent on the AMT that it would be cheaper to repeal the regular income tax.

A logical approach would be to reduce the AMT rates and eliminate the tax entirely for middle-income people, since they are innocent victims of a tax approach gone badly. One thought in this regard would be to have several rates that range from 15 percent to 25 percent for those that will still pay the tax. While changing the law will not help all middle-income people, for those it does help, it could help them big-time. Moreover, the changes could help a considerable number of middle and upper-middle-income families that are having trouble maintaining their standard of living.

Rethinking Sunset Tax Provisions

In the first Bush administration, three major tax laws were passed, and they will be phased out if nothing is done. This will take place because of their sunset provisions. These laws all reduced taxes, but if they were allowed to return to the way they were initially, it would be the equivalent of tax increases.

In the current political atmosphere, the administration and Congress will not allow major portions of these laws to lapse with nothing being done. This means major rewriting of the laws over the next several years, and one can bet that the current administration will want the rewriting done before the president's second term is over. As a matter of fact, the process is already starting. The obvious question here is when these tax laws are re-written, who will get the biggest benefits, and who will get hurt. This could be either good news or bad news for the middle class, but it may not be good news unless they exert their latent political power.

One might reasonably ask why the three major tax law changes in the first Bush administration had provisions that phase in, and then phase out, tax reductions? The answer is that in negotiations with Congress, the administration conceded to Congress that there would be a maximum dollar amount of tax reductions. Since the size of the administration's proposed tax reductions exceeded the agreed-upon total, it meant that techniques had to be devised for the tax reductions not to exceed the maximum amount agreed upon. The most talked about adjustments were estate taxes, where a series of reductions would take place, but ultimately the reductions would be eliminated.

A dollar ceiling approach to tax reductions is convoluted and illogical, unless of course you are a politician. Make it appear with rising budget deficits that the size of tax reductions are limited, but then at a later date with much less fanfare, add back tax reductions to what you wanted in the first place. As a matter of fact, in the rewriting phase, there is a good chance the overall tax reduction will be more than what the reduction had been initially if no dollar caps had been involved.

Do not presume, however, that in this rewriting phase the middle class will come out as winners. Part of the middle class has a strong political base, what with the AARP and the unions, but there are other members of the middle class, such as young and middle-age white-collar workers who do not have strong organized representation.

When these tax reduction opportunities present themselves, the question is whether the middle class will benefit in a fair and equitable way. Or, whether down the road, if others benefited more in this process, whether the middle class will ultimately have to ante up more in future taxes to meet an outsized budget deficit.

Adequate representation is not the only factor determining how the middle class will be treated in future negotiations. Many distractions can divert middle-class attention away from the rewriting of these laws. Excessive amounts of public attention on a major revamping of Social Security laws is an important diversion.

The Congressional Budget Office was asked by ranking members of the Senate Budget Committee, the Senate Finance Committee, the House Budget Committee, the House Ways and Means Committee, and the Joint Economic Committee to examine how effective federal tax law rates will change over the coming decade if the current law is not changed. That is, if the provisions of tax laws enacted in 2001, 2002, and 2003 follow the phasing in and phasing out provisions.

Tax legislation enacted in 2001, 2002, and 2003 is scheduled to phase in, phase out, and then sunset after 2010. As a result, federal tax rules will differ in every year from 2001 through 2011, and therefore, so will effective tax rates. The current provisions, and how they are handled, will have a different impact on people with different incomes, and because those provisions change from year to year, effective tax rates will rise or fall in patterns that vary over time and income groups. The Congressional Budget Office study was an attempt to determine the effective federal tax rates from 2002 through 2014. The study was called *Effective Federal Tax Rates under Current Law, 2001 To 2014*, and was published in August 2004.

Three major tax laws were enacted between 2001 and 2003. The first was the Economic Growth and Taxpayer Relief Reconciliation Act of 2001 (EGTRRA), which reduced rates, increased credits, and provided relief from marriage penalties and from the alternative minimum tax. It restructured tax rates and brackets, increased the child credit and the dependent care credit, and increased the earned income credit for married couples. All of these provisions sunset in 2011, and the provisions of individual tax law return to those in effect before 2001.

The second law was the Job Creation and Worker Assistance Act of 2002 (JCWAA), which increased depreciation allowances for some property and altered some provisions concerning operating losses. The third law was the Jobs and Growth Tax Relief Reconciliation Act of 2003 (JGTRRA), which accelerated some of the provisions in EGTRRA and temporarily increased exemption levels for the alternative minimum tax.

One of the main tasks assigned to the Congressional Budget Office in studying these three tax laws was to determine the effective federal tax rates for five income classes. The estimates were on an annual basis and ran from 2001 through 2014. The estimates assumed that nothing was changed in the phase-in, phase-out, and sunset provisions. By using this approach, Congress would have a starting point with respect to determining effective tax rates if there were no further changes in the laws.

It is evident that if tax reductions are phased out as the current law dictates, the effective tax rate for all income groups will rise. What is also evident is that the increase in effective tax rates for the lower and middle-income groups will rise more than for the high-income groups.

For example, in 2001, the effective tax rate for the lowest quintile was 5.4 percent, for the middle quintile 15.2 percent, and for the highest quintile 26.8 percent. If the laws change and expire based on current law, the lowest quintile effective tax rate would jump to 8.3 percent, the middle quintile tax rate would increase to 18.2 percent, and the highest quintile tax rate would edge up to 28.8 percent. Thus, without any changes in the three laws, low- and middle-income individuals should be aware they are starting from a competitive disadvantage of more built-in tax rate increases than for those in the higher-income bracket. Table 1 from the Congressional Budget Office (CBO) shows how the effective federal tax rates change for five different income groups from 2001 to 2014 if the current laws stand.

A New Approach to Simplifying and Reducing Taxes

The president is in the process of developing proposals to simplify the tax system, make temporary tax reductions permanent, and reduce taxes even more. His greatest successes will probably come in making some of the temporary tax reductions permanent, although even here, modifications and compromises will be necessary. Justification can simply be that if temporary tax reductions are not made permanent, they amount to a tax increase. Politicians who vote for raising taxes tend to ultimately do something else for a living.

President Bush, in trying to simplify the tax system, is no doubt thinking in broad terms. This could mean recommendations that would cut back on the increases in marginal tax rates and ultimately switch over to greater reliance on a consumption tax rather than an income tax. Simplifying the tax system is a worthy endeavor, but moving to a consumption tax has no broad-based support. Moreover, every time politicians try to make major changes in the tax system in the name of simplification, tax computations become more complicated.

The tax simplification recommendation we offer uses a very different type of approach than the path that politicians seem to follow. Our plan emphasizes a simplified way for individuals to compute their tax liability. After all, isn't that what tax simplicity is all about?

Let all people, irrespective of income, be able to compute their annual income tax liability using only a one or two-page form. What this approach involves is that all income would be fully taxed irrespective of how the income is generated, and no deductions, exemptions, or tax credits would be allowed. It would be gross income in the purest sense. Obviously, this would result in a higher level of taxable income than under the traditional computation approach.

Because the income level is higher, the tax rates applied could be lower. Moreover, the tax rates could be designed in a way where there are fewer marginal rate brackets and where most people would have a lower tax liability than if they computed their taxes in the traditional long form way. By using such an approach, the president could get tax simplification and tax reductions all rolled into one package. Think of the advantages for the overwhelming majority of American people all along the income spectrum.

In addition to bringing tax reductions for many, this would be an opportunity to cut back on a time-consuming, frustrating tax computation process that can be expensive. Of course, if individuals want to go through the arduous task of computing their tax liabilities on the current basis, or on both, that would be their prerogative.

We suspect that many individuals would probably be willing to pay somewhat more in taxes if they could reduce the time and aggravation of thinking about the computations, then actually doing the computations, and then worrying about whether they have filled out the forms properly. What a nice bonus it would be for the American people if they had a one or two-page form to fill out, and if the brackets were designed in a way where most people would get a tax reduction to boot. At least on the surface, it is hard to see what public groups would be against this type of proposal.

A Creative Approach to Expanding Health Care Insurance

As Thomas Geoghegan has pointed out, our incomplete system of employer-provided health insurance has three major flaws: It doesn't cover everyone, it doesn't cover everyone well, and it is becoming a drag on employment and our economy. Presently, health care costs can amount to 18 percent to 20 percent of payroll. Employers will hesitate to hire new full-time workers if it means taking on this kind of cost. As the cost of health insurance goes above this, it will put an even more serious drag on hiring—and on the competitiveness of American businesses. Our present system either hamstrings the ability of businesses to compete or encourages them to hire part-time and temporary workers. Neither is good for the well-being of American families or the national economy as a whole.[14]

Universal health care insurance provided by the government currently is not practical from a financial point of view, and the way the government spends money in other areas, it probably will never be practical. Yet, that does not take the government off the hook. We would argue that the government has at least a moral obligation to do all that it can to make sure that affordable health care is available to all Americans, irrespective of who provides the health care coverage and how it is paid for. There is something wrong with a society where so many people have inadequate or nonexistent health care coverage, and for many who have such coverage, the cost is eating them alive.

Let us look at the government's financial circumstances as they currently stand. In fiscal year 2004, it had a budget deficit close to 4 percent of GDP. Moreover, the deficit was even larger if the Social Security surplus is excluded. In fiscal years 2005 and 2006, the deficit as a percentage of Gross Domestic Product will probably be between 2.5 percent and 3.0 percent. For an economy that in 2006 will be five years into an economic recovery, that is a sad state of affairs.

This massive deficit should not be an excuse for the government being timid when it comes to significantly improving the health care situation in the United States. For the political party that addresses this issue aggressively, it should be a political opportunity. Yet, neither party is being overly aggressive in providing practical solutions, After all, this is not a problem for just a few Americans; it is a problem for many Americans, many of whom vote. Especially in need are those who are actively seeking but not finding jobs, those between jobs, and those whose companies do not provide coverage because the people are classified as part-time workers or consultants.

Since a primary goal of the authors is to present new ideas, we have a recommendation. The government could reward businesses that provide health care insurance and could penalize businesses that don't. The carrot would be lower income tax rates for those that meet the standards, and the stick would be higher income tax rates for those that don't. A firm above a certain size would need to meet a government-determined minimum insurance package in order to get the tax benefit and to avoid a tax penalty. Also, anyone who works twenty hours a week or more for a company would be covered, even if the company classifies them as part-time employees or consultants, as long as they don't have coverage elsewhere. Moreover, the coverage would need to extend for a meaningful period past their employment termination date.

As for small companies, they will not be penalized for failing to meet minimum health care insurance requirements. However, they could be rewarded in the form of a lower income tax rate for providing such benefits. Thus, in the case of large companies, it would be the use of the carrot and stick; in the case of small companies it would be just the carrot.

This proposal shows that a liberal historian and a conservative economist can join forces and be creative in a practical way. Both believe that half a loaf is better than no loaf at all, although they may look at what constitutes a loaf quite differently.

Finally, we applaud the companies that announced in January 2005 that they will sponsor health care coverage for the uninsured. Their program is expected to begin before the year is over and is intended to cover uninsured part-time and temporary workers, contractors, consultants, and early retirees who generally are not eligible for employer health plans. According to the *New York Times* (January 27, 2005), the sponsors will begin promoting their plan to about 3 million workers, or about 7 percent of the estimated 45 million uninsured Americans. The companies will not subsidize the coverage, but will help create a pool of potential participants that is sufficiently large to justify lower insurance rates than individuals would have to pay on their own. In our view, those firms involved in this type of program should get a tax break.

This type of approach will complement our carrot and stick approach. The sixty companies involved in this project are obviously public-spirited. Yet, there apparently are many companies around the country that need a financial nudge to get involved.

Social Security Recipients Need to Have More Payout Options

When it was determined that Social Security recipients should receive full benefits at sixty-seven years old and not sixty-five, the change was based on what was perceived to be the financial problems of the system. It had nothing to do with the needs of the people who receive the money, and how their circumstances, and problems, have changed. Couples marry later, have families later, their children go to college when their parents are older, and their own parents live longer and often require a considerable amount of financial assistance.

At the same time, the breadwinner situation has also changed. It is not uncommon for people to lose their jobs before they reach retirement age, and it has become difficult for them to find adequate, let alone comparable employment. Often their retirement packages have been watered down and typically don't start for a number of years, and they have difficulty finding adequate health care coverage at a price they can afford. What these circumstances mean for many families is that they are being squeezed financially before they reach the age of sixty-two, which is when they can start receiving partial Social Security benefits.

The obvious question here is: Why doesn't the government rethink the payout options for Social Security recipients, so they will have maximum flexibility in meeting their own particular needs? Let the people make the choices, not the government. Why aren't those politicians who think recipients should have a choice as to how Social Security funds are invested arguing for giving these individuals greater freedom of choice as to when they receive their funds?

Greater payout choices can be separated as an issue from total benefit costs for the entire Social Security program. Total benefit costs can be kept the same if viewed over an extended number of years, irrespective of how the payout laws are changed. Thus, any attempt to argue against the concept of greater payout flexibility on the basis of affordability makes no sense. This is the type of recommendation where the benefits to making the change—many being synergistic in nature—clearly outweigh any adversity. The only adverse factor of consequence we can think of are the administrative problems in instituting the new system.

There is no one magical approach with respect to payout alternatives. Yet, what is clear is that in order to meet the needs of as many American families as possible, the first option for payout should probably be when people reach their late fifties, and these options should extend out to when people reach their early seventies. For example, the earliest payout could start at 58, the next payout point could be 65, and the last payout point could be 72. Obviously, those wanting to start their payments at 58 would incur a considerable payout penalty, but if the wolf is at the door, it may be worth it to give up some long-term proceeds, especially if their retirement benefits do not kick in until they reach 60, 62, or 65 years old.

The Approach To Payroll Taxes Needs to Be Changed

Today's workers should finance today's retirees, and tomorrow's workers should finance tomorrow's retirees. Inevitably, tomorrow will be a more expensive proposition than today. Therefore, affordability for those paying must be continually weighed against the needs of those receiving. There is nothing wrong with today's workers paying for today's retirees, and tomorrow's workers paying for tomorrow's retirees, as long as the trade-off approach between the two does not change over time. It would be unfair to emphasize benefits for one generation and emphasize affordability for the next.

In order to measure the trade-off between paying taxes and receiving benefits, it helps if the tax inflows come from a single source; a proper tradeoff is difficult to determine if funding comes from a variety of sources. Fiscal conservatives should be attracted to any program where every year, specific benefits paid are matched against total revenues received from a specific tax source. This approach elevates the importance of tax affordability and should put pressure on legislators to make benefit increases more cost effective.

At present (2005), Social Security is running a good-size surplus, while Medicare and Medicaid are running large deficits. When looked at in combination, there is a large and growing deficit. From a financial point of view, if these three programs are funded primarily from one common source—payroll taxes—there is still likely to be a revenue shortfall. This gap will need to be closed, either by raising revenues or cutting back on outlays.

The set of tax increases and decreases recommended here is an attempt to be practical and fair. In the case of Social Security, Medicare, and Medicaid, the proposals would establish an approach where total taxes and benefits can be weighed against each other every year. The objective is to create a financial balance where official decisions are based on a trade-off between the pain of those paying the taxes against the needs of those receiving benefits. Currently there is no trade-off approach for even one of those programs, let alone all three.

The approach recommended is purely and simply a continuation of pay-as-you go, but with improvements. Payroll taxes are likely to cover Social Security benefits for another half century, and probably more. However, funding for Medicare is already insufficient, and the picture will deteriorate further when the full cost of prescription drug legislation hits in 2006. Moreover, there is no direct funding source for Medicaid.

One approach to help close the annual funding gap for these three programs is to remove the income ceilings for employer-employee taxes. Even though the so-called "crisis" of Social Security has been exaggerated, the much greater financial problems of Medicare and Medicaid have been largely ignored. The fiscal health of Social Security has not been helped by the fact that wage growth has been concentrated at the higher end of income, which, of course, is not hit by a payroll tax, except for part of Medicare. In 1983, 90.2 percent of earnings in covered employment were taxable; the covered share in 2002 was 85.4 percent. It is projected to fall to 83.8 percent by 2012.[15]

According to Dean Baker and David Rosnick, if the income ceiling were raised to $110,000, it would eliminate 40 percent of the projected shortfall. If we eliminate the ceiling altogether, this step alone would virtually guarantee solvency and full benefits over a seventy-five-year period. This is true whether one uses Congressional Budget Office projections or the more conservative ones proposed by the Social Security trustees. According to a 2005 memo by the Office of the Actuary for the Social Security Administration, removing the earnings cap on taxes and benefits improves the seventy-five-year actuarial balance by 1.7 percent of payroll, thereby eliminating 90 percent of the funding deficit forecast by the trustees. Removing the cap would completely eliminate the deficit forecast by the Congressional Budget Office, with its more plausible but still unduly conservative economic growth forecast.[16]

One consequence of the fact that the tax cap hasn't kept up with wage growth at the top is that the payroll tax has become an increasingly onerous burden disproportionately carried by the 90 percent of Americans who make less than the income ceiling. Three out of four households now pay more in Social Security taxes than in income taxes, while those who earn above the income ceiling basically get a tax break. From 1973 to 2000, Social Security and Medicare taxes grew 82 percent faster than incomes.[17]

In order to reduce the current pain inflicted on lower- and most middle-income people by the payroll tax, we propose that the first $3,000 of income in a year should be exempt from employee and employer payroll taxes. We are not wedded to the exact number of $3,000, but believe that a number in that area would help low and middle-income people in a meaningful way without significantly hurting those in the higher income brackets. If our proposal had been in place in 2005, all the people who earned under $93,000 (the $90,000 income ceiling plus the $3,000 tax exemption) would have received a reduction in their payroll taxes.

In the second George W. Bush administration, any tax increase proposal will be difficult to sell to the president because of his philosophical approach on the subject. The only way such legislation would have a chance of being accepted by the administration is if it is combined with other tax reductions such as those recommended in this book. When there are both tax increases and tax reductions, politicians then can classify the legislation as tax reform.

From the perspective of the authors, our task is to make logical proposals that from a political point of view have a chance of being acted upon. All of the proposals made in this book can stand on their own, and we surely hope that they all would be given a fair hearing. Having said this, we still believe that the most pressing non-defense problem is to make sure that Social Security, Medicare, and Medicaid are effectively and properly financed on an ongoing basis. It would be a mistake to concentrate just on Social Security when the problems for Medicare and Medicaid are far more pressing.

A New COLA Approach Is Needed for Social Security

The best COLA approach is one that is very generous to Social Security recipients and protects them from the vicissitudes of cost-of-living swings, and yet does not cause those paying the taxes to finance the COLA to be unduly burdened. Sounds like an impossible task, but that is not the case. The price index we use (based on personal consumption expenditures) is the same the Federal Reserve uses when measuring inflation. The Federal Reserve excludes food and energy, but we can hardly recommend that when it comes to COLA adjustments for the elderly.

Simply stated, price increases as measured by personal consumption expenditures (PCE) will be the only index used to determine annual benefit increases. There will be no average wage adjustments in the formula. In computing the annual COLA adjustment, every year 0.5 percent will be added to the PCE price increase in order to account for the fact that the elderly tend to have larger increases in their cost-of-living than the population in general, they are more subject to emergencies, and they have little financial ability to cope with emergencies. There would also be a minimum annual increase of 2 percent, even if the PCE in a year is below that number. This minimum rate will serve as a countercyclical stimulant when the economy is weak, and will provide the elderly with a degree of comfort about what will happen to the future of their Social Security payments. Later in the book, this topic will be covered in greater detail.

Conclusions

What is proposed in this book are sensible ways to maintain and grow some of our critical social programs in perpetuity. We endeavor to ask and answer what we believe to be the right questions, such as: What do we owe to one another? And what machinery can we devise to ensure that our common needs are justly met and paid for? The politics of recent decades has made it almost impossible to even ask these questions or propose solutions that require sacrifice and justly shared burdens. We are fast reaching a crossroads, much like the one in Herbert Croly's day. The "promise of American life" is being broken. According to Thomas Jefferson, "Every society has a right to fix the fundamental principles of its association." To do this will require innovative and bold thinking—a new public philosophy, a new nationalism— to renew that promise for this century. And action must come soon. As someone once said, you often don't see the bones until the tide goes out. By then, it's too late.

Chapter 5

HISTORY AND DIRECTION OF SOCIAL SECURITY, MEDICARE, AND MEDICAID

In the early twentieth century, both the states and the federal government began to recognize that in an increasingly industrialized economy, certain risks could best be met through a social insurance approach to public welfare. A contributory financing of social insurance programs would ensure that protection was available as a matter of right, as contrasted with a public assistance approach, whereby only those persons in need would be eligible for benefits.

Social insurance started with workers' compensation. A federal law covering civilian employees of the government in hazardous jobs was adopted in 1908, and the first state compensation law that was held constitutional was enacted in 1911. By 1929, workers' compensation laws were in place in all but four states. These laws made industry responsible for the costs of compensating workers, or their survivors, when the employee was injured or killed in connection with his or her job.

The Great Depression of the 1930s made federal action a necessity, as neither the states and local communities nor private charities had the financial resources to cope with the growing needs of the American people. Beginning in 1932 the federal government first made loans, and then grants, to states to pay for direct relief and work relief. Subsequently, special federal emergency relief and public works programs were implemented. In 1935, President Roosevelt proposed to Congress economic security legislation based on the recommendations of a specially created

Committee on Economic Security. On August 14, 1935, the Social Security Act became law.

Social Security

The law established two social insurance programs on a national basis to help citizens meet the risks of old age and unemployment. The first was a federal system of old-age benefits for retired workers who had been employed in industries and commerce (about 60 percent of the workforce); the second was a combination of federal and state systems of unemployment insurance. Initially the act provided monthly benefits to retired workers age sixty-five and over, and lump-sum death benefits to the estates of those workers.

The Social Security Act also included federal grants in aid to the states for the means-tested programs of old-age assistance and aid to the blind. These programs supplemented the incomes of persons who were either ineligible for old age and survivors' insurance or whose benefits could not provide a basic standard of living. The intent of federal participation was to induce states to adopt similar programs.

The Social Security Act established other federal grants to enable states to extend and strengthen maternal and child health and welfare services. These grants became the Aid to Families with Dependent Children program, which in 1996 was replaced by a new block-grant program called Temporary Assistance for Needy Families.

The old-age insurance program had not reached full operation before significant changes were adopted. In 1939, Congress made the old-age insurance system a family program when it added benefits for dependents of retired workers and surviving dependents of deceased workers. Benefits became payable in 1940, not in 1942 as originally planned. No major changes were made in the program until the 1950s, when it was extended to cover many jobs that previously had been excluded. In some cases this was done because experience was needed to work out procedures for reporting the earnings and collecting the taxes for persons in certain occupational groups.

The scope of the basic national social insurance system was significantly extended in 1956 through the addition of disability insurance. Benefits were provided for severely disabled workers aged fifty or older and for adult disabled children of deceased or disabled workers. In 1958 the Social Security Act was amended to provide benefits for dependents of disabled workers, similar to those already provided for dependents of retired workers. In 1960, the age-fifty requirement for disabled worker benefits was removed.

The 1967 amendments provided disability benefits for widows and widowers aged fifty or older.

Monthly cash benefits were increased ten times on an ad hoc basis, previous to the implementation of the first automatic cost-of-living adjustment (COLA) by the Social Security Amendments of 1972. Beginning in 1975, benefits have been automatically adjusted to keep pace with inflation. (Since 1975, there have been annual increases, except during calendar year 1983 when the adjustment was delayed six months.) The 1972 amendments tied the benefit increases to the consumer price index (CPI). The amendments also created the delayed retirement credit, which increased benefits for workers who retire after the normal retirement age.

The 1977 amendments changed the method of benefit computation to ensure stable replacement rates (Social Security benefits compared with earnings in the year before retirement). Earnings included in the computation were indexed to account for changes in the economy from the time they were earned.

The 1983 amendments made coverage compulsory for federal civilian employees and for employees of nonprofit organizations. State and local governments were prohibited from leaving the system. The amendments also provided for a gradual increase in the age eligibility—from 65 to 67—for full retirement benefits, beginning with persons who reached 62 in 2000. For certain beneficiaries, benefits became subject to income tax.

The only amendment after the major 1983 change took place in 1994. That amendment raised the threshold for the coverage of domestic workers' earnings from $50 per calendar quarter to $1,000 per calendar year. After 1995, this threshold of coverage rose in $100 increments, based on average wage increases. Tables 2 and 3 present Social Security and Disability Insurance receipts, benefits, and net differences. The data for Social Security began in 1937, and the data for Disability Insurance started in 1957.

Medicare

Medicare is a nationwide, federally administered health insurance program authorized in 1965 to cover the cost of hospitalization, medical care, and some related services for most people age sixty-five and over. In 1972, coverage was extended to those receiving Social Security Disability Insurance payments for two years, and to individuals with end-stage renal disease. In 2006, prescription drug coverage will be added.

Medicare consists of two separate but coordinated programs—Hospital Insurance (HI) Part A, and Supplementary Medical Insurance (SMI). The

SMI program is composed of three separate accounts—Part B, Part D, and the Transitional Assistance Account. Almost all persons aged sixty-five and over, or who are disabled and entitled to HI, are eligible to enroll in Part B and Part D on a voluntary basis by paying monthly premiums. Health insurance protection is available to Medicare beneficiaries without regard to income.

The Medicare program is the second-largest social insurance program in the United States, with 41 million beneficiaries and total expenditures of $281 billion in 2003. The Boards of Trustees for Medicare report annually to Congress on the financial operations and actuarial status of the program. Beginning in 2002, discussions of both the HI and SMI programs were combined into one report. The Office of the Actuary in the Centers for Medicare and Medicaid Services prepares the report under the direction of the boards.

The HI trust fund is financed primarily by payroll taxes paid by workers and employers. The taxes paid each year are used mainly to pay benefits for current beneficiaries. The SMI trust fund is financed primarily by transfers from the general fund of the U.S. Treasury and by monthly Part B and Part D premiums paid by beneficiaries. A detailed breakout of Medicare programs is presented in Tables 4 and 5.

Medicare Prescription Drug Legislation

On December 8, 2003, the Medicare Prescription Drug, Improvement and Modernization Act was passed into law. The centerpiece of the legislation was a new prescription drug benefit program. It was initially estimated by the government that from 2004 through 2013, the Prescription Drug legislation would cost Medicare $669 billion, and in 2013, the cost would be $112 billion. Since the initial estimate, it has been recognized both inside and outside government that the cost of the prescription drug legislation has been grossly underestimated.

The prescription drug legislation is very complicated, as witnessed by some of the following highlights. It will require a major educational effort on the part of the government to explain the options to the American people:

✓ A new Part D drug program was established. As a prelude to this program, a temporary plan was instituted, establishing Medicare-endorsed drug discount cards. Enrollment in the temporary plan began in May 2004 and allows access to discounts beginning in June 2004. This program then phases out as the drug benefit program becomes available in 2006. Card sponsors can charge up to a $30 annual enrollment fee. Beneficiaries whose incomes do not exceed 135 percent of the federal poverty level, and who do not have third-party coverage, are eligible for a subsidized enrollment fee, and for transitional assistance amounting to $600 per year.

✓ Beginning January 1, 2006, all Medicare beneficiaries (those entitled to Part A or who are enrolled in Part B) are eligible for subsidized prescription drug coverage under Part D. Beneficiaries may access the subsidized coverage by enrolling in either a stand-alone prescription drug plan or an integrated Medicare Advantage plan. The latter offsets Part D coverage alongside the Medicare medical benefit. While the part D program is voluntary, a late-enrollment penalty will apply for beneficiaries who fail to enroll at the first opportunity and who do not maintain credible coverage elsewhere. Credible coverage can be any external prescription drug coverage that meets or exceeds the actuarial value of standard coverage in Part D. Unlike Part B, beneficiaries must opt into Part D by affirmatively electing a plan with drug coverage.

✓ Part D coverage includes most FDA approved drugs and biologics. Drugs currently covered in Parts A and B will remain covered there. Basic Part D coverage can consist of either the standard or an alternative design that provides the same actuarial value. For 2006, standard Part D coverage is defined as having a $250 deductible, with 25 percent coinsurance for drug costs above the deductible, and below the initial coverage limit of $2,250. The beneficiary is then responsible for all costs until the $3,600 out-of-pocket limit is reached. For higher costs, there is catastrophic coverage that requires enrollees to pay the greater of 5 percent or a small co-pay.

✓ The drug benefit will feature a new beneficiary premium, which represents 25.5 percent of the cost of basic coverage on the average. For prescription drug plans, and the drug portion of Medicare Advantage plans, the premium will be determined by bids. The 74.5 percent federal subsidy to prescription drug plans and Medicare Advantage plans will consist of a direct subsidy and reinsurance. The reinsurance will reimburse plans for 80 percent of drug costs in the catastrophic range. Beneficiaries with low incomes and modest assets will be eligible for subsidies that eliminate or reduce their Part D premiums and cost-sharing.

✓ With the availability of Part D drug coverage and low-income subsidies in 2006, Medicaid will no longer be the primary payer for full-benefit dual eligibles. States are subject to a contribution requirement and must continue to pay into the Part D account in the SMI Trust Fund a portion of their estimated foregone drug costs for this population.

Starting in 2006, states must pay 90 percent of the estimated costs, with this percentage phasing down over a ten-year period to 75 percent in 2015.

How Social Security and Medicare Are Currently Funded

Four so-called trust funds are studied in this book, in addition to Medicaid, which does not fall into the so-called trust fund category. Old Age and Survivors Insurance (OASI) pays retirement and survivors' benefits; Disability Insurance (DI) is self-explanatory. They are often combined and referred to as OASDI. The other two previously mentioned trust funds have to do with Medicare. HI pays for inpatient hospital and related care, and SMI pays for physicians and outpatient services.

The major sources of funding for OASI, DI, and HI are payroll taxes on earnings, which are paid by employees, employers, and the self-employed. Those who are self-employed pay both employer and employee taxes. The payroll tax rates are set by law. The tax rates for OASDI apply to earnings up to a specified annual amount. HI taxes are paid on total earnings (see Table 6). SMI is financed mainly by payments from general government revenues and monthly premiums charged to beneficiaries. The SMI premium is based on a method defined by law, and it increases as the estimated cost of SMI increases.

In 2005, 10.6 percent was the tax rate for Social Security—5.3 percent paid by the employer and 5.3 percent paid by the employee. The total tax rate for disability was 1.8 percent; with the employer and employee each contributing 0.9 percent. Thus, the total tax rate for Social Security and Disability Insurance amounted to 12.4 percent, where it has been since 1990. The income ceiling subject to tax is $90,000 in 2005. This ceiling is increased every year. The automatic adjustment is based on increases in average wages.

In 2004 the tax rates for the Hospital Insurance portion of Medicare totaled 2.9 percent—1.45 percent paid by the employer and 1.45 percent by the employee. These rate levels have been in place since 1986. Until 1991, the income ceiling was the same as that for OASDI—$53,000. After 1991 the ceiling was raised sharply, and in 1995 it was removed entirely. When OASI, DI, and the HI portion of Medicare are combined, the total employer-employee tax rate is 15.3 percent. Table 6 presents the history of tax rates and maximum taxable earnings since 1937.

Medicaid

Medicaid is a government program that pays medical costs for low-income individuals. The program was instituted in 1965 and is jointly funded by the federal and state governments in order to help the states in providing long-term medical assistance. Federal statute presents over twenty-five eligibility categories for which federal funds are available. They can be classified into five groups: children, pregnant women, adults in families with dependent children, individuals with disabilities, and individuals sixty-five years old and over.

About 42 million people were enrolled in Medicaid in 2003. It covers about one-quarter of the country's children and is the largest single purchaser of both maternity and long-term care services. In 2003 the elderly and those with disabilities represented about 30 percent of Medicaid beneficiaries, but accounted for two-thirds of its spending. In 2005, Medicaid spending is estimated to be $322 billion, of which $182 billion will be the federal share.

Each state establishes its own eligibility standards; determines the type, amount, duration, and scope of services; sets the rate of payment for services; and administers its own program. The amount, duration, and scope of each service must be sufficient to reasonably achieve its purpose. States may place appropriate limits on Medicaid services based on such criteria as medical necessity or utilization control. With some exceptions, a state's Medicaid plan must allow recipients freedom of choice among health care providers participating in Medicaid.

The amount of total federal outlays for Medicaid does not have a cap. The federal government must match whatever a state provides (within the law) for its eligible recipients. However, reimbursement rates must be sufficient to enlist enough providers so that Medicaid care and services are available to the general public in that geographical area. The portion of the Medicaid program that is paid by the federal government is determined annually for each state by a formula that compares the state's average per capita income level with the national average. By law the percentage cannot be lower than 50 percent or greater than 83 percent.

Medicaid was a medical care extension of the federally funded income maintenance programs for the poor, with an emphasis on the aged, the disabled, and disabled children and their mothers. Over time, Medicaid has been diverging from its firm requirements that applicants needed to pass in order to be eligible for cash programs. Legislation now ensures Medicaid coverage to an expanded number of low-income pregnant women, poor children, and some Medicare beneficiaries who are not eligible for any cash-assistance program and would not have been eligible for Medicaid under the earlier rules. The most significant trend in service delivery is the rapid growth in managed-care enrollment within Medicaid. Table 7 presents the magnitude of Medicaid payments beginning with 1961.

Table 7 is especially important for a number of reasons. The amount spent by the federal government on Medicaid is huge. In 2003, Medicaid expenditures by the federal government were $161 billion—a huge amount by any standard. Moreover, in a period of roughly a decade, the amount spent by the federal government annually on Medicaid has virtually doubled. Remember, this is only the federal government's share of Medicaid. The federal government is matching what the states are spending. Looking ahead, it will be hard to hold down the growth of Medicaid spending by both the federal and state governments as the number of elderly increase, and so do the number who move down the ladder from Medicare to Medicaid.

Despite these impending circumstances, there is no financial plan on the part of either the federal or state governments to finance future Medicaid outlays. Since the federal government has much greater capabilities to raise future funds than do the states, it is the state governments that will feel most of the financial pain. This is already happening. It is little wonder that the pressure on state governments to cut back on Medicaid programs has already begun.

The handwriting is on the wall. It is only a matter of time before a financial crisis in Medicaid occurs, and the crisis will fall directly on the states. The next recession will surely bring about the inevitable, and then the key question will be whether the federal government takes over a growing part of Medicaid in order to fill the void? Or, worse yet, whether the benefit void continues, and then expands. In looking at the president's recent budget documents, there is nothing that indicates there is any provision for dealing with an impending Medicaid crisis.

It should be evident that the federal government cannot afford to sit on its hands and wait for what appears to be the inevitable. There are things that it can do if it uses some creativity. For example, have the federal government base how much it gives to a state in Medicaid payments on whether a state has devised specific and adequate funding sources for Medicaid.

The federal government would not dictate the sources to be tapped by states. Each state could choose its own approach to funding, as long as the amount involved was sufficient to meet federal government requirements. Also, the money raised by the states would have to be specifically earmarked for Medicaid spending. The money could not be diverted to other uses.

This is another one of those situations where a carrot and a stick approach can be used. If a state does not have specifically earmarked sources to fund Medicaid, then the federal government would not fully match a state's funding. However, if a state does have specifically earmarked sources, then the federal government would provide something extra.

If this type of approach were adopted, it would make financial life easier for states, especially during difficult economic times. Recessions are especially painful for low-income people, and recessions are difficult times for states to scrounge around and try to raise new money. If a systematic funding approach is already in place, it will be easier for states from both an economic and political point of view to raise additional money. Moreover, in a recession, it would be much appreciated by both states, and Medicaid recipients, if the federal government were to chip in something above the current split.

Where We Came From

Here we are in a new century. Economic growth is strong, the unemployment rate is declining, inflation is moderate, and interest rates are low. After rallying from its recent slump, the stock market is holding its own, financial institutions are on a sound footing, and U.S. economic growth is again the envy of the world. To be sure, some dark clouds are in evidence—such as the current account and budget deficits—but so far the rain has held off.

Contrast these circumstances with the early 1930s, when the Social Security system was implemented. The economy was in depression, the unemployment rate was well into double digits, the stock market had collapsed, financial institutions were in ruin, most savings had been depleted, and private pensions were few and far between. Pessimism reigned, and many people lived hand-to-mouth. Conditions were dire. The private sector was incapable of providing meaningful assistance. The elderly were especially hard hit. The only entity to turn to was the government; it was the only one with resources—it had the power to tax and borrow. It was under these circumstances that the Social Security system came into being.

It is easy for us to look back over seven decades and be critical of those who designed the Social Security system; but we forget that it was a different population then, with different needs. In a country racked by economic despair, a Social Security system that relied heavily on government borrowing was the only practical financing alternative at the time. The depressed state of the economy and the financial markets made it virtually impossible to create a system where tax inflows and investment earnings would be sufficient to meet benefit payments. A real trust fund with real investment would have been impossible. Under these circumstances, the government had no viable options.

Social Security has had little in the way of significant amendments since its inception; yet one has to say that the founders achieved what they set out to do. The government provided a safety net for the elderly who had no other place to turn. The founders of the system could not have anticipated the dramatic improvement in the prosperity of the country, and equally dramatic changes in life expectancy and the size of the population.

The Social Security program is not significantly different from its early years. This is due in good part to the advent of Medicare and Medicaid, which have addressed many of the financial needs not met by Social Security. Furthermore, legislators have been more willing to make changes in Medicare and Medicaid than in Social Security. That is the good news. The bad news is that an excessive amount of public and official attention has been devoted to "fixing" a Social Security system that is *not* in financial difficulty and is *not* going broke. Meanwhile, not enough attention is being paid to Medicare and Medicaid, where the deficits have spun out of control, and no attempt is being made to fund them properly. Properly funding any of these programs does not mean cutting benefits. Yet, in 1983, Congress did cut future benefits, based primarily on recommendations by the National Commission on Social Security Reform.

Down the road, another commission will surely be formed. It is hoped that, at that time, Social Security, Medicare, and Medicaid will be analyzed as a package, with considerable emphasis placed on funding, and on the relationship between benefits and what they cost the American taxpayer. Such an approach would go a long way toward helping the public understand the relationships and the proper funding of these programs.

Where We Are Now

The public pays too much attention to Social Security and not enough attention to Medicare and Medicaid. This is understandable, but questionable. If you pay into a system over a working lifetime, you believe you should get that money back, with interest, in your later years. The thinking is that, after all, it's your money. The attitude is different with respect to Medicare and Medicaid. They are viewed as programs funded primarily by the government. The personal attachment to the money is not the same as in the case of Social Security. The fact that one way or the other, Medicare and Medicaid are financed by taxpayers does not seem to be personal enough. This explains why Social Security is on the minds of almost all adult Americans, but that is not the case with respect to Medicare and Medicaid.

Unfortunately, the public does not fully understand these three programs. With Social Security, the problem seems to be a misunderstanding of how the system operates. The most commonly held misconceptions are that there is actual money in the Social Security Trust Fund, that ultimately the money will run out, and when that happens, retirees will no longer receive their benefits. When it is suggested that benefits should be cut, or that the age at which benefits payments start should be raised, some people feel that it is better to get something rather than nothing. Shame on those who propagate such suggestions.

The story that needs to be told is that Social Security is a pay-as-you-go system. The government is obligated to meet the benefit payments, and the money to meet these obligations can be raised any way the government chooses. It can come from employer-employee tax payments, other taxes, or it can come from borrowing. Thus, when it comes to recipients receiving benefits, the fact that there are nonexistent funds in a nonexistent trust account is not important.

Also pertinent in this analysis is that if the government were to pay Social Security benefits entirely from employer-employee tax payments, it could do so for a much longer period of time than is officially estimated. As a matter of fact, if annual real GDP growth should average about 3 percent, employer-employee taxes could probably fund Social Security benefits indefinitely. The system may be in need of a small adjustment of the sort that Congress has approved in the past, but it is also entirely possible (which Social Security actuaries acknowledge) that it is solvent as is. Ideology aside, the scale of the fixes would not require Social Security to abandon the role that was conceived for it in 1935. Thus, there is no reason to cut back on future Social Security benefits, and there is no reason to spend time, effort, and money devising an elaborate investment program that diverts funds that could directly pay current benefits.

With respect to Medicare and Medicaid, the funding problems are much more severe than generally realized. Thus, there are plenty of reasons to focus on the financing problems of these two programs—and it is better that these problems are addressed sooner rather than later. The main cause of these financing problems is that Medicare and Medicaid benefit payments are growing rapidly; only a portion of Medicare is funded by employer-employee taxes and by monthly payment from beneficiaries; the prescription drug program is likely to cost far more than expected, and none of Medicaid's benefits are funded by specific taxes. With Medicare and Medicaid deficits growing by leaps and bounds, this puts pressure on the government to limit other programs.

Where We Should Be Heading

At first glance one might say, let's spend more time and effort solving Medicare and Medicaid financing problems and less time worrying about Social Security. That is not the right approach. Why not look at the three programs together? Why not raise enough money every year through employer-employee taxes to finance Social Security, Medicare, and the federal government's part of Medicaid? Taxes paid in should be related to benefits paid out.

The more that taxes are directly related to benefits, the greater the pressure to prioritize when it comes to benefit increases. For example, would it have been worthwhile to pay 1 or 2 percent more in employer-employee tax rates in order to pay for a prescription drug program? If the answer is no, then what is the proper trade-off between higher taxes and new benefits? Asking the right question is paramount in order to arrive at the right answer.

The best way to look at these three programs is to view them as a package. After all, they are related both from an economic and social perspective. As a matter of fact, many individuals will receive payments from all three programs. Unfortunately, as Social Security and Medicare benefits for the elderly do not meet their needs, these people eventually end up a Medicaid recipient. This unfortunate progression puts a burden on the entire U.S. tax system, not to mention the fact that those in their twilight years who slip into poverty through no fault of their own deserve a better fate.

The approach recommended here is unique in that it looks at Social Security, Medicare, and Medicaid as a whole and places primary emphasis on affordability and proper funding. The centerpiece of the funding recommendations is a pay-as-you-go approach, with specific annual taxes paid to fund specific annual benefits. As of now, increases in benefits paid by Medicare and Medicaid seem unrelated to the cost borne by the taxpayer. Needs are not measured against tax burdens. The result is that there is little pressure to hold down the size of the programs or improve their quality.

If these three related areas were viewed as a package, one way of controlling this package on both the receipts and spending sides would be to adopt a Gramm-Rudman type of approach. For those who do not remember the basic thrust of Gramm-Rudman (which unfortunately was superseded in

1990 by much less effective legislation), if government spending were to be increased in discretionary areas, either taxes would have to be raised or benefits cut to pay for the new spending. These recommendations, if they had been in place, could have significantly improved the prescription drug legislation that was passed in late 2003.

With respect to prescription drug legislation, on a scale of one to ten, the desire to help the elderly would be rated a ten, the cost-effectiveness of the benefit package would be a five, and the funding of the program would be a one. Good intentions by themselves should not have been enough to pass this piece of legislation. The country is not rich enough to have programs based solely on good intentions that cost a great deal of money and are not properly financed.

Thus the passage of this legislation was a good-news bad-news proposition. First the good news. There was a need for broadly based prescription drug legislation because many people had either limited or no coverage, and the cost of prescription drugs had become onerous. The legislation that passed had bipartisan support, and that support continues. There were no sunset provisions, which meant that the program is permanent. The legislation was supported, and continues to be supported, by influential and well-intentioned groups such as the American Association of Retired People.

However, the bad news is not inconsequential. Little attention was paid to the costs and funding. Can Americans afford the package that was passed, especially when no specific funding source—or funding cost for that source—is specified? The legislation is complicated, which means that many will not understand the benefits or the costs. Complicated legislation today often leads to even more complicated amendments tomorrow. The greater the complexities, the less likely that the program will be cost-effective.

We now have in place a prescription drug program[1] where the cost is underestimated, and will become even more expensive as time goes on. Funding sources will be inadequate to pay for the program, and there are no checks and balances with respect to revenues versus benefits. If adequate revenue sources had been part of the original legislation, pressure would have been greater to make benefits more cost-effective. Simply put, the program should have been a trade-off between tax costs and benefit outlays.

Finally, think about what the approach to prescription drug legislation might have been if the recommendations made in this book were in place. The cost of the program would have been balanced against the amount of the increase needed in employer-employee tax rates. This would have put pressure on the legislators to come forward with their most cost-effective program. The politicians would not want to pass legislation where the political cost of raising tax rates would be greater than the political benefits from instituting the program. By having specific tax rate increases to pay for specific benefit increases, the costs and who pays them cannot be hidden. Moreover, if costs prove to be underestimated, the piper will ultimately be paid, since down the road, employer-employee tax rates will have to be raised.

Trade-offs are at the core of many of the recommendations in this book—who pays and how much versus who receives and how much. The basic philosophy is that the current generation of workers pays, and the current generation of retirees receives; the next generation of workers pays, and the next generation of retirees receives.

———————)((◐))(———————

Chapter 6

MISCONCEPTIONS AND MYTHS ABOUT SOCIAL SECURITY

It isn't only the average citizen who harbors misconceptions about Social Security. This is also the case with respect to many individuals in the public sector despite their assertion of expertise in this area. And many politicians— who should know better—are often the main offenders. This was evident during both the 2000 and 2004 elections, when the lack of understanding of this topic on both sides of the aisle was an embarrassment. It is one thing to propose questionable recommendations, but it is something else to have no real understanding of how the system works.

The Green Book, which is prepared by the Ways and Means Committee of the House of Representatives, explains in detail how the Social Security system actually works. It places considerable emphasis on cash coming into the government, and where the money is spent. It also explains why the Social Security trust fund is not a trust fund in the commonly thought sense. The information will surprise many readers. The following are some key quotes (italics added) from *The Green Book:*

> *Contrary to popular belief, social security taxes are not deposited into the Social Security Trust Fund.* They flow each day into thousands of depository accounts maintained by the government with financial institutions across the country; along with many other forms of revenues, these social security taxes become part of the government's operations cash pool.

Once these taxes are received, they become indistinguishable from other moneys the government takes in. They are accounted for separately through the issuance of federal securities to the Social Security Trust Fund—which basically involves a series of bookkeeping entries by the Treasury—*but the trust funds themselves do not receive or hold money. They are simply accounts.* Similarly, benefits are not paid from the trust funds, but from the Treasury. As the checks are paid, securities of an equivalent value are removed from the trust fund accounts.

When more social security taxes are received than are spent, *the money does not sit idle in the Treasury, but is used to finance other operations of the government.* The surplus is then reflected in a higher balance of securities being posted to the trust funds. Simply put, these balances, like those of a bank account, represent a promise that, if needed to pay social security benefits, the government will obtain resources in the future equal to the value of the securities. Federal securities issued to any federal trust fund represent permission to spend.

When the government issues a security to one of its own accounts, it hasn't purchased anything or established a claim against some other person or entity. It is simply creating an IOU from one of its accounts to another. Hence, the building up of federal securities in a federal trust fund—like that of social security—*is not a means in and of itself to accumulate assets.* It certainly has established claims against the government for the Social Security System is part of the government. *These claims are not resources the government has at its disposal to pay future social security benefits.*

The significance of having trust funds for social security is that they represent a long-term commitment of the government to the program. While *the funds do not hold "reserves" that the government can call on to pay social security benefits,* the balances of federal securities posted to them represent and have served as financial claims against the government—claims on which the Treasury has never defaulted, nor used directly as a basis to finance anything but social security expenditures.

The surplus social security taxes being collected today are not the means through which most of the future cost of the system will be met. Most of today's taxes are used to cover payments to today's retirees. The future costs to the system will largely be met through future taxation. The promise of future benefits rests primarily on the government's ability to levy taxes in the future, not on the balances of the trust funds.

Many things complicate any determination of the relationship of benefits to taxes for future retirees. Although social security tax rates and benefit formulas are set by law, they are not immutable. Since Congress has modified taxes and benefits many times since the beginning of the program, it is clearly inconsistent with the program's history to calculate taxes and benefits into the future on the assumption that these key elements will not change. There is little doubt they eventually will be altered. Changes would obviously affect the relationship of taxes to benefits. However, the nature of future changes is unknown, whereas current law is given.

Further complicating the issue is the nature of the program. *As a "social insurance" program, social security has both social and insurance goals. The social-goal features provide a design that deliberately gives a better return on taxes to some workers than to others. For example, the basic formula for calculating social security benefits is tilted to repay a higher proportion of earnings for lower-paid workers. Also, a complex array of dependents' benefits is available at no additional cost for workers with families.*

As with insurance, the exact relationship of social security benefits received to total taxes paid cannot be predicted for each and every worker. For example, workers who die before or shortly after retirement and leave no survivors may collect only a few dollars in benefits or perhaps none at all. Other workers may collect social security benefits for many years after retirement and receive benefits substantially greater than the value of their social security taxes. Workers who become disabled or die at an early age might have paid relatively little in social security taxes, but they or their families may receive benefits for many years, recovering the value of the worker's taxes many times.

Also, *there really is no "typical" social security beneficiary with a "typical" work history.* An "average" benefit can be the result of many different work histories and thus be based on different amounts of taxes paid. For example, because the benefit formula does not require that all earnings be used in the benefit computation, workers with gaps in their earnings history may receive the same benefits as other workers, but pay less in total taxes.

It is also readily apparent that past retirees recovered the value of their taxes very quickly. Payback times, however, have lengthened for workers retiring today, but they are still significantly shorter than those projected for future retirees. This is ameliorated somewhat by the projection that future retirees are expected to live longer, and thus collect benefits longer.

The concept of the program is that it serves social ends that transcend the calculation of which individual or generation obtains some sort of balance-sheet profit or loss. Pay-as-you-go retirement systems such as social security, by their very nature often provide large returns on the contributions of the initial generations. In the early years of such programs, the rate of workers to recipients is very high, allowing tax or contribution rates to be low. As the program matures, rates rise to reflect the increase in the number of beneficiaries. This is not unique to social security. Establishing benefit levels for early recipients in excess of what contributions would dictate is also found in private pension systems.

Providing "adequate" benefits to initial social security recipients that were essentially "unearned" in relation to their contributions to the system has been justified on the basis of social policy. Providing a minimum level of protection to

the first workers to participate in the system was considered more important
in a period of economic depression than concerns about excessive rates of
return on taxes paid.

*Besides, the social benefits of giving a measure of economic independence for the
elderly, and later for orphaned children, surviving spouses, and the disabled, are believed by many to be immense.* For example, younger workers are in large part
relieved from the financial burden of supporting their parents, and the elderly
are afforded an opportunity to live independently and with dignity.

Myths

The House Ways and Means Committee *Green Book* indicates how the
Social Security system works. After reading the previous quotes, it should be
evident that there are many misconceptions about the system. These misconceptions lead to other misconceptions, which in turn lead to improper
conclusions and policies. The following presents a brief summary of some of
the major myths.

1. ***The Social Security System needs to be saved.*** The Social Security system
   has no chance of failing—never did and never will—therefore, it does not
   need to be "saved." It is a pay-as-you-go system. The government has the
   power to tax, the ability to borrow, and it can use any source of funds
   available to pay Social Security benefits. Social Security payments come
   from the same tax-and-borrow pie as other government outlays, yet no one has
   expressed any concern that the government will be unable to raise enough
   money to meet military obligations or interest payments.

   Social Security accounts are only very slightly out of balance over the
   long-term. The Congressional Budget Office puts the 75-year shortfall at
   just four-tenths of 1 percent of the GDP. To put it another way, the cost of
   the Bush tax cuts over that same 75-year period will be three times larger
   than Social Security's financing gap.

   A slight increase in wage growth—1 percent point more than currently
   projected—would also eliminate most of the Social Security shortfall.
   Given our previous discussion about the wage stagnation and growing
   economic insecurity faced by American families, efforts to increase wage
   growth across the population—through minimum wages pegged to inflation, labor law reform, investment in early education and public infrastructure, and greater monetary policy sensitive to employment growth—
   would expand opportunity as well as place our entitlement programs on a
   sounder footing.

2. ***Social Security receipts are set aside in a trust fund.*** If you can find the
   money, let us know where it is. Every year Social Security tax inflows are

also used to help pay government obligations in general, such as military costs, interest on the public debt, and social programs. Nothing is saved and nothing is left over. When Social Security tax inflows are greater than Social Security outflows, the government recognizes it by the flick of a pen (or now, a computer key) and gives the trust fund a nonmarketable IOU from the Treasury. The so-called trust fund will then earn imputed interest in the form of more nonmarketable government IOUs.

3. *If there were no Social Security taxes and no trust fund, beneficiaries would not receive their money.* Wrong again. It wouldn't make a dime's worth of difference to those receiving benefits. Remember, Social Security is a pay-as-you-go system, and no one source is earmarked to meet Social Security outlays. If there were no Social Security taxes the government would find other revenue sources, such as raising other taxes or borrowing money. To make this point even stronger, suppose there were no Social Security taxes and the Treasury IOUs held by the so-called trust fund were torched or eliminated, with the flick of a computer key. Also assume that employers do not pay in regularly, employees do not pay in regularly, and the government announces there are no assets in the trust fund. What would all this mean to Social Security beneficiaries? Absolutely nothing! They would still get their money, as the government would do what it has to do in order to meet these obligations.

The whole notion of the Trust Fund has twisted the Social Security debate in damaging ways. Advocates of privatization seem to want to have it both ways with regard to the Trust Fund, and the supposed 'crisis' of Social Security. Today, when the payroll tax takes in more revenue than goes out in benefits, they declare the Trust Fund meaningless. Or worse, actually: its empty, and the American people have been sold a bill of goods. But then they argue that in 2018, when benefits supposedly start to exceed the payroll tax, we've got a crisis. Either the Trust Fund is meaningless (as we argue), or it isn't. One cannot say it is meaningless now, in order to raise fears about the viability of Social Security, and then suddenly invoke its sudden collapse in a few decades time as a justification for privatization. The idea of a non-existent Trust Fund has become so associated in the public mind with the privatization argument that some readers will undoubtedly wonder about our position on this. We are consistent. Privatization advocates are not. If Social Security is just a part of the budget, then there can't be a Social Security crisis. There can be a general budget crisis, of course, but Social Security won't be responsible. Unless we privatize part of it, that is.

Once we acknowledge that the Trust Fund doesn't matter, we can move away from the useless debate about the magical date when Social Security runs out of money, and towards how in the long run to make sure that tax revenues for Social Security are sufficient to pay for the benefits that are promised and distributed. This is why Social Security is a manageable problem: all we need to do is try to bring revenues and benefits into some kind of reasonable balance over the long-term. We offer concrete ways of doing this, without harming the elderly and their families.[1]

4. *A pay-as-you-go system cannot work indefinitely.* Pay-as-you-go is an excellent idea when the tax side imposes limits on the benefit side. It can also be an excellent idea if it induces the government to get rid of the trust fund concept and designates specific tax sources to meet specific needs, such as Social Security, Medicare, and Medicaid payments. If specific receipts are applied to specific outlays, this can counter unduly large and not-well-planned benefit programs.

5. *Benefits that individuals receive will be less than what they pay into the system.* Most recipients, to date, have received much more in benefits than what they paid in. This situation is not likely to change in the foreseeable future as people live longer after retirement. This is so, even though there will be some diminution of benefits as the age for receiving full benefits is extended under current law. Also, individual contributions are only part of the tax payments; employers pay an equal amount. On the benefits side, the payments made by the government contain some subsidies based on social considerations, such as payments to families. Some tax benefits also exist. Thus, not only should individuals have little concern about whether they receive benefits, they should have little concern that they are being shortchanged.

6. *It is important for Social Security payment increases to keep pace with wages.* Keeping pace with wages is not as important for beneficiaries as keeping pace with their living costs; it is the latter that strongly influences a beneficiary's standard of living. Some people, such as Federal Reserve Chairman Greenspan, have long recommended that a different index be substituted for wage increases in computing cost-of-living adjustments for Social Security recipients. While there is logic to such an approach, there is also a problem. What is substituted for the current approach must be acceptable to the general public, to vested interest groups, and to the politicians. Our proposal, which is a modified form of the price index for personal consumption expenditures, is an attempt to create an acceptable compromise for groups that have different agendas.

7. *The only way to fix Social Security is by further increasing the age when benefits start.* It is unnecessary to further cut future benefits by changing the age when benefits are first received. In 1983 future benefits were reduced by legislation that increased the age requirement for full payment, and there are proponents today who want to do the same thing again. Well-intentioned but misguided groups are searching for ways to lower future benefits above and beyond changing the COLA so that they meet future (but underestimated) payroll tax inflows. Little time is spent on other alternatives, some of which we document in this book.

8. *A conflict of interest exists between the young and the old with regard to Social Security reform.* Not so. The elderly and soon-to-be-elderly want to make sure they continue to receive their benefits. They have little interest in how the government finances the payments to them, but that does not stop their strong personal interest in having the system work properly for their children and grandchildren. It is true that the elderly are gaining political power because their numbers are growing more rapidly than the rest of the population. Yet, taking advantage of other groups is not part of their agenda. Those who favor privatization of Social Security have long argued that self-interested seniors represent the greatest obstacle to their reform ideas. It is true that seniors (according to polls) consistently oppose privatization more than any other age group. They want the size of their benefits (and how they are taxed) maintained on an uninterrupted basis. But of course, they have little to gain one way or the other from privatization reforms undertaken now, since none of the plans currently under consideration apply to people over the age of 55. Self-interest alone, then, clearly doesn't explain their opposition. A better explanation is that as one ages, the possibility of having to live out your sunset years in poverty becomes vivid and real. This gives rise to some degree of sympathy for those who might suffer this fate, now or in the future. This sympathy, of course, naturally extends to their own children and grandchildren, and fears for their future. The elderly want a system where all groups—such as their children and grandchildren—ultimately benefit. The kind of empathy expressed by our nation's elderly, hard won over the years, is both promoted and embodied by Social Security itself. It shouldn't be dismissed. They know what they are talking about.

Feeding Confidence Fears

It is hard to understand where this sudden "crisis" talk with regard to Social Security came from without understanding the politics and philosophy behind the idea of privatization. Pessimism about the ability of our government to honor future obligations may have justifiably increased over the past few years, but the reasons have little to do with Social Security. What has changed, of course, is that the Federal government has a huge deficit—and with no end in sight. Social Security has been run well; but much of the rest of our government has not. So why are we talking about a Social Security crisis?[2]

Some people, both inside and outside the government, have a goal of shrinking government down to the smallest level possible. That is their goal, and privatizing all or part of Social Security is a means to an end. One approach being used is to try to convince the American people via the media that Social Security is in crisis and that should be taken as a fact. Of course, it isn't a fact.

Politicians and other observers tend to talk as if the trustees' seventy-five year projections were precise. Social Security's own actuaries don't claim such certainty, of course. For this reason, they make three different projections of economic and demographic data. They have also changed them frequently, and their accuracy leaves something to be desired. In 1994 the system was supposed to go bust in 2029, according to the Social Security trustees.[3] Back on May 15, 2000, when soon-to-be-president George W. Bush made a major speech on partial privatization, he used an exhaustion date of 2037. In the trustees' annual report published in March 2004, the so-called exhaustion date for the trust account was 2042, and now a Congressional Budget Office study indicates that 2052 is the best estimate for the exhaustion date. The "doomsday date" continues to be shifted frequently and always farther into the future. It gets shifted into the future because the data and facts require it to be shifted that way. Moreover, there is more shifting into the future to come.

Much of our reasoning is based on the following, which we will present in greater detail in the next chapter. The trustees' estimates made in 2004 assume 3.6 percent real GDP growth in 2005, with the growth rate gradually slipping to 2.2 percent by 2013. They then estimate that annual growth will slip to 1.8 percent by 2015, and stay there until supposedly the trust fund is exhausted. The average annual growth between now and the exhaustion date is 2.0 percent.

In contrast, in the years from 1960 to 2004, the average annual growth rate in GDP was 3.3 percent. While it is optimistic to think that a growth rate of 3.3 percent could be duplicated, it should be pointed out that Chairman Greenspan of the Federal Reserve believes that in recent years there has been an underlying improvement in productivity, and it is productivity that is the linchpin that allows economic growth to take place. Maybe the Social Security trustees should ask the Federal Reserve to present them with estimates of long-term economic growth rates and use those numbers in computing Social Security revenue inflows.

An administration trying to convince people that market investments are the place to be will first need to refute the unduly low economic growth forecasts of the Social Security trustees. Up to this point, they have not done it. Obviously, if the economic growth rate slumps to only 1.8 percent and stays there, the one place not to be invested would be the stock market. In our view, the trustees' economic growth forecast is grossly underestimated and the stock market will probably do reasonably well, but so will payroll tax revenues and the financial state of the Social Security system.

Another factor to consider is that a good performance of the stock market over a long time does investors little good if they have to take out their money when the stock market is weak and declining. It also does the country little good if people are taking their money out under such circumstances because it could lead to cumulative downward momentum in equity prices. For nonsophisticated investors, in deciding what to do, they will not have time, patience, and knowledge on their side.

Moreover, when money is taken out of the stock market by Social Security recipients when the market is not doing well, it is likely the economy will not be doing well. This means the budget will not be doing well, and neither will the size of Social Security payroll tax inflows. At that point the key question will be whether the government will bail out Social Security recipients that have made bad investments, and if so, how will the government do it?

Our view is that there is nothing wrong with limiting the size of government, but if some meaningful form of Social Security privatization takes place, then the government will somewhere down the line be more involved, not less involved, in the affairs of individuals. Privatizing some part of Social Security now will at some point lead to new government programs, not fewer ones.[4]

Furthermore, it has become common practice to argue that our changing demographics have doomed the Social Security Trust Fund. The aging of the population will leave us with too many retirees for too few workers. While this is important, it should be pointed out that the trustees built this adversity into their estimates. It therefore doesn't make sense to double-count these demographic adversities, especially when using overly pessimistic economic forecasts as well.

Finally, while the demographic problem is real, it is more manageable than many realize. First, the trustees predict a sharp rebound in longevity, even though improvements in mortality have slowed significantly in the past decade. Second, it is true that in 1950 there were sixteen workers paying in to Social Security for every worker drawing benefits, and that by the time the baby boomers begin to retire, the ratio will be two to one. However, most of this transition happened before the mid-seventies, and this trend has slowed noticeably. To put it another way, while the ratio of people of working age to those either under twenty or over sixty-five will decline from 1.5 today to 1.2 in 2050, the latter number still remains an easier burden than what working Americans faced in 1965. Most observers also believe that the trustees have underestimated the impact of future immigration. They predict that it will taper off sharply. Given the steady and increasing flow of immigrants in recent years, and the predicted shortage of adult workers, an increase seems more likely. In fact, substantial immigration could eliminate the Social Security shortfall all by itself. If the immigration doesn't materialize, the worker shortage should boost wages, which could also eliminate the fiscal gap. The demographic doomsday scenario is exaggerated.[5]

What Crisis?

Despite the facts, many Americans believe the Social Security system is on the verge of collapse, and if it is not saved, they will never get their money. When officials talk about the need to "save" the system, they are adding to this misconception. Yes, the financing of the system needs to be reexamined along with the financing of Medicare and Medicaid, but the Social Security system does not need to be saved because it is not on the verge of collapse. Yet, trying to explain the true Social Security picture to the American people, and even to many politicians, is an uphill battle.

Unfortunately, the "trust fund" analogy has contributed to the perception of crisis. As Dean Baker suggests, Social Security is in crisis "in the same way that a car headed westward in the middle of Kansas faces a crisis. If it doesn't stop or turn, the car will eventually fall into the Pacific Ocean, but it's hard to get too worried about the possibility." We agree.[6]

As Paul Krugman of the *New York Times* has pointed out, there are only two ways that Social Security would be unable to pay full benefits in 2018: if Congress votes specifically to repudiate the trust fund, and therefore not honor its debts to retirees (a political impossibility), or if the nation is in a general fiscal crisis and is unable to honor any of its debt.[7]

Ultimately, however, the assurance that workers will get their benefits rests on the faith and credit of the government's promise to do so—in other words, on our willingness as a society to keep our promises to one another. Since we have a representative democracy in which politicians are held accountable both by elections and the rule of law, this shouldn't be an issue.

Chapter 7

GOVERNMENT CANNOT LEGISLATE INVESTMENT SUCCESS

After the bear market in stocks in 2000 and 2001, partial privatization proposals receded into the background. After the stock market recovery, especially in 2003 and 2004, such proposals reemerged. It is amazing how bear and bull markets in stocks can influence privatization proposals. What should be clear is that bull markets tend to create false optimism while bear markets create excessive pessimism.

The time period used to measure performance is very important. In the long run there are good and bad time periods for the stock market. The same is true for stocks in individual industries and companies, although their specific performance often does not mirror the general performance of the market. This means that the period from when a person starts making long-term retirement investments and stops making those investments is of paramount importance with regard to their performance. Remember, most individuals have little flexibility as to when they retire. Tell the people who retired in 2000 and 2001 during a major stock market meltdown, who had to withdraw considerable amounts of money to live on, that they made wise investment decisions. Almost all high-tech investors are still licking their wounds.

Equity Investments and the Safety Net

The constant emphasis on returns misunderstands the purpose of Social Security and the role it plays in the lives of most Americans. Social Security was intended to be a safety net—a kind of retirement insurance. Social Security benefits do not run out, are guaranteed by the full faith and credit of the U.S. government, and are pegged to inflation. People cannot necessarily live well on Social Security benefits alone, but they will last as long as you do. The purpose of Social Security is not to help people get rich, it is to help guarantee that the elderly can live the rest of their lives with dignity.

There are other means for Americans willing to undertake greater risk for greater reward, and we should consider making those investment vehicles more attractive and broadly available. But Social Security was designed to provide a baseline protection against the risks and vicissitudes of the market economy. If private accounts don't do as well as anticipated, there could be a hole in the safety net that could put millions of Americans at risk. Low- and moderate-income people would be especially vulnerable; the results could be catastrophic. Lower returns than privatizers claim are actually a logical implication of the low profit growth projections of the Social Security trustees, coupled with the relatively high price-to-earnings ratio in the stock market at present. This is especially true if one takes mutual fund fees and administrative costs into account. Using more realistic estimated returns, analysts at Goldman Sachs concluded that privatization under the probable Bush plan is likely to leave families worse off than under the present system.[1] Yale economist Robert Shiller came to the same conclusion.[2] All private account proposals include cuts in expected benefits for those who choose to divert a portion of their payroll tax contributions. Many also include the use of progressive price indexing, which would reduce expected benefits for the majority of American workers. Given the growth of economic insecurity, the privatization of risk, and the soundness of the Social Security system as a whole, this kind of 'reform' strikes us as unnecessary and counterproductive.

Good Regulatory Rules Do Not Guarantee Good Investment Results

One of the authors of this book was on the board of a family of mutual funds for over three decades, and it is clear to him that you can have all the rules and regulations you want, but they will not guarantee investment success. Rules and regulations are created to keep investment managers on the straight and narrow and have them follow proper governance approaches. It is the performance of the markets and the investment managers that will determine success.

When politicians tell the American people that only safe investments will be allowed in privatized investments and that no speculation or day-trading will take place, they are overpromising. If mutual funds were to make such claims in their current advertising, they would have major regulatory problems.

Finally, it should be pointed out that the devil is in the details when it comes to rules and regulations. If you don't think so, have the proponents of privatization answer the following questions:

- ✓ Would investors be allowed to place money in current portfolios, or would a whole new series of investment funds have to be devised?

- ✓ Could equity fund managers aggressively trade their portfolios?

- ✓ Would there be quality and size standards in the securities purchased?

- ✓ Could the fund manager invest in foreign securities?

- ✓ Could currency risks be taken, and what hedging approaches would be allowed?

- ✓ Could a fund manager be allowed to trade in options and futures, and make investments in derivatives?

- ✓ Could money be placed in index-type investments, and if so, which ones?

- ✓ Could the managers hold large cash positions?

- ✓ Could convertible issues be bought, and if so, would there be a maximum?

- ✓ Would the size of purchases or sales of securities be limited because of their influence on the market's direction and momentum?

- ✓ Who would have the power to hire or fire the investment managers, and how long would it take?

- ✓ How much of the operating results would be made public, and what would be the time lag?

- ✓ Could the managers be paid on the basis of current industry standards?

- ✓ Would there be operating cost restrictions?

- ✓ Could the fund managers charge load and marketing fees?

- ✓ Would there be a limit on annual management fees?

- ✓ Could managers receive bonuses for good performance?

- ✓ Who would monitor the trading procedures and operations?

- ✓ Who would monitor the investment managers for improper pricing of securities and collusion?

- ✓ Would soft-dollar payments for research be allowed?

- ✓ Would it be proper for public officials to "talk up" the stock market, especially before an election?

✓ Who would be the regulator, or regulators, and how would the chain of command work?

✓ In a litigious society, how can we control the legal costs and unnecessary cases?

✓ Finally, who would be responsible to the American people if things go terribly wrong since, more likely than not, those who created partial privatization would be out of office? Whatever the flaws of publicly run programs, elected officials are theoretically accountable.

Will Low- and Middle-Income People Be Taking Excessive Risks?

Our present retirement savings system has three components presented in an ascending order of risk: Social Security benefits, employer-provided pensions, and private savings. Low- and middle-income Americans are less likely than others to have assets of any consequence in pensions and private savings. The number of workers covered by employer-provided defined-benefit plans has dropped precipitously in recent decades; today it is very uncommon for most Americans below the median income to have access to such plans. They are also less likely to be employed by companies that offer defined-contribution plans, less likely to choose them when offered, and less likely to have family budgets that allow them to make good use of these plans.

The only component of this tripartite retirement savings system that is guaranteed, pegged to costs, and lifelong is Social Security. Privatization will introduce risk into the one part of the system that doesn't have it presently. It will also involve future cuts in guaranteed benefits. The further down the income scale one goes, the more families need and value security over risk—and the more important those guaranteed benefits become. Thus, privatization of Social Security can do disproportionate harm to those who can least afford it.

The risk that investing inherently involves is of course greatly exacerbated by the relative knowledge (and risk tolerance) of the investor, and the timing of when the investments are drawn on or liquidated. Who is to properly advise low- and middle-income people as to whether they should make their own investment decisions, and if so, how they should invest their funds? If they decide to make such investments, a considerable number are likely to be either overly aggressive or overly conservative. This is something they don't have to worry about under the current Social Security system.

Our experiences with 401(k)'s and private account options offered to state and county employees over the past few decades would seem to indicate that most Americans—not just the poor and the uneducated—either make poor investment decisions when given the chance, or prefer not to be given the chance at all. One-quarter of those eligible to participate in a 401(k) choose not to do so, often passing up an employer match. Less than 10 percent of those who do participate contribute the maximum.

According to Alice Munnell, formerly of Clinton's Council of Economic Advisers, most 401(k) investors don't diversify, don't rebalance their portfolios in response to aging or market returns, and over invest in company stock. Moreover, most Americans lack sufficient financial experience, education or time to learn how to watch out for their own interests. Indeed, in 2001 the Labor Department made a rule change that allows investment companies to hire independent advisory firms to manage 401(k) accounts for individual investors.

Much of the logic of partial or full privatization of Social Security seems to be based on the assumption that the shift towards individualized defined-contribution plans in the private sector over the past few decades has been a success. In fact, as was discussed in Chapter Three, the privatization of risk has only been a success for corporate employers. It has been a disaster for individual workers and their families. The practical reality of 401(k)'s, for example, is that only the affluent have been able to take full advantage of them. By encouraging the private sector shift towards individualized defined-contribution accounts through tax breaks and subsidies, the Federal government has essentially subsidized the savings of the well-off, while greatly increasing the degree of economic insecurity faced by most American families. Fewer workers are now covered by pension plans of any kind than twenty-five years ago, and those pensions have become less valuable. Stagnant wages and the collapse of personal savings have made things even worse.

In IRA, Keogh, and 401(k) investments, if things go wrong, there is still Social Security to fall back on. In periods of recessions and stock meltdowns, which typically occur more often than once in a decade, will government bail out retirees and their families? If Social Security goes wrong or disappears, what is there for lower- and middle-income people to fall back on? As long as wages remain stagnant, the costs of housing, child rearing, and health care remain high, the trend of individualizing risk in the private sector continues, and we do little to renew opportunity for the great middle, the answer for millions of Americans will be . . . nothing. Individualized accounts can never match the investment returns and economic security of a large common fund that is managed solely in the interests of its contributors, and that pools risk. Privatization is a bad deal for working families.

Social Security Is a Family Program

Social Security is not just a retirement program. It is also a family insurance program, which disproportionately benefits those on the bottom half
of the income scale. Remember that Social Security also provides survivors
and disability insurance. Public discussion of Social Security and privatization tends to focus almost exclusively on elderly retirees, but nearly one-third
of all beneficiaries receive support through survivor and disability components of the program. What will happen to them, when an ever-growing
percentage of revenues generated by the payroll tax are withdrawn from the
program to fund private accounts?

Social Security provides more benefits to children than any other social
program, roughly $16 billion annually. More than 5 million children either
directly receive benefits or do so indirectly as members of households that
receive them. Those receiving survivors benefits number 6.7 million, of whom
1.9 million are children. An additional 8 million receive benefits because they
were working and became disabled or because they are family members of a
disabled worker. One in five of them are children.

According to the National Center for Children in Poverty, in the after-
math of the 9/11 attacks, most of the children who lost a parent, as well as the
surviving parents who stayed home to care for these children, qualified for
survivor benefits from Social Security. Most workers disabled in the attacks—
and their children—qualified for disability benefits under the program. The
first checks arrived in early October 2001, quickly and efficiently, with no
stigma—a promise kept.[3]

Children who receive disability or survivor benefits tend to come from
more financially vulnerable families than other American kids. Why?
Working-class parents are more likely to work in more dangerous surround-
ings and have inadequate health care coverage, making disability, or even
death, a greater possibility than for others. Fathers are more likely to die
during their working lives than mothers, leaving many kids in female-headed
households. African-Americans and Latinos are more likely than whites to
need these protections. These insurance protections have kept millions of
middle- and low-income families and their children from falling into poverty
because of death or disability. Each year, Social Security keeps one million
children out of poverty.[4]

Unlike welfare and other means-tested programs, which tend to be
under-funded and have benefit time limits, survivor and disability protection
through Social Security is an entitlement—a universal right, basically. While
these benefits are of the greatest use to poorer citizens, they are in fact
available to all. Ninety-six percent of all American workers hold jobs covered

by Social Security; 97 percent of workers aged 20 to 49 are eligible for survivor protection, and 91 percent of covered workers aged 21 to 64 have worked long enough to acquire long-term disability protection.[5]

Social Security is the primary source of life and disability insurance for many families; for some, it is the only source. It is especially critical for families headed by younger workers. Thirty percent of all twenty-year-olds, after all, will become disabled during their working lives, and one out of seven of them will die before retirement. Younger workers who become disabled or die would not be able to accumulate sufficient assets in private accounts to provide the same level of insurance protection currently offered by Social Security. Just over half of all private sector workers have employer-provided life insurance, and even fewer have long-term disability coverage through their jobs. In terms of price and coverage, survivors and disability benefits through Social Security offer far more than private insurance ever could—but only as long as the pool of citizens paying in remains large and broad. With privatization, how will we fund these insurance programs?[6]

An Adverse Ripple Effect Is Possible If Privatization Goes Wrong

The government loses tax receipts when payroll taxes are reduced. This loss will eliminate rather quickly the annual Social Security surplus. The government would then have to fill this financial void by such means as raising taxes, cutting benefits, or borrowing. Moreover, partial privatization would mean that Social Security benefits paid out by the government would be reduced for people after their retirement, with individuals hoping their privatized income will fill the void. There is no guarantee that the void will be filled, especially if people are unlucky enough to begin their retirement when there is a stock market meltdown.

Generations to come could find themselves saddled with the debt incurred to pay for privatization. Economist Alan Blinder, former vice chairman of the Federal Reserve Board of Governors, calculates that the transition costs of the most widely used model of Social Security privatization would be $6.5 trillion over the first twenty years. According to the CBO, it would increase the budget deficit every year until 2050. One wonders whether the bond market will choke on all this debt, which in turn will boost intermediate- and long-term interest rates. This result would obviously hurt both the housing market and the affordability of housing, especially for low- and middle-income people.

An additional danger is that partial privatization of Social Security is likely to set in motion an unraveling process. For the more radical advocates of privatization, this is precisely the point. As Benjamin Page and James Simmons have argued, the minority of Americans (mostly young and high income) who will tend to benefit from private accounts—and who have political influence—will eventually try to push Congress for the privatization of a larger and larger share of payroll tax contributions.

This is even more likely to take place if progressive price indexing is included in the Administration's ultimate reform proposal, since those with above average incomes will see drastic reductions in their benefits. Under this indexing scheme, proposed by investment executive Robert Pozen, benefits for about 70 percent of workers would be indexed predominantly to prices rather than to increases in average wages. For most retirees, this would mean significantly lower benefits than those promised under current law. Those with no other sources of retirement income would quickly experience a sharp drop in living standards when they stop working. Those with ample resources may come to see Social Security as a bad deal for them, and seek ways to opt out of the program.

Encouraging those at lower risk of economic catastrophe out of a risk pooling arrangement (which is what Social Security is, after all) tends to weaken what makes such pooling beneficial and effective. Economists refer to this as *adverse selection*.[7] This is precisely what a reform plan that includes both carve-out private accounts and progressive price indexing will do, by making the system unattractive to all but low-earning Americans. The likely end result, in this scenario, is that Social Security will become yet another miserly welfare program for the poor. Its mild redistributive effects—arguably the only real political and moral justification for the regressivity of its revenue source—will be drastically reduced. Benefit cuts will be much easier to accomplish politically, if only the very poor receive them. The burden on what is left of Social Security to help those who most need the program will become heavier. The entire system may unravel. It would represent a major and unnecessary change in the philosophy of the program. As Robert Ball, former commissioner of Social Security once put it, "through Social Security we recognize that we're all in this together." Private accounts will weaken that commitment.[8]

Discussions about Social Security have been couched almost entirely in individual terms, as if retirees have no spouses, children, or grandchildren. The "logic" of privatization, its moral impetus, leans in this direction. But one consequence of speaking about the issue in this way is that we tend to ignore the possible effects that privatization might have across generations. Changes that might appear to help one generation may actually do them harm while rendering other generations worse off. This isn't abstract; it involves American families caring for their children, and for their grandparents. As the National

Center for Children in Poverty has recently argued, the generation that will perhaps be most immediately threatened by changes in Social Security is the current generation of parents. Already squeezed, they worry about paying for their children's education and saving for their own retirement. If investment volatility and benefit cuts leave their own parents in need, privatization will have an enormous ripple effect across generations that will exacerbate family insecurity, with nothing gained.[9]

What Would a True Ownership Society Look Like?

The idea of an ownership society, of course, is a great one. Most Americans would support such an idea, if it offered what most of us expect ownership to provide: a sense of security, belonging, and empowerment; a stake in the future, and in the ongoing American project. To put it in an older language—that of Franklin Roosevelt's Four Freedoms—'ownership' to most of us offers the possibility of liberation from want and fear. The kind of ownership President Bush's approach seems to advocate, however, has a different meaning: what is owned is the risk. In this ownership society, you are on your own. Geoffrey Nunberg of the Center for the Study of Language and Information at Stanford University puts it well: "Nowadays, being asked to feel 'a sense of ownership' in your job doesn't usually mean you're being given managerial control, much less an equity stake in the business; it's more a question of feeling your own neck is on the line. The Bush Social Security program," Nunberg concludes, "comes to pretty much the same thing."[10]

We can do better. The notion of encouraging people to save and build wealth is a sound one. But the ownership society under discussion presently both underestimates and misunderstands the obstacles to creating a nation of wealth holders. There are other options, and many of them have already been tested. We have a number of instruments already in place to encourage the ownership of assets, but most of them are aimed primarily at the upper middle class and the wealthy. The higher the income and the bigger the mortgage, the more one benefits from being able to deduct home mortgage interest and property taxes, for example. This tax expenditure was worth $98 billion in 2004. Contributions to savings plans like Keogh's, IRA's, and 401k's are deductible, which also tends to disproportionately benefit the well off—to the tune of $113.8 billion in 2004. This is money well spent, to be sure—but why not open it up to more families, and direct the money where it will do the most good?

A goal should be to help the non-wealthy build assets, and increase national savings. The 2000 Gore presidential campaign, for example, proposed something called a universal 401(k). Democratic Congressional leaders are likely to put a similar idea forward, if plans for privatization are defeated. Advocates of universal 401(k)'s agree that we can do more to encourage savings and ownership, but dispute the necessity (and wisdom) of gutting Social Security in order to do it. Opportunity, rather than fear and risk, is a more just and efficient way of expanding ownership and effective freedom. The idea is that the Federal government would create inducements for low and moderate-income citizens, with the greatest incentives going to those who need the most help.[11]

Another idea for furthering ownership and effective freedom is the creation of Individual Development Accounts (IDA's), also sometimes referred to as 'stakeholder accounts.' The idea first emerged in the late 1980s largely as an antipoverty measure—an alternative to traditional assistance programs that was designed to promote independence among the poor. Since 1990 some 500 different experimental projects have been established, involving more than 20,000 IDA holders. Conducted by the Corporation for Enterprise Development and the Center for Social Development, the results have been promising. Based on this success, the federal government included money for IDAs in the welfare reform bill of 1996. Two years later, Congress created a five-year, $125 million demonstration, designed to create roughly fifty-thousand IDAs.[12]

While the notion of such accounts began as an antipoverty measure, its potential applicability is much broader. In April 2005, for example, Great Britain will begin making every one of its newborns an "owner" from birth, by setting up a personal trust fund of about $500 (more, for those from poorer families). Relatives are encouraged to add to the trust fund, which accumulates tax-free. Building on the success of the IDA experiments as well as the British experience, policymakers and academics in the U.S. have toyed with a variety of different versions. With support across divisions of party and ideology, Nebraska senator Robert Kerrey proposed what he called "KidSave Accounts" in the late 1990s. Under Kerrey's proposal—available to all, not just to the poor—the federal government would contribute a $1,000 stake at birth for every American child, and $500 per year for five years. The money would be invested and would grow until the child reached the age of twenty-one. At this point, it was estimated, in the neighborhood of $20,000 would be available for college tuition, to start a business, or to purchase a home.[13]

Others have proposed larger sums. Bruce Ackerman and Anne Alstott, in their influential book *The Stakeholder Society,* have put forward the most far-reaching proposal. They argue for an $80,000 stake for every American citizen at the age of twenty-one. Financed by a 2 percent tax on all wealth above $80,000, the money could be used for college tuition, to start a business, or to purchase a home. Aside from unemployment benefits and a minimal citizen's pension for retirees and the disabled, they argue, this stake would replace much of the welfare state, and build a true ownership society.

There is a reason, of course, that so many of these ideas were first proposed during Clinton's second term: the federal budget was in surplus. Clearly, we are not living in the same world now. If we wish to truly build an ownership society, we will either have to put it off until we've gotten our fiscal house in order, or we will have to come up with creative (and honest) ways to find the revenue. Given the shifting of the tax burden downward over the past few decades, Ackerman and Alstott propose a tax on wealth directed specifically to stakeholder accounts or universal 401(k)'s for the overwhelming majority of our young people. Leon Friedman has proposed completely eliminating the estate tax, in favor of a 1 percent net worth tax levied on the top 1 percent of American households. Most European countries have levied general taxes on wealth for years; Switzerland, for example, uses marginal rates of 0.05 to 0.30 percent after exempting the first $100,000 per household. According to Edward Wolff, such a tax (exempting homes and middle class levels of other assets) would have raised $52 billion in the U.S. in 1998. Only 8.5 percent of families would have paid more than $300.[14]

These approaches are no doubt too radical for the American people. Yet, approaches that have been presumed radical have been tried before and worked very well. The Serviceman's Readjustment Act of 1944—the G.I. Bill—was our last great program aimed at young adults. In the waning days of World War II, with the Great Depression a very recent memory—and its re-emergence a widespread fear—it was widely understood as an expression of common citizenship. Placed alongside our proposal for universal pre-school, some form of wealth-building accounts for young people would constitute a kind of social inheritance, provided to each new generation by the most privileged members of the generations that preceded them, in recognition of the social cooperation necessary for a market society to work.

If we want to talk about an 'ownership society' and renewing liberty for a new century, perhaps we need to broaden our horizons and look at approaches that many would consider radical. The origin of the word 'radical' is to 'get to the root' of something, after all. Is this politically realistic right now? Probably not. But if we intend to take the idea of an 'ownership society' seriously, perhaps we need to put all our cards on the table. At the very least, it's something to consider once we've gotten our fiscal house in order.

What should be evident from this discussion is that from the point of view of both the individual and society, the upside potential for the stakeholder approach is far greater than for partially privatizing Social Security. Correspondingly, the downside risk for a stakeholder program is modest, but the downside risk for privatizing Social Security is huge and incalculable.

Chapter 8

BIG BUDGET DEFICITS: NOT GOOD FOR STOCKS AND PRIVATIZATION

P rivatizing of Social Security means allowing individuals to pay less in the way of employment taxes. This, of course, means that the government gets less in the way of revenues. With less in revenues, the budget deficit rises, and this would be from an already unduly high and unacceptable level. The higher the deficit moves, the more upward pressure there will be on interest rates, and higher interest rates tend to dampen economic growth. Slower economic growth will retard business profits and dividends, and lower profits and dividends will hurt stock market performance. With a weaker stock market performance, the return for equity holders will suffer, which means those investors who divert funds from payroll taxes will suffer.

Social Security Privatization Adds To the Budget Deficit

Of course, that would not be the only way that investors who try to take "advantage" of privatization will suffer. In order to gain the opportunity to invest in stocks, they will have to forgo part of their future Social Security benefits. This means they will have one sure loss of future income, with a good chance that their equity returns will not fully compensate for what they gave up in benefits.

An excessive budget deficit hurts the economy in general, and equity investors in particular. It diverts savings to finance a budget deficit instead of using it in more productive ways, especially in the private sector. It will add to inflation unless there are corresponding offsets in monetary policy and the dollar. It can make people feel that an administration does not have its house in order if it cannot control its finances, which in turn tends to place other administration policies under a cloud. Finally, when the next recession comes, what policy flexibility will there be to get the country out of its economic malaise? Needless to say, these factors are not good for any stock market investor, and especially not good for those who have forgone sure income for something much more tentative.

It should not be inferred that we are long-term bears on the economy and the stock market. However, we do want to point out that a huge budget deficit creates all kinds of problems that will limit the size and consistency of economic growth, and limit the ability of the government to use countercyclical stimulation when necessary. This is not good news for those who are counting on a steady stream of income to help them in their twilight years, especially since they often have little control over when they retire and when their emergencies occur. Nor is it good news for privatization proponents who assume the return on stocks will exceed the return on lost Social Security income by enough to more than compensate for the additional risks.

It Makes a Difference Who Finances
Our Budget Deficit

In 2004, foreigners financed virtually our entire budget deficit. Yet, over the long run, the U.S. cannot count on foreigners to continue to do this. As a matter of fact, in 2005 there are already signs that foreigners will buy less U.S. Treasury debt than they did in the previous year. Assuming that this trend continues, the amount of our budget deficit financed by our own people will need to increase. In order for the reader to understand the importance of this analysis, it is necessary to dig into the facts.

In the last three fiscal years, official and private foreign investors have financed almost all of the U.S. budget deficit. In the period from September 2001 through September 2004 the budget deficit was $945 billion. During that period, foreigners added $856 billion to their holdings of U.S. Treasury securities. Also during this period, the Federal Reserve added $165 billion to its outright holdings. Since these two groups added more to their holdings than the size of the deficit, it means that private domestic investors actually liquidated Treasury securities (see Table 10).

When domestic private investors have to buy substantial amounts of Treasury securities to cover a large budget deficit, this puts upward pressure on interest rates. This is because these investors need an inducement to buy, and typically the answer is higher interest rates. Obviously this did not happen in the last three years, when domestic investors were not needed to cover the budget deficit. This should help explain why the budget deficit of almost $1 trillion in the last three fiscal years brought about almost no upward pressure on intermediate- and long-term interest rates. Those who realize how good a deal this is for the U.S. also need to realize that this scenario will not continue indefinitely.

The combination of huge U.S. budget and trade deficits puts downward pressure on the U.S. dollar, and foreign investors do not like the idea of investing in assets where there is concern of further depreciation. In the last three fiscal years—2002, 2003, and 2004—the budget deficits were $158 billion, $377 billion, and $413 billion respectively. In the last three calendar years—2002, 2003, and 2004—the trade deficits were $422 billion, $497 billion, and $617 billion respectively. Thus the combined budget and trade deficits for this three-year period were an unconscionable $2.5 trillion!

Looking to the next three years, the budget deficit will remain unduly high as spending continues to grow at more than two times the rate of inflation. Foreign trade deficits will move noticeably higher, primarily because the U.S. consumer has an insatiable appetite to buy inexpensive goods from abroad. The combined total for the twin deficits from 2005 through 2007 are likely to reach an even more unconscionable $3.5 trillion! Under these circumstances, the administration should do more than keeping its fingers crossed that foreigners will not continue to diversify away from the dollar, and away from U.S Treasury securities.

This change in budget financing circumstances will increasingly put the Federal Reserve, and its new chairman, in a difficult policy position. In recent years the Federal Reserve has indicated that the dollar and budget policies are the responsibility of others. Thus, the Federal Reserve has made changes in its overnight federal funds target rate based almost entirely on domestic economic considerations. This could change, and it may not be by choice. There is a good chance that the budget, the trade deficit, and the dollar will become more important considerations in monetary policy deliberations.

Ability of the Treasury Market to Finance Revenue Shortfall from Privatization

On January 11, 2005, Treasury Secretary Snow admitted to a group representing government securities dealers that partial privatization could mean $100 billion to $150 billion per year of additional Treasury financing for the next decade. He didn't talk about the following decade. His primary interest at the meeting was to find out whether the market could handle such a large amount. It should be no surprise that the dealers thought it could be done. However, they did not indicate at what price.

The Treasury market being able to take down this huge additional amount of securities is one thing; investors being able to absorb the securities without major adverse effects is another matter. It is likely that domestic private investors would have to come out of the closet and buy a large portion of Treasury issues, even if partial privatization of Social Security does not take place. The need to attract these buyers would put upward pressure on interest rates. Moreover, since current Treasury financing has already inundated major maturity sectors out to ten years, it is likely that a considerable part of the new $100 billion to $150 billion per year in financing needed to cover partial privatization would be in maturities longer than ten years. The Treasury has already intimated that it will issue 30-year bonds beginning in 2006 ($20 billion to $30 billion per year), and this is not related to privatization financing. When privatization financing is added on, it could mean that a manageable amount of bond financing could turn into an excessive burden on the long end of the Treasury market. Needless to say, going from virtually no financing out past ten years to a large amount will put upward pressure on long-term interest rates.

No one is smart enough to know exactly how much intermediate- and long-term interest rates would rise because of the financing of partial privatization of Social Security. Much will depend upon the size of the budget deficit and how much domestic investors will be induced to buy Treasury securities. Yet, one thing is for sure, and that is that rate increases in the intermediate- and long-term markets would not be inconsequential because of partial privatization.

If this scenario were to play out, it could create major headaches for the Federal Reserve and its policies. The housing market and business borrowing are significantly influenced by the level of intermediate- and long-term interest rates, and needless to say, higher rates would do damage to both sectors. The Federal Reserve could be put in a position where increases in Treasury rates, and their impact on housing and plant and equipment spending, could cause a considerable slowdown in the economy. These are not the kinds of headaches that a soon-to-retire Federal Reserve chairman would like to have in the last few months of his central bank career.

Chapter 9

LET'S TALK POLITICS

Allow us to quote Marx—Groucho, that is: "Politics is the art of looking for trouble, finding it everywhere, diagnosing it incorrectly, and applying the wrong remedies." Are we seeing this in the current administration's policies that try to head us down the road to privatization of Social Security? Unfortunately, it is hard for Americans to truly understand the risk and rewards of the privatization recommendations when the administration is using the bully pulpit to convince, not enlighten, the American people.

In this chapter we will outline the nature and specifics of the partial privatization proposal that is likely to come from the Bush administration in the coming months. This is a more complicated undertaking than one might expect, because the administration has been holding its cards close to the vest. Most close observers believe that they will ultimately offer a variation on Plan 2 from the Bush-appointed Social Security commission.

Next, we talk about the Democratic Party's approach—or the lack thereof—to Social Security, and we will discuss the role of the American Association of Retired People (AARP) in the political process. We will discuss some of the obstacles President Bush faces in attaining his reform objectives, and what should follow if his efforts fail. Finally, we will argue that the public debate about Social Security, in the end, is really about philosophy, not numbers. It is about how we talk about government, and what we think the legitimate and effective role of government is in fostering opportunity, freedom, and ownership. Social Security inspired a great deal of alarm and heated rhetoric in some quarters when it was first created, because it involved a fundamental reordering of a portion of the economy, and basic changes in the relationship between citizens and their government. Privatization, in whatever form, proposes a similar reordering. We should be talking about it at this level, with an appropriate degree of seriousness, humility, thoughtful deliberation, and care. In terms of its impact on the daily lives of Americans, now and in the future, Congress probably hasn't considered such an important issue since the civil rights laws of the mid-sixties. This is no time to play politics. Getting this wrong could fundamentally alter the future of the nation.

President Bush and Social Security Privatization

To understand the true picture of where the Republicans stand on Social Security, it is necessary to go back before the 2000 election and see where George W. Bush stood on this topic, and to look at the changes in his thinking since that time. What is clear is that the president and his party have not significantly changed their views on Social Security in general, and on partial privatization in particular.

The president's benchmark statement on Social Security was made on May 15, 2000, in a speech at the Rancho Cucamonga Senior Center in California. He had not yet officially received the Republican nomination, but his campaign for the presidency had already begun. Interestingly, his initial comments sounded as if he were a Democrat extolling the virtues of the current Social Security system. However, as he continued to speak, he sounded as if he had made a U-turn with respect to his thinking. The following are key quotes from his speech:

> Sixty-five years later, we can declare: Social Security is the single most successful government program in American history. Without it, more than half of all seniors would live in poverty. For millions—for parents and grandparents with little or no savings—it is the difference between destitution and dignity. Social Security is a defining American promise, and we will not turn back. This issue is a test of government's capacity to give its word and keep it, to act in good faith and to pursue the common good.

Yet, later in the speech, his approach and comments changed drastically. We quote:

> We are nearing Social Security's greatest test. Eight years from now, the massive baby-boomer generation will begin drawing benefits (2008). Their

lives will be long and healthy. And, within two decades, there simply won't be enough younger workers to pay the benefits earned by the old. If we do nothing to reform the system, the year 2037 will be the moment of financial collapse. The system will be insolvent, with deficits in the trillions of dollars, requiring either a massive cut in benefits or a massive increase in taxes.

Reform should include personal retirement accounts for young people—an element of all the major bipartisan plans. The idea works very simply. A young worker can take some portion of his or her payroll tax and put it in a fund that invests in stocks and bonds. We will establish basic standards of safety and soundness, so that investments are only in steady, reliable funds. There will be no fly-by-night speculators or day trading. And money in this account could only be used for retirement, or passed along as an inheritance.

Let me be clear. Personal accounts are not a substitute for Social Security. They involve only a limited percentage of the payroll tax, so the safety net remains strong. Let me say again: For those who are retired, or near retirement, there will be no changes at all to your social security. But we can and must give younger workers the option of new opportunities.

The basic points are clear: According to the administration, Social Security is in crisis, and some form of privatization must be part of the solution. On May 2, 2001, after George W. Bush had taken over the reins of government, he named a so-called bipartisan commission to study Social Security reform and to develop a plan to let workers invest some of their payroll taxes in private accounts. The cochairman of the commission was former New York senator Daniel Patrick Moynihan, a Democrat, who had long urged partial privatization. All other members of the new commission also happened to support partial privatization.

While the committee may have been bipartisan in that both Republicans and Democrats were members, the litmus test was that members had to be in favor of some sort of privatization. Thus, bipartisan membership was not nonpartisan membership. Unfortunately, stacking the membership deck hardly created a free flow of ideas and aggressive interchanges. To understand how the deck was stacked, all the reader has to do is look at the following, which is what the commission was asked to do. They were requested to make recommendations using six guiding principles:

✓ Modernization must not change Social Security benefits for retirees or near-retirees.

✓ The entire Social Security surplus must be dedicated only to Social Security.

✓ Social Security payroll taxes must not be increased.

✓ The government must not invest Social Security funds in the stock
   market.

✓ Modernization must preserve Social Security's disability and survivors
   programs.

✓ Modernization must include individually controlled, voluntary
   personal retirement accounts that will augment Social Security.

Public hearings started on June 11, 2001, and finished on December 11, 2001. The commission released its final report on December 21, 2001, and the report was revised on March 19, 2002. The ultimate recommendation was for allowing lower-income workers to place up to 4 percent of their wages into their own accounts, up to a cap of $1,000. That same dollar cap would also apply to people at higher income levels. This was the old foot-in-the-door approach. On October 3, 2002, the Senate Committee on Finance held a hearing on the final report.

History shows that the commission's recommendations went nowhere. Part of the reason was that government, and the American people, had other things on their minds such as homeland security, terrorism, and the military conflicts in Afghanistan and Iraq. Also, the plunge in the stock market, especially in 2001, was hardly a selling point for partial privatization of Social Security. Yet even if these post-9/11 events had not taken place, the president's Social Security recommendations would not have become law. Broad support both inside and outside the government was lacking.

Despite the lack of success in passing his Social Security reforms, President Bush came back in December 2004 with a so-called summit that supported the same type of thing he had recommended in his first administration, except the level of privatization would be even greater. There was no semblance of either nonpartisanship or bipartisanship. As a matter of fact, he seemed to remove the pretense that this summit had a bipartisan base. Apparently he believed that his strong showing in the 2004 presidential election along with working majorities for the Republicans in both the House and the Senate were sufficient to carry his Social Security reform legislation over the top.

The summit was held on December 15, 2004, and occurred over two days. There were two primary topics—Social Security reform and tax reductions. Participants came almost entirely from administration advisers, cabinet secretaries, and approximately three dozen corporate and financial executives. Almost all of the businesses represented would in some way benefit from the tax reduction or Social Security reform proposals. There was not even a scintilla of an attempt to make this a bipartisan summit. Being in favor of tax reductions and some privatization of Social Security appears to have been the litmus tests for being invited to the summit. On the basis of this analysis, one can argue that the purpose of the summit was to drum up support among powerful people for the president's recommendation on these two items.

On February 2, 2005, President Bush delivered his State of the Union address. In that speech he made some comments with respect to his upcoming Social Security proposals. Nonetheless, the administration at that time had been reluctant to put forward a detailed plan, largely for political reasons. The Cato Institute—a longtime advocate of privatization—gathered together from the State of the Union address, White House briefings, and White House fact sheets a summary outline of the parameters of the program, and in early February 2005 presented the following on its website:

There will be no changes in the current system for people who were born before 1950—those who are 55 and older now. If you were born in 1949, or before, you would not be impacted by any of the changes envisioned by the president for Social Security.

The system will initially operate much like the Thrift Savings Plan for government employees. Workers would have a choice from a small number of broadly diversified funds with a life-cycle fund as the default. Funds would be managed by the private sector on a contractual basis and administered by the federal government. Early estimates by the Social Security Administration indicate that administrative fees could be kept as low as .3 percent annually of assets under management.

Yearly contribution limits would be raised over time, eventually permitting all workers to set aside 4 percentage points of their payroll taxes in their accounts. Annual contributions to personal retirement accounts initially would be capped at $1,000 per year in 2009. The cap would rise gradually over time, growing $100 per year, plus growth in average wages. By 2014 about half of American workers would be able to privately invest 4 percent of their wages.

To ease the burden of transition costs, the accounts would be phased in according to the age of the work force. The first year of the program (2009), those born between 1950 and 1965 could enter the system. The second year, those born before 1978 could enter. And, in the third year of implementation, all eligible workers would be able to participate in personal accounts if they chose.

Participants would not be permitted, under the system, to have pre-retirement access to their personal accounts. The accounts will be held and protected to fund benefits when they hit retirement age. They would not be permitted to make loans to themselves through the accounts, nor would they be permitted to borrow against them.

Accounts would belong to workers and be fully inheritable.

A Growing Storm of Resistance

Most Democrats in Congress as well as some Republicans are resisting the president's Social Security approach. So is the powerful AARP. Congressional Democrats are not likely to present a detailed Social Security plan, but rather, they will wait and see what the president proposes. When these proposals are made, the Democrats will then do battle with the president on many of his recommendations. Privatization and cutbacks in benefits are two areas they will most aggressively fight.

This does not mean that Democrats in Congress are fully satisfied with the current Social Security system. Rather, they would like to make revisions in Social Security, but in the context of the way it is currently structured. Their highest priority is likely to be to minimize the possibility of the Social Security system going terribly wrong after seven decades of being very right. Moving down the road toward privatization enhances the risks of things going wrong—terribly wrong.

It should come as no surprise therefore that the president's Social Security program is already running into considerable resistance in Congress, and that is before many of the specifics of the program have been detailed. Almost all Democrats, and some Republicans, will try to block the legislation. In arguing against the legislation, those people who fight it are likely to point out that the president's budget record leaves a great deal to be desired, and his Social Security proposal will make the budget deficit worse. They will also argue that the Social Security estimates used by the president to show what bad shape Social Security is in are not only questionable, but some have already been proven wrong.

Finally, they can also argue against the questionable logic and soundness of the president's specific Social Security proposals. But of course, it is one thing to stop bad legislation. It is another to propose good legislation. Opposition to private accounts will be led by two entities: the Democratic Party and the AARP. Let's review their positions on the issue.

The Democrats

The Democrats' approach to Social Security, beginning with 2000, is difficult to comprehend. In contrast to the Republicans, who have maintained the same Social Security message, the Democrats appear to have changed their position on this issue. Part of this may be explained by the fact that the Democrats have been out of power since the 2000 election, and that Gore's and Kerry's advisers and their ideas were not exactly the same. With two losses in a row, it is unclear whose ideas, if any, were dominating Democratic thinking.

The disappearance of the budget surplus also seems to have put a crimp in their sails, since the proposals offered by the Gore campaign in 2000 can no longer be funded without tax increases of some sort. Democrats, in effect, have been on the defensive on this issue in recent years. This is not exactly the situation the Democrats want to be in since they traditionally believe that they are the champions of the middle class.

From an analytical perspective, the most useful way of explaining the changes in the Democratic Party's approach to Social Security is to look at its platform in 2000, and again in 2004. They are very different. Quoting from the 2000 party platform:

> We now have an extraordinary opportunity to maintain Social Security. In addition, we can reform it—not the wrong way—with proposals such as raising the retirement age, but the right way—with fiscal discipline and by making it fairer for widows, widowers, and mothers. . . .
>
> To build on the success of Social Security, Al Gore has proposed the creation of Retirement Savings Plus—voluntary, tax-free, personally controlled, privately managed savings accounts with a government match that would help couples build a nest egg of up to $400,000. Separate from Social Security, Retirement Savings Plus accounts would let Americans save and invest on top of the foundation of Social Security's guaranteed benefit. Under this plan, the federal government would match individual contributions with tax credits, with the hardest-pressed working families getting the most assistance.

In 2004, whether they intended to or not, the Democrats seemed to downplay the relative importance of making major changes in Social Security. The platform was forty-three pages in length, and Social Security came in under the heading of "Standing Up for the Great American Middle Class." This heading was on page 24, and Social Security was addressed on page 26; amazingly, it covered only one paragraph, which stated the following:

> We are absolutely committed to preserving Social Security. It is a compact across generations that has helped tens of millions of Americans live their retirement years in dignity instead of poverty. Democrats believe in the progressive, guaranteed benefit that has ensured that seniors and people with disabilities receive a benefit not subject to the whims of the market or the economy. We oppose privatizing Social Security or raising the retirement age.

We oppose reducing the benefits earned by workers just because they have also earned a benefit from certain public retirement plans. We will repeal discriminatory laws that penalize some retired workers and their families while allowing others to receive full benefits. Because the massive deficits under the Bush Administration raided hundreds of billions of dollars from Social Security, the most important step we can take to strengthen Social Security is to restore fiscal responsibility. Social Security matters to all Americans, Democrats and Republicans, and strengthening Social Security should be a common cause.

Nice words, but where is the detail and the substance? Where is the guidance to party members? What an incredible difference between the Social Security part of the platform in 2000! In 2000 the platform had an aggressive approach with respect to adding to benefits, especially for the middle class. Moreover, no specifics were presented in the 2004 platform to make the program more fiscally responsible.

In that platform, the Democratic Party dropped out of sight with respect to concrete proposals to reform Social Security. The Democrats went from detailed Social Security recommendations in 2000 to no detailed recommendations in 2004, and what they had to say in their platform about Social Security was the one paragraph, buried late in the document. The comment by Kerry that "I have a plan" was a day late and a dollar short.

One can argue that this lack of emphasis by the Democrats on reforming Social Security—and not having a logical and specific plan to do so—contributed toward John Kerry's defeat. In contrast, the Republicans stayed with virtually the same Social Security recommendations in both 2000 and 2004, with the key element being partial privatization. And now President Bush has made it the centerpiece of his second-term domestic agenda.

The AARP's Position

When it comes to major Social Security reform, it is highly unlikely that it will happen without the blessing of the AARP. The AARP is a membership organization of about 35 million that serves people fifty years of age and older. It provides a wide range of benefits, products, and services for its members. These benefits are listed on the AARP website and also in its magazine.

Simply put, there is no other organization in the U.S. that has the breadth and the power to represent people fifty years old and over. Moreover, with the aging of the population, its power and influence will only increase. Since Social Security reform is a key item for the elderly, and those soon to be elderly, the power of AARP is magnified even more.

What we have found is that when AARP supports legislation, the executive branch will applaud the wise judgment of the AARP. When the AARP is moderately against legislation, or the legislation is not viewed as all that important to the elderly, the executive branch tends to downplay, or ignore, the comments of the AARP. However, when the AARP aggressively attacks a proposal, and that proposal is of major importance to the elderly, the executive branch's main line of attack is to call into question the motives and political leanings of AARP. That currently is what is happening with respect to the Bush administration and the AARP on the issue of Social Security reform.

In 2003 the Bush administration was more than willing to accept the support of the AARP for its prescription drug legislation. One can argue that if the AARP had been aggressively against the prescription drug legislation that was proposed, it would not have passed. At that time the Bush administration had no problem with AARP's motives or power base. It was a right-thinking group. Now, however, with the AARP vehemently against the Bush proposal on partial privatization of Social Security, the administration is attacking it as a left-thinking group.

Yet, if a group or an individual represents others, the goal is to improve the state of the people it represents, and that includes fighting those whose policies risk losing previous benefits. It is not a matter of political leanings or motivations, it is a matter of doing what you think is right for the people you represent, irrespective of whether politicians will classify the approach as liberal or conservative. Was the AARP conservative-leaning and correct when it supported the prescription drug legislation, but now it is liberal-leaning and thinking wrong because it is against the administration's Social Security proposals?

In any event, the competing sides on partial privatization of Social Security are now joined in battle. On January 4, 2005, the AARP took out a full-page add in the *New York Times*. Quoting from that ad:

> Let's not turn Social Security into Social Insecurity. While the program needs to be strengthened, private accounts that take money out of Social Security are not the answer and will hurt all generations. There are places in your retirement planning for risk, but Social Security isn't one of them. Call your legislators . . . and urge them to oppose private accounts that put Social Security at risk.

Social Security Privatization and the 2006 Congressional Elections

What the Bush administration needs to remember is that it is now one year until the next congressional elections, and if it wants to maintain its domination in Congress, it needs to consider offering a meaningful olive branch to the AARP on Social Security reform. The president needs to realize that he was reelected for his leadership capabilities, especially in the international area, and that he ran against a disorganized Democratic Party whose candidate did not appeal to a broad spectrum of Americans and who did not focus on "gut" domestic issues.

In the 2006 congressional elections the key domestic issue is likely to be Social Security reform. Thus there will be congressional candidates who will win or lose based on their views on Social Security reform. Politically speaking, the president is playing with fire. As of this writing (Summer 2005), despite aggressive campaigning by the president, public support for Social Security privatization—never strong to begin with—is eroding. While opinion polls show that voters are worried about the solvency of Social Security, the more they hear about the president's reform ideas, the less they like them.

Since the 2004 election, it appears that the more voters learn about the facts of privatization, the less they seem to like it. A *Washington Post*–ABC News poll taken in March 2005 found that barely a third of the public approves of the way that President Bush is handling Social Security—the lowest level yet recorded for the president. A majority (58 percent) said that the more they heard about privatization plans, the less they liked them.

A March 2005 survey conducted by the *New York Times* and CBS News indicated that the deficit in particular worried many citizens. Most of those who expressed skepticism about privatization did so in part because of their concerns about the deficit. Respondents who disapproved of how Bush was managing the deficit totaled 60 percent, including 48 percent of conservatives. The focus on Social Security has, if anything, aggravated concern about the budget deficit. This is not good news for the president or his agenda. A survey taken by the Pew Research Center for the People and the Press the same month found support among young people for private accounts declining as well. Those respondents aged 18 to 29 who claimed to be following the public debate closely were more than twice as likely as their peers to oppose President Bush's reform proposals. Karl Rove hoped Social Security reform might be a way to bring younger voters into the Republican Party. It may well backfire.[1]

Equally disturbing for the president should be a Gallup Poll taken in early 2005 which found that those making $30,000 to $50,000 per year opposed privatization by 19 points; people making more than $75,000 support it, though only by 2 points—suggesting that working-class people generally oppose it, while more affluent people are evenly split. In this regard it should be pointed out that House Republicans who have expressed public reservations about privatization tend to represent working-class districts in places like Wisconsin, West Virginia, Kentucky, Alabama, and Louisiana. A 2001 study by the National Committee for an Effective Congress found that, of the 88 congressional districts that Republicans won from Democrats between 1994 and 2000, 59 had incomes below the national average. Among the 46 seats that the Democrats won from Republicans, 29 represented districts with incomes above the national average.

This situation creates a political dilemma for the president. Pressure Republican representatives from lower-income districts to vote for the president's privatization plan and they could lose their seats to Democrats in 2006. If that happens, the president will find it much more difficult to get his agenda through Congress in the last two years he is in office.

The constant talk of 'crisis' by the President and Republican officials may be having an ironic effect politically, by making Americans more aware of economic risk in their own lives, and of the value of government in mitigating it. According to *Business Week*, a growing number of Americans from across the political spectrum are worried that "the country's web of public and private social protections is fraying." Polls seem to indicate increasing support for a government guaranteed minimum standard of living for retirees, and a strong reluctance to see it solely as an issue of individual responsibility. Members of "Safety Net Nation," as the magazine refers to them, reject both traditional liberalism and conservative free-market approaches.

Mostly white, male, with average incomes and slightly below average educational attainment, 'Safety Net Nation' represents roughly one-fifth of the electorate. Most of them voted for President Bush in 2004, and they have leaned towards the Republicans in recent elections. But the language of crisis with regard to Social Security has heightened anxiety among this "risk-averse cohort."

As Democratic pollster Stanley Greenberg put it, "what happened is that Bush gave the nation an extended tutorial on risk, and that came on top of growing awareness of the risk shift from private institutions to individuals." The result, he concluded, "is a collapse in support for Social Security reform." Alice Munnell, former Clinton Administration economic adviser, concurs: "people have not done a very good job with 401(k)'s, and it weighs on them. I don't see any sign that they're dying to take on still more of this kind of responsibility. The Social Security debate may be testing the limit of the swing to individualism we have seen for the last twenty to thirty years." The political stakes of this are enormous. It offers the possibility of a profound political realignment in favor of the Republican Party similar to the one instigated by Social Security's creation in 1935. But it also provides the Democrats with an opportunity to redefine their core beliefs, and use them to speak to the lives of ordinary citizens.[2]

Budget Deficit Could Sink the Privatization Proposal

The size of the budget deficit is daunting. In fiscal year 2004 the budget deficit was $413 billion, which was an unduly large number for the third year of an economic recovery. In fiscal 2005, the deficit appears likely to be between $320 billion and $330 billion, but meaningful further improvement will be harder to come by. As a matter of fact, it can be argued that when President Bush's administration ends in 2008, there is a good chance the deficit will be in the area of $300 billion. Incidentally, this performance would be a far cry from Office of Management and Budget's politically influenced deficit estimate of only $228 billion for fiscal 2008 that was made on July 30, 2004.

Needless to say, the budget numbers on the president's watch have not been sterling. Some of the blame he has received is misplaced, and some is not. In this regard, it is important to discuss in some detail what has happened since President Bush's first term in office, which began in early February 2001.

What the data show is that the first major impact the Bush administration had on the budget was in June 2001 with the passage of the Economic Growth and Taxpayer Relief Reconciliation Act. Up to that point it was a Clinton administration budget. In the twelve months ended June 30, 2001, the budget was in surplus by $229 billion. In the twelve previous months there was a surplus of $207 billion. Thus, at the time the Bush administration put its first major imprint on the budget, which was about five months after taking office, the president had inherited a surplus of roughly $200 billion. However, he also inherited some dark clouds on the economic horizon. These were circumstances and events that not only were going to eliminate the budget surplus, but put the budget well into deficit no matter who was in office.

In the middle of 2001 the stock market was in the throes of a major decline, nonfarm employment had already begun a downward trek, corporate profits were sliding, and the Federal Reserve had belatedly moved from an overly restrictive monetary policy in the second half of 2000, to a neutral policy by the middle of 2001, and finally to an accommodative policy by the end of 2001. These changes by the monetary authority were too little, too late, especially since major changes in monetary policy work with a considerable time lag. With the budget surplus causing a drag on economic growth in 2000 and in the first half of 2001, this meant that monetary and fiscal policies were not well positioned to help a sliding economy and stock market. Obviously these were not the best set of circumstances—and then came 9/11.

Tax cuts and government spending increases were needed after 9/11. The question was, what form should they take, and what should be the magnitude involved? In this regard, the president gets high marks for the timely nature of his proposals, but he gets much less generous marks for the specific recommendations. The tax reductions could have been designed in a way to better stimulate the economy than the ones proposed and passed, and the same could be said for the spending increases.

Yet, whatever the flaws in the administration's proposals, they were accentuated once they reached the halls of Congress. Both parties elevated pork barrel legislation to a new level. Spending bills had more ornaments than a Christmas tree, and the tax reductions seemed to spread like wildfire into areas that helped companies and industries, but fell short on what they provided to many Americans. The most obvious examples of good intentions gone awry were the prescription drug legislation passed in December 2003, and business tax reductions passed just before the 2004 elections.

Given all of the previously mentioned factors, it is virtually impossible to exactly apportion the blame for the budget missteps and mistakes. The cast of characters would be considerable. This leaves us with the problem of determining how much of the adverse budget picture should be placed at the president's doorstep. What we can say with some conviction is that currently there would be a good-size budget deficit even if President Bush had handled everything properly. It would have been an accomplishment on the part of the president if the budget deficit for fiscal year 2004 had been held to $200 billion or about half of the $413 billion deficit that took place. The result is not something to brag about.

Irrespective of who should get blamed for what, the reality of the situation is that the president is currently saddled with an unacceptably large budget deficit, and the budget has moved from a moderate surplus to a huge deficit on his watch. The total swing has been over $½ trillion—from a $200 billion surplus to a deficit that is currently over $300 billion. Thus, the size of the deficit, and his performance in budget deficit management will not help the president when it comes to his Social Security privatization request, where the budget deficit would be pushed even higher, and in a major way.

Is a Mandate to Govern a Mandate to Privatize Social Security?

Some have argued that President Bush should get his way when it comes to legislation because he, and the Republican Party, received a mandate to govern. Yet, a mandate to govern is not a mandate to pass all kinds of legislation, especially if the public is cool to, or against, what is being proposed. This is a problem with respect to partial privatization of Social Security. Simply put, a mandate to govern is not a mandate to partially privatize the Social Security system. Moreover, the population would be even more against the president's likely proposals if it were fully educated on how the current system really works, and on the potential problems and risks for making major changes.

One might wonder why partial privatization of Social Security is so high on the president's list of things to do. Maybe it is the ideologues who have convinced him that it is the right thing to do. This is despite the fact that the CBO indicates that it will be the middle of the twenty-first century before there is a financial crisis in Social Security, and we believe that forecast is overly pessimistic, especially if real economic growth averages around 3 percent per year. Moreover, the financing of Medicare and Medicaid is a far more pressing problem, along with the financial squeeze on many middle-class Americans. Medicaid especially is in dire straits, since neither the federal government nor the states have specific funding programs for that program, and many states are already looking for ways to cut back on Medicaid spending.

Finally, in President Bush's second term in office, the number of items on his plate is mind-boggling—the war in Iraq, terrorism, nuclear proliferation, budget and trade deficits, energy shortfalls, economic growth, immigration, border safety, Medicare, Medicaid, and major appointments, especially in the judicial area. The middle-class squeeze isn't going away; neither are education reform and racial issues. He will need to deal with these problems despite a divisive political split in the country, where it is difficult to get people to compromise on any issue. As a matter of fact, it is difficult to get people on one side of an issue to even listen to people on the other side. Given all of these factors, his prioritizing of issues could prove to be the biggest problem of all, and his priorities should not involve partial privatization of Social Security.

Authors, such as ourselves, have the luxury of sitting back and pontificating without the daily pressures that exist for our national leaders. This gives us the advantage of being above the fray, so to speak, and from that vantage point we can make judgments that some problems are likely to receive too much attention and others too little. People like ourselves can perform a useful public service by pointing out the need to rebalance priorities, to pay more attention to problems that are neglected, and to make judgments as to the proper role of government in people's daily lives.

If There Is a Political Stalemate on Social Security Reform, What Then?

At the time of publication of this book (mid-2005), the final outcome of Social Security reform is unclear. What we do know is that our ideas, with respect to trying to solve the combined problems of Social Security, Medicare, and Medicaid, are not on the front burner for the current administration. Moreover, there is still a great deal of educating to be done to convince people that Social Security, Medicare, and Medicaid should be viewed together, and that Medicare and Medicaid have far more serious problems than Social Security.

From strictly a procedural point of view, there are several legislative hurdles that Social Security reform would have to surmount. One is to get the legislation through committees in both houses. The next is to get the legislation passed by both houses. If these hurdles are overcome, then a joint committee of both houses has to resolve the differences in the bills passed by both houses. Even that is not the end of the process. The president may consider vetoing the legislation if it does not achieve what he wants or if he finds sections in the legislation that are totally unacceptable. A this point, we are not even close to step one. There is not even a bill, and what is being designed currently is a work-in-process situation.

This is President Bush's second attempt at Social Security reform. In this regard he has some advantages and disadvantages compared with the last time. On the advantage side, he is an incumbent with a power base, he has had time to add to and arm-twist potential supporters, and he has refined his arguments with respect to why partial privatization is necessary. In addition, he claims that he has a mandate, and he can benefit from the fact that the Republicans have much larger majorities in both the House and Senate. As a matter of fact, in the previous Senate there was a time when the Republicans had no majority at all.

Yet, his opponents are powerful and have not been asleep. They also have an advantage in that the more the public understands about the problems with Social Security, the more it will realize that privatization is a bad idea. People can point to the fact that recent Social Security surpluses have been larger than the administration expected, and that the so-called doomsday date has been extended by both the Social Security Trustees and the CBO. Also in the opponents' favor is that the budget deficit will rise substantially when payroll tax inflows decline and future benefits are likely to be cut. Finally, opponents are taking advantage of the division among Republicans and the ranks of partial privatization proponents as to what the proposal should entail and how they should proceed.

The differences between the two sides have already reached a point similar to what occurred during the national election in 2004 when no price was too high to get a candidate elected, even if it meant speaking half truths, or no truths at all. Many in the media have joined the battle, both in terms of how they present their stories and how they slant their editorial comments. Similar to the election, it is almost considered an act of disloyalty if you turn your back on party loyalties.

Assuming that Social Security reform grinds to a halt—as we anticipate it will—the question is whether the ball will be dropped by the administration and Congress for another day and another time? Just because the president does not get his way on privatization should not freeze Social Security reform. In this regard, we have several proposals in mind that we designed in order to avoid the polarization that currently exists.

President Bush's Social Security proposals are a rush to judgment. He is in a hurry to change a system that has worked well for seven decades, and even under his overly pessimistic forecast, it would not be in crisis for almost three decades. The proper approach would be to use the remainder of 2005 and 2006 to look at the problems of Social Security, Medicare, and Medicaid on a combined basis, and then come up with recommendations that will alleviate the financial burden that will drown the budget in red ink. This would still leave President Bush with almost two years to pass comprehensive new legislation. In this regard, we offer the following recommendations:

✓ The Federal Reserve would be requested by the president to make annual GDP forecasts into the distant future. It would then take these annual GDP forecasts and transform them into annual estimates of Social Security payroll tax receipts. The purpose of this approach is to find out, as we believe to be the case, that future payroll tax receipts are being substantially understated by the Social Security Trustees. The

Federal Reserve would use only one best-guess forecast, compared with three by the Social Security Trustees (they emphasize the middle one). It is our belief that even the optimistic forecast of the trustees is too pessimistic.

✓ At the same time the Federal Reserve is making revenue forecasts, the Social Security Trustees would be making annual Social Security benefit forecasts. Only their best-guess forecast would be presented. This would be based on all the current laws, and therefore would include the current cost-of-living (COLA) approach, where average wage increases play an important role in the formula. Wage increases have brought about COLA increases for Social Security recipients that are very generous.

✓ Additional COLA approaches should be tried by the trustees to see if it is possible to design an approach that is very generous for Social Security recipients, would have some added Social Security benefits not in the current COLA approach, but that in the long run would reduce the size of COLA increases. We believe we have come up with an answer, and would like to see the trustees compare the performance of the current COLA approach with our approach, as well as with other approaches, like progressive price indexing.[3]

✓ We do not consider Progressive Price Indexing a viable option, even though the President seems to embrace the idea. It is not a COLA concept; rather, it is a redistribution of COLA income. Different types of COLA's for different people is the approach used, with higher income people receiving the COLA that provides the smallest benefits. This approach just happens to fit in well with privatization, where surpluses will quickly turn into deficits and where the President will be looking for inducements for higher income people to take the private account option, since their COLA income in their Social Security accounts would be significantly reduced.

✓ We call our COLA formula "PCE Price Plus." The approach uses an index that is applied to personal consumption expenditures (PCE). The PCE index is published by the government in its GDP and personal income and consumption releases. The Federal Reserve believes the PCE price changes are the most accurate way of measuring inflation. It believes it is superior to the CPI as a measurement of prices because the PCE approach takes into consideration the consumer's substitution of one product for another.

✓ Since the elderly have to contend with a higher cost of living than the general population, since they have little flexibility to adapt to financial adversity, and since certainty of income is so important, we have added two items to the index. One is to add 0.5 percent to the PCE increase every year, and the second is to guarantee that the COLAs increase at least 2 percent for Social Security recipients every year.

✓ At the same time the Federal Reserve and the Social Security Trustees are working on their projects, the CBO would estimate annual federal government outlays for Medicare and Medicaid. The number of years estimated by the CBO would be the same as the number of years estimated by the Federal Reserve and the Trustees in their respective areas.

✓ The Federal Reserve, the Social Security Trustees, and the CBO would combine their estimates into one report. The primary estimate made would be cash coming in each year for Social Security and Medicare (there are no federal receipts designated for Medicaid), compared with cash going out for Social Security, Medicare, and Medicaid. The combined results should give a clear picture of the financial state of Social Security, Medicare, and Medicaid. It would also answer some questions as to whether, and when, annual Social Security tax inflows would fall short of annual benefit payments, and whether a change in receipts estimates, and a change in the COLA, would make a major difference. We think that it would.

Social Security Privatization: A Few Thoughts on Philosophy

Critics of privatization have spent a great deal of time explaining how both the Social Security "crisis" and the "solution" of privatization rest on faulty numbers. So have we. Arguably, however, the numbers are beside the point. Like tax cuts, for many conservatives Social Security "reform" is about philosophy, not math. Privatization is not intended to deal with Social Security's long-term financing imbalance; for that, the Bush administration prefers some form of benefit cuts. Public confusion about this serves the privatization cause, by linking two issues that really are separate. Privatization is related to "saving" Social Security only in the sense that it is supposed to provide the "spoonful of sugar" to make the benefit cut "medicine" go down.

Most privatization advocates, in fact, are quite up front about this. "Social Security reform is not, at bottom, an economic issue with moral overtones," wrote Jonathan Rauch in the *National Journal* earlier this year. "It is a moral issue with economic overtones." Conservative columnist George Will agrees that the "philosophic reasons for reforming Social Security are more compelling than the fiscal reasons."[4] Peter Wehner, Bush's director of strategic initiatives, made this clear in a February 2005 memo published in the newsletter *Congress Daily,* when he conceded that without benefit cuts, privatization would do little to address the system's "fundamental structural problem." Private accounts have different virtues, Wehner explained. "Our goal is to provide a path to greater opportunity, more freedom, and more control for individuals over their own lives. That is what the personal account debate is fundamentally about." "For the first time in six decades," he concluded, "the Social Security battle is one we can win—and in doing so, we can transform the political and philosophical landscape of our country."

In other words, Social Security privatization is a philosophical debate about the role of government (and perhaps about the legitimacy of progressive redistribution), not a mathematical debate about how to make Social Security's outflows match its inflows. The numbers don't add up, but for those most committed to privatization, that is really beside the point. We agree in part, and that is why we've tried to engage the issue both philosophically and pragmatically. We believe that popular opposition will stop privatization from getting through Congress in the near term, but much of that opposition is motivated by fear and anxiety. Fear and anxiety can stop bad things from happening, but they cannot make good things happen. For that, the American public will need to be convinced by ideas as well as facts.

While the privatization of risk in recent decades reflected shifts in the private sector, it was also part of a larger political (and philosophical) strategy within the Republican Party to encourage the creation of a parallel system of private individual accounts that could eventually be portrayed as a viable alternative to Social Security. While one rarely hears this today, for a half century Social Security was generally referred to as the "third rail" of American politics. Even at the height of Reagan's influence, it would have been political suicide for the GOP to attempt a frontal assault on the program. Instead, Republicans in Washington chose to "carve out a competing policy path, one that would slowly undermine support for Social Security and preserve the idea of privatization for the day when it was politically ripe."[5]

This strategy was well described in the fall 1983 issue of the journal published by the conservative Cato Institute, the intellectual redoubt of Social Security privatization advocates for decades. The authors called for the creation of a coalition of those that would "reap benefits from the IRA-based private system," including the "banks, insurance companies . . . that will gain from providing such plans to the public." By approaching the issue in this way, they continued, "we may be ready for the next crisis in Social Security." Their plan called for a campaign to "achieve small legislative changes that embellish the present IRA system, making it in practice a small-scale private Social Security system." From there, "the natural constituency for an enlarged IRA system must be . . . welded into a coalition for political change." Running alongside this effort would be a form of "guerrilla warfare against both the current Social Security system and the coalition that supports it." The reason for designing a private IRA system, they concluded, "is purely political." The article, notably, was entitled "Achieving a 'Leninist' Strategy."[6] The pro-privatization wing of the Republican Party began to follow the Cato playbook. As early as 1983, it began to play up publicly the fiscal crisis of the program, question whether young Americans could rely on it in the future, and raise the necessity of drastic reform. The GOP is reaping the fruit of this political investment presently.

There can be no question that many advocates of partial privatization believe that such reforms will save a Social Security system that is in crisis. As we have shown, their beliefs are based on demonstrably false assumptions. But as stated above, "saving" Social Security is really beside the point for many other privatizers. They see "partial" privatization as the first step in a likely unraveling of the Social Security program, which they believe is an unjustified and unaffordable expansion of government power. It is in this sense that Social Security privatization is a "philosophical" issue rather than an economic one.

The more politically aware among them also conclude that by criticizing and then essentially eliminating Social Security, they will have also eliminated the single greatest example of effective "big government" in the lives of most Americans. Once that is accomplished, the Democratic Party ceases to have much to claim for itself. This is a plausible and historically informed analysis. Politically it's quite brilliant, on a scale with the political brilliance that inspired Social Security in the first place. As Thomas Frank has pointed out, with Social Security's guaranteed benefits, workers can look forward to a time of relative leisure and complete freedom from the boss. Under privatization, all bets are off. Retirement would now be mainly tied "to the size of your portfolio, which in turn is tied to your willingness to work—longer hours, and on the boss's terms." The market itself might become the "third rail" of American politics, Frank concludes, with its priorities becoming the nation's priorities, and its demands increasingly hard to refuse. This would leave very little political space for the kind of bold leadership and government initiatives that helped to build the post–World War II middle class. Is this what we want?[7]

When Social Security was created in 1935, it helped to bring about a tectonic shift in American politics and ideas, as well as in the lives of individual citizens. It provoked a profound national debate about the responsibilities of democratic government, the material conditions of freedom in a modern industrial economy, and the relative importance of luck and personal responsibility in the economic fortunes of American families.

Making powerful use of the language of freedom, Franklin Roosevelt forged a new political order that lasted well into the post-World War II era. Social Security is its centerpiece. One of the virtues of President Bush's aggressive agenda on the subject is that it has opened these issues for debate once again. Free market conservatives have longed for such a discussion for decades; armed with a vision of freedom that places individual choice and independence from government at its center, their philosophical approach has essentially framed public discourse for two decades. Their ideas are powerful and persuasive. They've effectively held together an otherwise divergent coalition between economic interests seeking lower taxes, less regulation and the privatization of risk, and moral traditionalists. Partial privatization of Social Security would be their greatest political victory.

However, as Alice Munnell observed above, Americans may be reaching the limits of their willingness to tolerate the society and economy that the conservative vision (and globalization) seems to be creating. In a more objective sense, the excessive tilt towards individualism may be putting a strain on our ability to sustain and reproduce our way of life, and even on the legitimacy of many of our core institutions and constitutive commitments.

This is a propitious time politically. The overreaching of the Administration on this issue has provided a golden opportunity for Democrats to re-articulate their vision of freedom and its necessary preconditions for another era. The New Deal order was built on the ability of liberal Democrats (and many moderate Republicans) to deliver on the American Dream for the great American middle class. President Bush and the Republican Party, to their credit, are thinking on this scale. Democrats aren't. They should be. The nation would benefit from genuine debates about ideas, rather than partisanship based merely on power, resources, and opinion polls. Democrats have done the nation a service by holding the line against private accounts and insisting that the financial future of Social Security is a separate question. But what happens next? The relationship between freedom and security has been at the heart of modern liberalism. If they cannot affirm that philosophy today with concrete proposals, they may find themselves in the minority for a generation.

In his second Inaugural Address, President Bush issued a ringing call for freedom at home and around the world. He talked mostly about foreign policy, but also referred to the "broader definition of liberty" that he saw at work in programs like the Homestead Act, Social Security, and the G.I. Bill. Citizenship and freedom, he argued, are rooted in the independence that stems from ownership. "By making every citizen an agent of his or her own destiny," the President argued, "we will give our fellow Americans greater freedom from want and fear." The echoes of Roosevelt are unmistakable.

More powerful, however, was his evocative account of the conservative notion of freedom. As William Galston pointed out recently in his brilliant dissection of the speech, Bush essentially made the case that conservative individualist means are now better suited to serve classic liberal ends "than are New Deal programs of social solidarity." Partial privatization of Social Security, as well as the other pieces of the President's 'Ownership Society,' promises not only freedom from want and fear, but also freedom of individual choice, and freedom from dependence on government. While we are deeply skeptical about these claims, it is an undeniably powerful vision.[8]

What does freedom mean in the twenty-first century? And what, in Galston's words, are "the means needed to make it effective in our own lives?" For most of the twentieth century, as we discussed in Chapter Three, liberals took the lead in defining and expanding freedom by insisting that sometimes it can only be advanced through an active government. In recent decades, liberals have almost completely ceded the notion of freedom to conservatives. This is certainly an historical irony, as well as a political mistake. Social Security is the quintessential example of how public power can advance freedom in people's lives. Because of Social Security's creation the elderly no longer had to depend on others—or charity—for basic subsistence. They could be economically self-sufficient. It gave them freedom. Liberals, Galston argues, "seldom talk about Social Security or other programs in terms of freedom." He believes they would gain from doing so. So do we, but our primary concern is the larger point: freedoms often have conditions for their effective exercise, and sometimes government has to act to ensure broad access to those conditions.[9]

Will privatization enhance individual freedom, as some advocates argue? Will it provide a greater degree of independence? That depends upon what, in the real world, you think allows people to be free. If you think that any reduction in the size, authority, or capacity of government constitutes a victory for freedom, then you might answer "yes." This struck Franklin Roosevelt as a rather complacent attitude toward the future of capitalism and liberal democracy, unsupported by history and overly dismissive of our ability to collectively redeem our national ideals. We are more than just consumers. Dollars don't deliberate, seek common ground, or express empathy. We are also citizens. According to philosopher Benjamin Barber, privatization is a kind of reverse social contract: It dissolves the bonds that tie us together. The social contract "takes us out of the state of nature; it asks us to give up a part of our private liberty to do whatever we want, in order to secure common liberty for all."[10]

Privatization returns us to that state of nature. Ostensibly that is a kind of freedom. But is it the kind of freedom we want? One in which we now have the freedom to get whatever we can, but lose the common power to secure everything to which we have a right? Ultimately it promises an acceleration of the trend toward risk privatization, leaving families and individuals to cope on their own with the "hazards and vicissitudes" of economic life. It is an odd position for a political party supposedly dedicated to family values to take. Surely debt, bankruptcy, and economic anxiety threaten the viability and stability of American families more than gay marriages and Super Bowl halftime shows do. Kick out the last stable leg of the nation's retirement stool and you are likely to increase risk, decrease the risk-taking on which innovation depends, and make millions of Americans a little less free.

————)((()))(————

Chapter 10

FORECASTING BY THE TRUSTEES: FLAWS AND RECOMMENDATIONS

I n their annual report, the Social Security Trustees place a great deal of emphasis on when the trust funds will run out of money. The fact that these are not real trust funds and that they have no money seems to be beside the point. Moreover, even if these forecasts had any meaning or value, the previous estimates have been significantly wide of the mark. To be blunt, since 1997 the trustees' estimates have been abysmal.

Inaccurate Estimates

In the 1997 report, the trustees estimated that the Social Security and Disability Trust Funds would be exhausted by 2029; in the 2004 report the exhaustion date was 2042. To arrive at a thirteen-year revision in a period of seven years is incredible. This makes one wonder how far off their estimates might be over a period of seventy-five years.

What should be of even greater concern regarding the quality of the trustees' estimates is that in June 2004, the CBO made a forecast that the exhaustion date would be 2052, ten years further out than the trustees' forecast made only a few months earlier. Moreover, in arriving at this conclusion, the CBO used relatively conservative economic growth forecasts. The following are quotes from the annual reports of the Board of Trustees, 1997–2004:

1997—Although the combined trust funds are well financed over the next 10 years, the OASDI program is not in close actuarial balance over the full 75-year projection period and therefore does not meet the long-term solvency test. The estimated actuarial balance is a deficit of 2.23 percent of taxable payroll over the next 75 years, based on the intermediate assumptions. The combined OASI and DI Trust Funds would become exhausted in 2029 without corrective legislation.

1998—Although the combined trust funds are well financed over the next 10 years, the OASDI program is not in close actuarial balance over the full 75-year projection period and therefore does not meet the long-term solvency test. The estimated actuarial balance is a deficit of 2.19 percent of taxable payroll over the next 75 years, based on the intermediate assumptions. The combined OASI and DI Trust Funds would become exhausted in 2032 without corrective legislation.

1999—The assets of the combined OASI and DI Trust Funds are expected to continue growing over the next several years, based on the intermediate assumptions. By the end of 2021, the assets are estimated to reach $.46 trillion in nominal dollars. The assets are then estimated to decline until the funds are exhausted in 2034.

2000—Although the combined trust funds are well financed over the next 10 years, the OASDI program is not in close actuarial balance over the full 75-year projection period and therefore does not meet the long-term solvency test. The estimated actuarial balance is a deficit of 1.89 percent of taxable payroll over the next 75 years, based on the intermediate assumptions. The combined OASI and DI Trust Funds would become exhausted in 2037 without corrective legislation.

2001—Under the intermediate assumptions the combined OASDI Trust Funds are expected to become exhausted in 2038, one year later than projected in last year's report. The projected actuarial deficit is 1.86 percent of taxable payroll, 0.03 percent smaller than last year's report.

2002—Under the intermediate assumptions the combined OASDI Trust Funds are expected to become exhausted in 2041, three years later than projected in last year's report. The projected actuarial deficit is 1.87 percent of taxable payroll, 0.01 percent larger than last year's report.

2003—Under the intermediate assumptions, the OASDI cost rate is projected to decline slightly and then remain flat for the next several years. It then begins to increase rapidly and first exceeds the income rate in 2018, producing cash-flow deficits thereafter. Despite these cash-flow deficits, trust fund interest earnings and assets will allow continuation of full benefit payments until 2042, when the trust funds will be exhausted.

2004—Under the intermediate assumptions the combined OASI and DI Trust Funds are projected to become exhausted in 2042.

Tables 11, 12, and 13 document the misestimates made by the trustees. These tables indicate that receipts were underestimated and spending was overestimated. Thus, both errors moved the numbers in the same direction, which meant the surplus was much larger than expected. The biggest surprise in the data was the large overestimation of benefit costs that was made in the 1997 report. By 2003, spending was overestimated by $27 billion. On the basis of this performance, one should not bet the family farm on benefit forecasts seventy-five years out.

The underestimation of receipts ($15 billion for 2003) was also consequential. This was the result of an unduly conservative real GDP growth forecast of 2 percent from 1998 through 2004. From the beginning of 1998 through 2004, actual GDP growth averaged over 3 percent, or roughly 50 percent more than the official forecast made in 1997. And, there was even a minirecession during that period.

In looking behind the receipts misestimates, the primary reason for the error is easy to determine. It was due to gross underestimation of productivity increases from 1998 through 2003. In this period the Trustees estimated a 1.3 percent annual advance; the actual advance was 3.3 percent. Moreover, in 2004 the productivity performance was still at about 3 percent. Forecasts and actual data are presented in Table 14.

Some of the earlier productivity estimates made by the trustees were difficult to find. It was not until 2001 that the economic assumptions table published in the trustees' report included specifically stated productivity increases. In the 1997 report, the verbal commentary indicated that the 1998 estimate for productivity growth was approximately 1.3 percent.

If there is good news from a forecasting perspective, it is that the trustees' productivity estimates are no longer *ridiculously* low; they are just low. In 2004, the annual productivity increase for the next decade is estimated by the trustees to be 1.7 percent; a more reasonable estimate is an increase of about 2.5 percent.

An Inappropriate Forecasting Approach

Every year the Social Security Trustees make what they call short-range (ten years) and long-range (seventy-five years) revenue and benefit estimates. The estimates are based on current law and assumptions about the factors that affect the income and outlays of each fund. Assumptions include economic growth, wage growth, inflation, unemployment, fertility, immigration, and mortality as well as factors that relate to disability and the cost of hospital and medical services.

Alternative sets of economic and demographic assumptions are developed to show a range of possibilities. Intermediate or middle-of-the-road assumptions reflect the trustees' best estimates. Then there are low-cost and high-cost forecasts. The low-cost forecast is the most optimistic, and the high-cost forecast is the most pessimistic. Divergent economic and demographic assumptions account for the differences.

Every year, based on new experiences and new information, the assumptions are reexamined and the forecasts revised. Unfortunately, the revisions tend to be inadequate, and there is no evidence of any comprehensive rethinking. This would require a zero-base budgeting approach. Zero-base budgeting means that all assumptions and forecasts are reworked on a regular basis, and this is reflected in new forecasts that are not just a fine-tuning of old forecasts.

In arriving at what they call their short-range forecast of ten years, the trustees supposedly measure the adequacy of the Old Age and Survivors Insurance (OASI), Disability Insurance (DI), and Hospital Insurance (HI) trust funds by comparing assets at the beginning of a year to projected benefit payments for that year. Using this approach, OASI, DI, and HI funds are considered financially adequate over this so-called short-range period.

The trustees' approach is different with respect to the long-run seventy-five-year outlook, where an actuarial balance concept is used. The actuarial balance is the difference between annual income and costs, expressed as a percentage of taxable payrolls over a seventy-five-year period. As for the Supplemental Medical Insurance (SMI) portion of Medicare, the trustees apply a less stringent asset test because financing is provided by beneficiary premiums and general revenue payments (as well as Treasury borrowings). Each year, the asset test is automatically adjusted to expected costs. Thus, in a general sense, SMI financing is accounted for throughout the long-range projection period.

Tables 15, 16, and 17 show official forecasts with respect to direct receipts and outlays for OASI, DI, HI, SMI, and Medicaid. We have devised these tables to make the numbers more understandable, to indicate where the main problems lie, and to show the magnitude of the difficulties. Table 17 is the most interesting; it shows that a combined deficit of over $600 billion is less than a decade away. That is more than the size of the entire U.S. budget deficit in fiscal year 2004. Therefore, it is hoped that the government and the American people will recognize the magnitude of this problem and deal with it sooner rather than later.

A More Realistic Time Frame Needed

Imagine it is 1929 and you are asked to forecast what a prospective Social Security program would look like in 2004. Unless you were clairvoyant, you could not have come close to imagining what the U.S. would be like in 2004. Of course, in 1930 you would have had a chance to make a new seventy-five-year forecast. Would that extra year have given you any greater insight as to what would be happening seventy-five years later? Not a chance. As a matter of fact, the events that occurred in that extra year probably would have made the forecast worse. In 1929 the economic bubble burst, and the hyper stock market crashed. In 1930 it was all doom and gloom and a recession. Moreover, irrespective of what happened in any specific year around that time, forecasters would have gained no additional insight into the state of the U.S. economic and social fabric in 2004 or 2005.

Despite the impossibility of long-term insights, every spring the trustees of the Social Security system publish a report that contains a seventy-five-year forecast on everything from economics to demographics. The 2005 forecast goes out to 2080. Frankly, the forecast might as well be out to 2180, because the insights for both those years are about the same—nonexistent! No human is clairvoyant enough to make a forecast out three-quarters of a century.

What needs to be done is to arrive at a reasonable time frame to forecast Social Security inflows and outflows. Anything that is well short of seventy-five years would be better than what we have now. A much more reasonable approach would be for the trustees to make an annual forecast for each of the next five years, and also for the tenth year and the twentieth year. Thus, seven specific years would be forecast.

The seven time periods chosen are an attempt to stretch the forecasting envelope as far as possible without entering the sheer guesswork zone. Conceptually, this type of approach sounds easy, but practically speaking, that is not the case. Trade-offs are complicated by the fact that it is possible to forecast farther out for demographics than for economics. The use of a twenty-year maximum estimate would be a compromise. Demographic estimates can have considerable validity more than two decades out, but in a rapidly changing world, economic forecasts for two decades are little more than a guess. One decade may be about as far out as an economist can see, and then only in the broadest of terms.

In making annual economic forecasts for the next five years, the presumption is that current data and trends provide enough information to make reasonable estimates. After five years, the benefits from current statistics begin to fade. Thus, the forecast for ten years out is an approximation, and twenty years out is a rough guess. If a twenty-year forecast is a rough guess, what is a seventy-five-year forecast?

The ten-year and seventy-five-year annual forecasts represent major flaws in the trustees' approach. Yet, these are not the only problems. Too much emphasis is placed on the performance of the nonexistent trust accounts, their nonexistent investments, and their nonexistent earnings. Discussions of meaningless crossover points as to when the so-called trust accounts move into deficit, and when they supposedly reach oblivion, do nothing but mislead and unnecessarily frighten the American people. Instead of this misleading approach, the trustees' annual report should concentrate on estimates that compare the cash revenues coming in versus the cash benefits going out. This would apply to Social Security and Medicare, both individually and as a package.

A New Way for Reporting Data

In order to solve financial problems, it is first necessary to organize data in a useful way. Social Security, DI, Medicare, and Medicaid data need to be presented in a manner that will facilitate analysis and determine the best financing approach. To start the process, tables have been developed by the authors that show annual receipts, spending, deficits, and surpluses for these programs. The numbers are then combined so people can understand the magnitude of the problem. Table 18 provides the necessary data.

Using this approach, the first sign of an overall deficit problem appeared in 1976, when the shortfall for Social Security, Medicare, and Medicaid jumped to almost $17 billion, from $8 billion in the previous year. By the time the 1983 Social Security Commission was formed, the deficit for the programs had swelled to $53 billion. (These numbers show cash coming in and cash going out; they do not include imputed interest on nonexistent investments.) Legislative changes made in 1983 helped reduce the combined deficit through 1989. Then the upward trek in the combined deficits began.

Since 1961 in the case of Medicaid, and since 1967 in the case of SMI, which is when these programs began, their combined deficits have moved relentlessly higher. This is because SMI is underfunded by recipient contributions, and Medicaid has no direct financing. The 1983 changes did nothing to help the SMI portion of Medicare and did nothing to help Medicaid; thus, these two areas have eventually dominated the deficit numbers. In 2004, net cash flow for Social Security, DI, Medicare, and Medicaid amounted to a deficit of $243 billion. As recently as 2000, the deficit was a mere $98 billion.

In 2004, Social Security ran a surplus of $46 billion, and DI had a surplus of $1 billion. The HI portion of Medicare had a deficit of $13 billion, while the SMI portion of Medicare had a shortfall of $101 billion. Medicaid had a deficit of $176 billion, and this is all expenses since there are no offsetting tax receipts. Table 18 shows the performance of these programs since their inception.

Looking ahead, unless something is done, the combined annual shortfall for these programs is likely to exceed $600 billion in less than a decade, and this is despite a likely Social Security surplus. Unfortunately, most Americans are not aware of this situation. This is because the data dealing with these programs have not been well advertised, and have not been presented in a useful and understandable way.

Yet, there will be a day of deficit reckoning for these programs, and that could start in 2006, when analysts realize the additional taxpayer burden from the prescription drug legislation. The legislation is expensive compared with what Medicare beneficiaries will receive. A prescription drug bill was turned into an omnibus spending bill. Taxpayers will pay for a full loaf, and Medicare beneficiaries will receive half a loaf.

Specific Reporting and Forecasting Recommendations

The following recommendations are a more detailed presentation of the preceding commentary. The recommendations are primarily technical in nature, but one should not assume they are of marginal importance. They are needed to replace current approaches and techniques that have been around for ages and outlived any usefulness they might have had in the first place. Remember, bad bookkeeping and bad forecasting can lead to bad programs and bad results:

✓ *Trustees should publish annual cash inflow and outflow reports for Social Security, Medicare, and Medicaid.* Data should be published separately for each program, and then presented in a combined format. Past data and forecasts would both be presented. The forecasts would show tax rates needed to cover future benefits costs. Errors in past forecasts would also be shown and explained. The more you have to advertise your past mistakes, the more careful you are likely to be in making your forecast.

✓ *Forecasting techniques need to be sharpened, and time periods limited in order to achieve credible forecasts.* The trustees should make only one economic forecast, not three. Annually updated forecasts should be for every year within a five-year time frame, followed by a ten-year forecast and a twenty-year forecast. Thus, a total of seven separate years will be forecast. Twenty years may seem too far ahead to make educated estimates, but they would be a significant improvement over the current system that makes guesses seventy-five years out. It should be troubling that three-quarters of a century from now, none of those making current forecasts will be around to take the credit or the blame.

✓ *Economic forecasts should relate more closely to recent underlying changes in the economy.* The last five years should be used as a guide for economic forecasts over the next five years and provide useful information for ten- and twenty-year forecasts. This approach is especially important when it comes to estimating productivity gains, which serve as the foundation for economic growth. Making marginal changes in incorrect economic forecasts is not a good forecasting technique. How long will it take before the trustees realize that they are using out-of-date and underestimated productivity forecasts?

✓ *Each year, the CBO should publish an analysis devoted to documenting the annual cash inflows and outflows for Social Security, DI, Medicare, and Medicaid.* The study would also include updated forecasts. The numbers for each individual program would be presented, and then combined for analytical purposes. The CBO would be chosen for this task rather than the Office of Management and Budget (OMB), because the CBO tends to be less partisan, and typically less political. Therefore, it can be less political in how it handles the analysis, and its estimates can serve as a check and balance against forecasts by the Social Security Trustees and the OMB.

✓ *The Social Security Trustees should take on a new and more proactive role.* The American people are not well served by the trustees fine-tuning bad estimates on irrelevant items. There is a need for creativity when it comes to improving the current Social Security and Medicare systems, and it is the trustees that need to provide much of this creativity. More time should be spent on problem-solving, and less time devoted to making extensive and detailed forecasts on trust fund items that tend to mislead and confuse the American people.

✓ *Get rid of the term "trust fund" for Social Security and Medicare.* It conveys the image of funds being held in trust for a later date, which is not the case. The main impediment to getting rid of the trust fund designation is that some politicians would find it embarrassing to admit that money has not been set aside for future obligations and that there is no "lockbox." It should be made clear to the public that it has an ongoing priority claim on government funds, irrespective of how the money is raised. The Social Security and Medicare programs are financed on a pay-as-you-go basis, and whether they run surpluses or deficits is immaterial when it comes to whether people will receive their benefits. Taxes are collected from many sources and ultimately they wind up in general revenues, which are used to finance outlays. Thus, even when Social Security inflows exceed outflows—which is currently the case—the funds are neither saved nor invested. Rather, they are commingled with other government funds and used to meet all types of government outlays.

Chapter 11

SOCIAL SECURITY AROUND THE WORLD

Two related problems have had a strong adverse influence on privatized Social Security programs around the world. One is very high administration costs, and second are pensions that are inadequate to sustain even a minimally decent retirement. In some countries, a third problem can be added— high budget deficits. The UK may be the best example of missteps; these missteps started a quarter century ago and have not been rectified.

High fees levied on Britain's private accounts were so out of control— absorbing 20 to 30 percent of individual pension savings—that the government had to impose a "charge cap" on investment companies. The British Pensions Commission estimates that at least 75 percent of Britons with private pension accounts will not have enough savings to provide "adequate pensions" at retirement. "Those who think Mrs. Thatcher's privatization solved the pension problem" the commission concluded, "are living in a fool's paradise." American Social Security is now looked at with some envy in Britain, by retirees and policymakers alike.

The story in Chile is that privatization has had some success, but this compares with a previous system that was inadequate. The Chilean approach is a form of mandatory private insurance. It was adopted in 1981 and replaced a social insurance system that began in 1924. The centerpiece of the 1981 system is that individuals choose a pension fund management company. At retirement, individuals may make withdrawals from their individual accounts (which are regulated to guarantee income for their expected life span), or they can buy an annuity from a private insurance company, or they can opt for a combination of both.

Chile adopted the current system because of concerns that individuals would not receive adequate retirement funds. This was especially important for a country that, in 1981, lacked a broad array of private pension plans and other retirement alternatives that would provide an adequate financial safety net for the elderly. Ironically, but not surprisingly, the Chilean government is now putting in a substantial amount of funds in order to "provide subsidies for workers failing to accumulate enough capital to provide a minimum pension," according to a study conducted by the U.S. Federal Reserve and presented in a February 3, 2005 *Wall Street Journal* article.

That same article also presented the experiences of other countries with respect to privatization of Social Security–type accounts. The picture wasn't rosy; many of the countries were plagued with problems of complexity, high administrative costs, inadequate benefits, and limited popular support. In no case that we are aware of did a country that had a reasonably effective system before privatization improve its situation in a meaningful way after privatization. Moreover, quite a few countries were worse off than before.

The success gap between the U.S. and other industrialized countries when it comes to Social Security has widened in recent years in favor of the U.S., especially against nations that have tried privatization. It is little wonder that many countries that have gone down the privatization path wish they had not done so.

Social Security Needs and Capabilities Are Different

The U.S. situation is special because the country is special. Its capabilities are unique, and so are its needs and desires. It is an industrialized country of 300 million people that has extensive borders. It is the only superpower in the world, and it feels obligated to exert its influence and power. It's geography is varied and so is its population. The population is aging but there is a large amount of immigration (legal and otherwise) composed of many young people, which adds great uncertainty to the demographic and economic outlook. The country has been a democracy for over two centuries and has never significantly deviated from a capitalistic approach. It has had incredible resiliency to bounce back from adversity, whether it be wars, recessions, or major social conflicts. There is a toughness to the people when a crisis develops and it is recognized as such.

The U.S. economic story is also special. It dwarfs other countries in terms of the size of its GDP and its dollar growth. It has by far the most developed money and capital markets in the world. It has substantial amounts of natural resources, although these are not always used in the best way. It is the innovative leader of the world when it comes to research, development, and new products. The productivity of its private sector is the envy of the world. Pure and simple, it is by far the brightest star in the world's economic galaxy.

Yet, even though the U.S. is so special in a positive way, it is also has special problems and needs. The efficiency of government leaves a great deal to be desired, on the federal and state and local levels. Huge budget deficits are more acceptable than they should be, but the sheer wealth of the country has, to this point, deflected the importance of the problem. The U.S foreign trade deficit is unacceptably large because imports of consumer goods and oil are so large. There is no real energy policy, but again, like the budget and trade deficits, the wealth of the country seems to cover over major problems. The country is lacking a cohesive immigration policy and is just starting to deal with shortcomings in its intelligence and homeland security systems, and its military capabilities are being stretched in a world of terrorism and religious fanatics. These are pressing problems that gain the daily headlines and need to be addressed in a timely fashion.

Unfortunately, what does not gain headlines, and on the surface does not seem to be as timely when it comes to solutions, are the daily problems many Americans face who are just trying to make ends meet. The overwhelming majority of these people are not malingerers or malcontents. Most of the younger ones are trying to pick themselves up by their own bootstraps, but in a fast-moving industrialized society, a considerable number can be left behind. Most of the older generation no longer have the capability to improve their economic lot; all they can do is hunker down and further suppress their standard of living. Thus, the U.S. is special, not only because of its capabilities and wealth, but also because of the magnitude of some of its problems.

Thus, when the U.S. looks at how other countries deal with their poor, their middle class, their minorities, and their elderly, the solutions vary greatly. The U.S. has more assets in almost every conceivable way, but it also has a disturbing amount of liabilities. Simply put, the U.S. is different; it is bigger in every conceivable way, and studying how other countries deal with their economic problems is interesting, but not really applicable.

Therefore, we wonder why so many people place so much emphasis on figuring out a *proper* way to solve daily domestic economic problems. Isn't the objective to solve problems in *the most practical and logical way*? To many, the method seems to matter more than the results. Otherwise, how can one explain why these people make it sound as if Social Security is on the verge of crisis—which is clearly not the case—and then look to other countries who have used some sort of privatization to address their problems. This is despite the fact that there is no other country in the world that has had the same degree of success for seven decades with its Social Security system. How desperate can people be if the best example they can find that some sort of privatization is the answer to the U.S.'s Social Security problems is what has happened in Chile?

Available Information on Social Security Worldwide

The Social Security Administration publishes the most complete data when it comes to foreign social security–type programs, in a report called *Social Security Programs throughout the World.* It was first published sixty-five years ago. The report is divided into four volumes and is published at six-month intervals. Each volume is dedicated to a geographical region: Europe, Asia and the Pacific, Africa, and the Americas. These books are the result of a cooperative effort between the Social Security Administration and the International Social Security Association (ISSA). The ISSA was founded in 1927 and is a nonprofit organization that brings together institutions and administrative organizations from nations around the world.

The research and the writings are now contracted out to the ISSA. It does its research primarily through numerous country-based correspondents. It uses its Social Security Worldwide Database and other types of information to update its reports. A few political jurisdictions have been excluded because they have no social security system, or have not released information regarding their social security legislation.

The ISSA presents four summary tables in its publications. Most countries are represented, and we have chosen a select group that would be of primary interest to our readers. The information is presented in Tables 19, 20, 21, and 22. The titles are: Types of Social Security Programs; Types of Mandatory Systems for Retirement Income; Demographic and Other Statistics Related to Social Security, and Contribution Rates for Social Security Programs.

The information presented is simplified since there is only so much that can be put in a table. The cost factor and cost efficiency cannot be determined. Neither can affordability of the programs, their successes or failures in addressing the needs of the people, the proportion of the population the programs cover, and whether the programs are designed and managed by a democracy or a dictatorial government.

How long the programs have been in existence in their current form, how frequently major revisions have been necessary, and whether the programs are improving or deteriorating are also unanswered questions. Equity and fairness cannot be determined, and finally, it is very difficult to determine from the numbers whether a country is doing its best with the resources it has at its disposal.

Chapter 12

SOME PARTING THOUGHTS

In writing our book, it should be clear to the reader that almost all of the recommendations are a means to an end. The legislative proposals are not an end in themselves. Using this type of approach, we found we were quite flexible when it came to recommendations. If others have better ways to improve the state of the American people, then bring those ideas forward. Let's use their ideas and recommendations if they are better than ours. We take pride in authorship, but no more than that. It is also paramount that the American people and public officials are on the same page when it comes to the facts. Neither the American people nor the politicians should be afraid of the facts, whatever they may turn out to be.

For the purposes of reform, Social Security, Medicare, and Medicaid should be seen as parts of a larger whole. We also believe that these programs cannot and should not be separated from the larger questions of opportunity and economic insecurity affecting millions of Americans. While we disagree with many of its policy components, President Bush's advocacy of an "ownership society" should be taken seriously. It raises serious questions not just about how we finance entitlement programs (or whether we should have them at all), but also about what is needed to create and sustain the material conditions of the American Dream for another century.

The freedom and well-being of American families is heavily dependent upon the opportunity structure that they encounter at different points in their lives. That opportunity structure is shaped by a wide variety of social factors. Historically, government action has been critical for creating, shaping, and expanding it. If we put ideology aside, now may be a good time to reexamine this opportunity structure. Is it still working for the majority of Americans? If not, what will make it work?

We have argued that rising insecurity in the great American middle should be taken seriously and cannot be separated from this larger discussion. These are fundamental questions, of course. Honest conversations about our mutual commitments, by necessity, entails an equally direct conversation about what we can afford. We have suggested a few programs—and in keeping with our general approach, how we might pay for them. Perhaps we can afford more than is generally believed, but we may need a new way of talking about government, and to one another, to bring this about. American history may be a useful guide for a new nationalism, that openly and honestly tends to the roots of the institutions that ground our community.

Finally, this is a book about policy, first and foremost. It is the product of an experiment, in a sense: an effort to work across generations and political beliefs, to find what is essential and defensible. We haven't found any kind of magic bullet here. Some of what we have argued, advocated, and critiqued will disappoint or even anger people across the political spectrum. But that is precisely the point. Being a citizen in a representative democracy entails an honest deliberation, then persuasion, and finally compromise.

In the first chapter of the book we expressed our intention to use two ideas to guide our work: If we make commitments to one another, we must be honest about which ones can be kept; and efforts to solve social problems through government should, whenever possible, try to lift us all up from the bottom. Some of our ideas are more political and economically feasible than others, but they should receive serious consideration. Franklin Roosevelt once described his approach to governance in the following way: "Take a method and try it. If it fails, admit it frankly, and try another. But by all means, try something."

Appendix I

SOCIAL SECURITY, MEDICARE, AND MEDICAID: FACTS AND HISTORY

Listed in this appendix is everything you might want to know about the history and details of Social Security, Disability, Medicare, and Medicaid. This information should give you a solid background as to how, when, and why these programs evolved. In Appendix II, Tables 23 and 24 indicate the increases in the number of beneficiaries for Social Security and Disability Insurance. Tables 25 and 26 relate to Medicare enrollment and the number of Medicaid recipients. Table 27 shows the states that are attempting cost containment:

The Social Security Act

Title I	Grants to States for Old-Age Assistance
Title II	Federal Old-Age, Survivors, and Disability Insurance Benefits
Title III	Grants to States for Unemployment Compensation Administration
Title IV	Grants to States for Aid and Services to Needy Families with Children and for Child-Welfare Services
Title V	Maternal and Child Health Service Block Grant
Title VI	Temporary State Fiscal Relief
Title VII	Administration
Title VIII	Special Benefits for Certain World War II Veterans

Title IX	Miscellaneous Provisions Relating to Employment Security
Title X	Grants to States for Aid to the Blind
Title XI	General Provisions, Peer Review, and Administrative Simplification
Title XII	Advances to State Unemployment Funds
Title XIII	Repealed
Title XIV	Grants to States for Aid to the Permanently and Totally Disabled
Title XV	Repealed
Title XVI	Grants to States for Aid to the Aged, Blind, or Disabled
Title XVI	Supplemental Security Income for the Aged, Blind, or Disabled
Title XVII	Grants for planning Comprehensive Action to Combat Mental Retardation
Title XVIII	Health Insurance for the Aged and Disabled
Title XIX	Grants to States for Medical Assistance Programs
Title XX	Block Grants to States for Social Services
Title XXI	State Children's Health Insurance Program

Source: Compilation of the Social Security Laws, Social Security Online.

Development of U.S. Social Security Programs

1935	Social Security Old-Age Insurance; Unemployment Insurance; and Public Assistance programs for the needy, aged, and blind (replaced by the SSI program in 1972); and Aid to Families with Dependent Children (replaced with block grants for Temporary Assistance for Needy Families in 1996).
1934	Railroad Retirement System
1937	Public Housing
1939	Social Security Old-Age and Survivors Insurance
1946	National School Lunch Program
1950	Aid to the Permanently and Totally Disabled (replaced by the SSI program in 1972)
1956	Social Security Disability Insurance
1960	Medical Assistance for the Aged (replaced by Medicaid in 1965)
1964	Food Stamp Program
1965	Medicare and Medicaid Programs
1966	School Breakfast Program
1969	Black Lung Benefits Program

1972   Supplemental Security Income Program

1974   Special Supplemental Food Program for Women, Infants, and Children (WIC)

1975   Earned Income Tax Credit

1981   Low-Income Home Energy Assistance

1996   Temporary Assistance for Needy Families

Source: Social Security Programs in the United States, p. 6.

Important Dates for Social Security

June 8, 1934	Federal legislation to promote economic security was recommended in President Franklin D. Roosevelt's Message to Congress.
June 29, 1934	President Roosevelt created the Committee on Economic Security to study the problems related to economic security and to make recommendations for a program of legislation.
Jan 17, 1935	The Committee on Economic Security's recommendations were introduced in the 74th Congress.
Apr 19, 1935	The Social Security Act was passed in the House of Representatives 372 to 33.
June 19, 1935	The Social Security Act was passed in the Senate by a vote of 77 to 6.
Aug 14, 1935	The Social Security Act became law with President Roosevelt's signature.
Aug 23, 1935	The Senate confirmed the president's nomination of the original members of the Social Security Board, John G. Winant, Chairman; Arthur J. Altmeyer, and Vincent M. Miles.
Oct 14, 1936	The first Social Security field office was opened in Austin, Texas.
Nov 9. 1936	The Baltimore office for record-keeping operations opened in the Candler Building.
Nov 24, 1936	Applications for Social Security account numbers were distributed to the Post Office.
Jan 1, 1937	Workers began to acquire credits toward old-age insurance benefits.
Jan 1937	First applications for benefits filed. Ernest Ackerman, a retired Cleveland motorman, was among the first to apply.
Mar 11, 1937	First Social Security benefits paid (one-time payment only).

July 1, 1939	Under the Federal Reorganization Act of 1939, the Social Security Board was made part of the newly established Federal Security Agency.
Aug 10, 1939	The Social Security Amendments of 1939 broadened the program to include dependents and survivors benefits.
Jan 31, 1949	Ida May Fuller became the first person to receive an old-age monthly benefit check.
Nov 19, 1945	In a special message to Congress, President Truman proposed a comprehensive, prepaid medical insurance plan for all people through the Social Security system.
Jul 16, 1946	Under the President's Reorganization Plan of 1946, the Social Security Board was abolished and the Social Security Administration was established. Arthur J. Altmeyer was appointed as the first commissioner.
Aug 28, 1950	President Truman signed the 1950 Social Security Amendments.
Sep 1, 1954	Social Security Amendments established a disability "freeze" to help prevent the erosion of a disabled worker's benefits.
Aug 1, 1956	The Social Security Act was amended to provide monthly benefits to permanently and totally disabled workers aged 50–64 and for adult children of deceased or retired workers, if disabled before age 18.
June 30, 1961	The Social Security Amendments of 1961 were signed by President John Kennedy, permitting all workers to elect reduced retirement at age 62.
Jul 30, 1965	President Lyndon B. Johnson signed the Medicare Bill in the presence of former President Truman, who proposed this legislation in his message to Congress in 1945.
Dec 30, 1969	President Nixon signed the Federal Coal Mine Health and Safety Act. Monthly cash benefits were provided coal miners who became totally disabled because of black lung disease, and for the dependents and survivors.
Jul 1, 1972	President Nixon signed into law P.L. 92-336, which authorized a 20% cost-of-living adjustment (COLA) effective September 1992, and established the procedures for issuing automatic annual COLAs beginning in 1975.
Oct 30, 1972	Social Security Amendments of 1972 signed into law by president Nixon—creating the Supplemental Security Income (SSI) program.
Jan 1, 1974	SSI program went into operation as a result of the Social Security Amendments of 1972.

Mar 9, 1977	HEW reorganization plan published in Federal Register, creating the Health Care Financing Administration to manage the Medicare and Medicaid programs.
Jun 9, 1980	President Carter signed the Social Security Amendments of 1980. Major provision involved greater work incentives for disabled Social Security and SSI beneficiaries.
Aug 13, 1981	The Omnibus Budget Reconciliation Act of 1981 made major changes in Social Security, SSI, and AFDC. These included: a phasing out of students' benefits; stopping young parents benefits when a child reached 16; limiting the lump-sum death payment and changes in the minimum benefit.
Jan 20, 1983	The National Commission on Social Security Reform sent its recommendations for resolving the Social Security program's financial problems to the President and Congress.
Apr 20, 1983	President Reagan signed into law the Social Security Amendments of 1983.
Oct 9, 1984	Disability Benefits Reform Act of 1984 signed by President Reagan.
Jun 6, 1986	President Reagan signed the Federal Employees Retirement System (FERS) Act, which established Social Security coverage for federal employees hired after December 31, 1983.
Feb 20, 1990	The Supreme Court held in Sullivan vs. Zebley that substantial parts of the SSI regulation on determining disability for children are inconsistent with the Social Security Act.
May 17, 1994	SSA's Internet site was launched on the World-Wide Web (SSA Online at http://www.ssa.gov).
Mar 31, 1995	SSA became an independent agency.
Apr 19, 1995	The Alfred P. Murrah Federal Building in Oklahoma City, Oklahoma, was bombed, killing 168 individuals, including 16 SSA employees.
Aug 22, 1996	President Clinton signs welfare reform bill.
Dec 8–9, 1998	The first-ever White House Conference on Social Security was held in Washington, D.C.
Dec 17, 1999	President Clinton signed the "Ticket to Work and Work Incentives Improvement Act of 1999."
Apr 7, 2000	President Clinton signed into law a bill eliminating the Retirement Earnings Test (RET) for those beneficiaries at or above normal retirement age.

Source: Brief History of Social Security Pamphlet, Social Security Administration, August 2000.

Important Dates for Medicare

Jul 30, 1965	Authorized under Title XVIII of the Social Security Act, Medicare was enacted to cover the elderly. Seniors were the population group most likely to be living in poverty; about half had insurance coverage.
1966	Medicare was implemented and more than 19 million individuals enrolled on July 1.
1970	Over 20 million older Americans were enrolled in Medicare.
1972	Medicare coverage was extended to the disabled and to those with permanent kidney failure. Two million new individuals subsequently enrolled in the program.
1977	The Health Care Financing Administration (HCFA) was established to administer the Medicare and Medicaid programs.
1980	Coverage of home health services was broadened. Medicare supplemental insurance, also called "Medigap," was brought under federal oversight. More than 28 million individuals were enrolled in Medicare.
1982	While managed care plans could participate in the program since its inception, the Tax Equity and Fiscal Responsibility Act of 1982 (in provisions implemented in 1985) made it easier and more attractive for health maintenance organizations to contract with the Medicare program by introducing a risk-based option.
1983	A new perspective payment system (PPS) for hospitals was implemented to slow the growth of hospital spending and preserve the life of the Hospital Insurance Trust Fund. The PPS, in which a predetermined rate is based on patients' diagnoses, was adopted to replace cost-based payments.
1988	The Medicare Catastrophic Coverage act was enacted to include an outpatient prescription drug benefit and a cap on patient liability.
1989	The Medicare Catastrophic Coverage Act was repealed after higher-income elderly protested new premiums. A new fee schedule for physician services was enacted.
1990	Additional federal standards for Medicare supplemental insurance policies were enacted.
1996	The Health Insurance Portability and Accountability Act of 1996 (HIPAA) was enacted to amend the Public Health Service Act, the Employee Retirement Income Security act of 1974 (ERISA), and the Internal Revenue Code of 1986 to provide for improved continuity or "portability" of group health plan coverage and group health insurance provided through employment or through the individual insurance market (not connected with employment).

HIPAA also allowed HCFA to regulate small and individual private health insurance markets. The act created the Medicare Integrity Program, which dedicated funding to program integrity activities and allowed HCFA to competitively contract for program integrity work. Furthermore, HIPAA enacted national administrative simplification standards for all electronic health care transactions.

1997   The Balanced Budget Act of 1997 included the most extensive legislative changes for Medicare since the program was enacted:

Established as Part C of the Medicare program Medicare+Choice creating an array of new managed care and other health plan choices for beneficiaries, with a coordinated open enrollment process.

Developed and implemented several new payment systems for Medicare services to improve payment accuracy and to help further restrain the growth of health care spending.

Tested other innovative approaches to payment and service delivery through research and demonstrations.

Expanded preventive benefits.

1998   The Internet site www.medicare.gov was launched to provide updated information about Medicare.

1999   Medicare's hundreds of computer systems, with nearly 50 million lines of computer code, achieved Y2K readiness on schedule and under budget. Payments to health care providers for treating Medicare beneficiaries were uninterrupted and timely. The toll-free number, 1-800-MEDICARE (1-800-633-4227), was available nationwide. The first annual Medicare & You handbook was mailed to all Medicare beneficiary households.

1999   The Balanced Budget Refinement Act (BBRA) made substantial investments to meet the needs of our nation's hospitals and their patients.

2000   Medicare served 39 million seniors and disabled Americans. Medicare trustees estimated that Medicare would be solvent through 2025. The Benefit Improvements and Protection Act of 2000 made additional investments to providers and expanded preventive benefits.

2003   The Medicare Prescription Drug, Improvement, and Modernization Act of 2003 (signed into law on December 8, 2003), introduced the most sweeping changes to Medicare since the program's enactment in 1965. The law includes significant changes that affect beneficiaries, physicians, and other health care professionals. Part D of SMI, which begins in 2004, will initially provide access to prescription drug discount cards and transitional assistance to low-income beneficiaries. In 2006 and later, Part D will provide subsidized access to drug insurance coverage on a voluntary basis for all beneficiaries and premium and cost-sharing subsidies for low-income enrollees.

Source: Centers for Medicare and Medicaid Services, Medicare's Milestones.

Important Dates for Medicaid

Jul 30, 1965	The Medicaid program, authorized under Title XIX of the Social Security Act, was enacted to provide health care services to low-income children deprived of parental support, their caretaker relatives, the elderly, the blind, and individuals with disabilities.
1967	The Early and Periodic Screening, Diagnostic, and Treatment (EPSDT) comprehensive health services benefit for all Medicaid children under age 21 was established.
1972	The newly enacted Federal Supplemental Security Income program (SSI) provided states with the opportunity to link to Medicaid eligibility for elderly, blind, and disabled residents.
1981	Freedom of choice waivers (1915b) and home and community-based care waivers (1915c) were mandated. States were required to pay hospitals treating a disproportionate share of low-income patients additional payments (called disproportionate share hospitals or DSH).
1986	Medicaid coverage for pregnant women and infants (aged 1 year or under) whose family income was at or below 100 percent of the federal poverty level (FPL) was established as a state option.
1988	The Qualified Medicare Beneficiary (QMB) eligibility rule required states to provide Medicaid coverage for pregnant women and infants whose family income was at or below 100 percent of the FPL. The criteria established special eligibility rules for institutionalized persons whose spouses remained in the community to prevent "spousal impoverishment."
1989	EPSDT requirements were expanded. Medicaid coverage of pregnant women and children under age 6 whose family income was at or below 133 percent of the FPL was mandated.
1990	The Medicaid prescription drug rebate program was enacted. The Specified Low-Income Medicare Beneficiary (SLMB) eligibility group was established to provide Medicaid coverage for children ages 6 through 18 whose family income was at or below 100 percent of the FPL.
1991	DSH spending controls were established, provider donations were banned, and provider taxes were capped.
1996	The Temporary Assistance for Needy Families (TANF) block grant replaced the Aid to Families with Dependent Children (AFDC) entitlement program. The welfare link to Medicaid was severed and enrollment (or termination) of Medicaid was no longer automatic with the receipt (or loss) of welfare cash assistance.

1997	The Balanced Budget Act of 1997 (BBA) created the State Children's Health Insurance Program (SCHIP). Under this new state-based program, new managed care options were established. DSH payment limits were revised.
1999	The Ticket to Work and Work Incentives Improvement Act of 1999 (TWWIIA) expanded the availability of Medicare and Medicaid for certain disabled beneficiaries who return to work. The Medicare, Medicaid, and SCHIP balanced Budget Refinement Act of 1999 stabilized the SCHIP allotment formula and modified the Medicaid DSH program.
2000	The Benefits Improvement and Protection Act of 2000 (BIPA) modified the DSH program and modified SCHIP allotments. Other related legislation improved Medicaid coverage of certain women's health services.

Source: Centers for Medicare and Medicaid Services, Medicaid's Milestones, 2003.

Appendix II

THE TABLES

TABLE 1 Effective Federal Tax Rates and Shares Under Current Tax Law, Based on 2001 Incomes, by Income Category, 2001 to 2014

Income category	2001	2002	2003	2004	2005	2006	2007	2008	2009	2010	2011	2012	2013	2014
					Total Effective Federal Tax Rate									
Lowest Quintile	5.4	5.3	5.2	5.2	5.5	5.6	5.7	5.8	5.9	5.8	7.8	8.0	8.1	8.3
Second Quintile	11.6	11.6	11.0	11.1	12.0	12.1	12.3	12.4	12.4	12.3	14.2	14.4	14.5	14.7
Middle Quintile	15.2	15.0	14.5	114.6	15.6	15.7	15.9	15.9	16.1	16.1	17.6	17.8	18.0	18.2
Fourth Quintile	19.3	19.1	18.5	18.5	19.6	19.8	20.0	20.1	20.4	20.5	21.8	22.0	22.2	22.4
Highest Quintile	26.8	25.4	24.4	23.8	26.3	26.5	26.5	26.4	27.1	27.1	28.5	28.6	28.7	28.8

Source: *Congressional Budget Office, Effective Federal Tax Rates Under Current Law, 2001 to 2014, August 2004.*

TABLE 2 Breakout of Social Security(millions of dollars)

Year	Tax Receipts	Benefits	Net	Year	Tax Receipts	Benefits	Net
1936	-	-	-	1972	35.132	34,541	+591
1937	265	-	+265	1973	40.703	42,170	−1,467
1938	387	5	+382	1974	47,778	47,849	−71
1939	503	14	+489	1975	55,207	54,839	+368
1940	550	16	+534	1976	58,703	62,140	−3,437
1941	688	64	+624	**Transition**			
1942	896	110	+786	**Quarter>**	**15,886**	**16,876**	**−990**
1943	1,130	149	+981	1977	68,032	71,271	−3.239
1944	1,292	185	+1,107	1978	73,141	78,524	−5,383
1945	1,310	240	+1,070	1979	83,410	87,592	−4,182
1946	1,238	321	+917	1980	96,581	100,615	−4,034
1947	1,459	426	+1,033	1981	117,757	119,413	−1,656
1948	1,616	512	+1,104	1982	122,840	134,655	−11,815
1949	1,690	607	+1,083	1983	128,972	148,312	−19,340
1950	2,106	727	+1,379	1984	150,312	155,846	−5,534
1951	3,120	1,498	+1,622	1985	169,822	165,422	+4,400
1952	3,594	1,982	+1,612	1986	182,518	174,364	+8,154
1953	4,097	2,627	+1,470	1987	194,541	182,055	+12,486
1954	4,589	3,276	+1,313	1988	220,337	192,541	+27,796
1955	5,081	4,333	+748	1989	240,595	204,648	+35,947
1956	6,425	5,361	+1,064	1990	255,031	218,957	+36,074
1957	6,457	6,515	−58	1991	265,503	236,120	+29,383
1958	7,138	7,875	−737	1992	273,137	251,317	+21,820
1959	7,418	9,049	−1,631	1993	281,735	264,582	+17,153
1960	9,671	10,270	−599	1994	302,607	276,291	+26,316
1961	11,104	11,185	−81	1995	284,091	288,617	−4,526
1962	11,267	12,658	−1,391	1996	311,869	299,985	+11,884
1963	13,117	13,845	−728	1997	336,729	312,880	+23,849
1964	15,242	14,579	+663	1998	358,784	324,274	+34,510
1965	15,567	15,226	+341	1999	383,559	332,383	+51,176
1966	17,556	18,071	−515	2000	411,677	347,894	+63,783
1967	22,197	18,886	+3,311	2001	434,057	367,702	+66,355
1968	22,265	20,737	+1,528	2002	440,541	383,970	+56,571
1969	25,484	23,732	+1,752	2003	447,806	396,597	+51,209
1970	23,396	26,267	−2,871	2004	457,120	411,157	+45,963
1971	31,354	31,101	+253				

Source: Historical Tables, Office of Management and Budget, Fiscal Year 2006, Table 13.1, pages 274–285.

TABLE 3 Breakout of Disability Insurance (millions of dollars)

Year	Tax Receipts	Benefits	Net	Year	Tax Receipts	Benefits	Net
1956	-	-	-	1980	16,628	14,899	+1,729
1957	332	-	+332	1981	12,418	16,853	−4,435
1958	911	168	+743	1982	20,626	17,399	+3,227
1959	878	339	+539	1983	18,348	17,588	+760
1960	970	528	+442	1984	15,763	17,735	−1,972
1961	1,005	704	+301	1985	16,348	18,654	−2,306
1962	1,004	1,011	−7	1986	17,711	19,526	−1,815
1963	1,058	1,171	−113	1987	18,861	20,421	−1,560
1964	1,124	1,251	−127	1988	21,154	21,395	−241
1965	1,156	1,392	−236	1989	23,071	22,516	+555
1966	1,530	1,721	−191	1990	26,625	24,306	+2,319
1967	2,204	1,861	+343	1991	28,382	26,871	+1,511
1968	2,651	2,088	+563	1992	29,289	30,360	−1,071
1969	3,469	2,443	+1,026	1993	30,199	33,588	−3,389
1970	4,063	2,778	+1,285	1994	32,419	36,823	−4,404
1971	4,490	3,381	+1,109	1995	66,988	40,201	+26,787
1972	4,775	4,046	+729	1996	55,623	43,231	+12,392
1973	5,381	5,162	+219	1997	55,261	45,367	+9,894
1974	6,147	6,159	−12	1998	57,015	47,680	+9,335
1975	7,250	7,630	−380	1999	60,909	50,424	+10,485
1976	7,686	9,222	−1,536	2000	68,907	54,210	+14,697
Transition				2001	73,462	58,159	+15,303
Quarter>	**2,130**	**2,555**	**−425**	2002	74,780	64,202	+10,578
1977	8,786	11,135	−2,349	2003	76,036	69,789	+6,247
1978	12,250	12,214	+36	2004	77,625	76,212	+1,413
1979	14,584	13,428	+1,156				

Source: Historical Tables, Office of Management and Budget, Fiscal Year 2006, Table 13.1, pages 274–285.

TABLE 4 Breakout of the Hospital Insurance Portion of Medicare (millions of dollars)

Year	Social ins and retirement receipts	Benefits	Net	Year	Social ins and retirement receipts	Benefits	Net
1966	893	-	+893	1985	44,871	47,710	−2,839
1967	2,645	2,508	+137	1986	51,335	48,867	+2,468
1968	3,493	3,736	−243	1987	55,992	49,804	+6,188
1969	4,398	4,654	−256	1988	59,859	51,862	+7,997
1970	4,755	4,804	−49	1989	65,396	57,317	+8,079
1971	4,874	5,442	−568	1990	68,556	66,722	+1,834
1972	5,205	6,108	−903	1991	72,842	68,486	+4,356
1973	7,603	6,648	+955	1992	79,108	80,584	−1,476
1974	10,551	7,806	+2,745	1993	81,224	90,535	−9,311
1975	11,252	10,353	+899	1994	90,062	101,350	−11,288
1976	11,987	12,267	−280	1995	96,024	113,402	−17,378
Transition				1996	104,997	123,908	−18,911
Quarter>	**3,457**	**3,314**	**+143**	1997	110,710	136,010	−25,300
1977	13,474	14,906	−1,432	1998	119,863	135,299	−15,436
1978	16,668	17,415	−747	1999	132,268	129,286	+2,982
1979	19,874	19,898	−24	2000	135,529	127,698	+7,831
1980	23,217	23,793	−576	2001	149,651	139,082	+10,569
1981	30,340	28,909	+1,431	2002	149,049	145,308	+3,741
1982	34,301	34,344	−43	2003	147,186	151,967	−4,781
1983	35,641	38,102	−2,461	2004	150,589	163,765	−13,176
1984	40,262	41,461	−1,199				

Source: Historical Tables, Office of Management and Budget, Fiscal Year 2006, Table 13.1, pages 274–285.

TABLE 5 Breakout of the Supplementary Medical Insurance Portion of Medicare (millions of dollars)

Year	Premium Income	Benefits	Net	Year	Premium Income	Benefits	Net
1966	-	-	-	1985	5,524	21,808	−16,284
1967	647	664	−17	1986	5,699	25,166	−19,467
1968	698	1,390	−692	1987	6,480	29,932	−23,452
1969	903	1,645	−742	1988	8,756	33,677	−24,921
1970	936	1,979	−1,043	1989	11,548	36,854	−25,306
1971	1,253	2,035	−782	1990	11,494	41,450	−29,956
1972	1,340	2,255	−915	1991	11,807	45,458	−33,651
1973	1,427	2,391	−964	1992	12,748	48,595	−35,847
1974	1,704	2,874	−1,170	1993	14,683	52,398	−37,715
1975	1,901	3,765	−1,864	1994	16,895	57,997	−41,102
1976	1,937	4,671	−2,734	1995	19,243	63,482	−44,239
Transition				1996	18,931	67,167	−48,236
Quarter>	539	1,269	−730	1997	19,142	71,115	−51,973
1977	2,193	5,865	−3,672	1998	19,427	74,808	−55,381
1978	2,431	6,852	−4,421	1999	20,160	78,972	−58,812
1979	2,636	8,259	−5,623	2000	20,515	87,169	−66,654
1980	2,928	10,144	−7,216	2001	22,308	97,471	−75,163
1981	3,319	12,345	−9,026	2002	24,427	106,901	−82,474
1982	3,831	14,806	−10,975	2003	26,835	121,740	−94,905
1983	4,227	17,487	−13,260	2004	30,341	131,595	−101,254
1984	4,907	19,475	−14,568				

Source: Historical Tables, Office of Management and Budget, Fiscal Year 2006, Table 13.1, pages 274–285.

TABLE 6 Tax Rate and Maximum Taxable Earnings*

	OASDI				Medicare			
Years	% Employer	% Employee	% Total	Maximum Earnings	% Employer	% Employee	% Total	Maximum Earnings
1937–49	1.00	1.00	2.00	$3,000	-	-	-	$3,000
1950	1.50	1.50	3.00	3,000	-	-	-	3,000
1951–53	1.50	1.50	3.00	3,600	-	-	-	3,600
1954	2.00	2.00	4.00	3,600	-	-	-	3,600
1955–56	2.00	2.00	4.00	4,200	-	-	-	4,200
1957–58	2.25	2.25	4.50	4,200	-	-	-	4,200
1959	2.50	2.50	5.00	4,800	-	-	-	4,800
1960–61	3.00	3.00	6.00	4,800	-	-	-	4,800
1962	3.125	3.125	6.25	4,800	-	-	-	4,800
1963–65	3.625	3.625	7.25	4,800	-	-	-	4,800
1966	3.85	3.85	7.70	6,600	.35	.35	.70	6,600
1967	3.90	3.90	7.80	6,600	.50	.50	1.00	6,600
1968	3.80	3.80	7.60	7,800	.60	.60	1.20	7,800
1969–70	4.20	4.20	8.40	7,800	.60	.60	1.20	7,800
1971	4.60	4.60	9.20	7,800	.60	.60	1.20	7,800
1972	4.60	4.60	9.20	9,000	.60	.60	1.20	9,000
1973	4.85	4.85	9.70	10,800	1.00	1.00	2.00	10,800
1974	4.95	4.95	9.90	13,200	.90	.90	1.80	13,200
1975	4.95	4.95	9.90	14,200	.90	.90	1.80	14,200
1976	4.95	4.95	9.90	15,300	.90	.90	1.80	15,300

TABLE 6 (continued)

Years	OASDI				Medicare			
	% Employer	% Employee	% Total	Maximum Earnings	% Employer	% Employee	% Total	Maximum Earnings
1977	4.95	4.95	9.90	16,500	.90	.90	1.80	16,500
1978	5.05	5.05	10.10	17,700	1.00	1.00	2.00	17,700
1979	5.08	5.08	10.16	22,900	1.05	1.05	2.10	22,900
1980	5.08	5.08	10.16	25,900	1.05	1.05	2.10	25,900
1981	5.35	5.35	10.70	29,700	1.30	1.30	2.60	29,700
1982	5.40	5.40	10.40	32,400	1.30	1.30	2.60	32,400
1983	5.40	5.40	10.80	35,700	1.30	1.30	2.60	35,700
1984	5.70	5.70	11.40	37,800	1.30	1.30	2.60	37,800
1985	5.70	5.70	11.40	39,600	1.35	1.35	2.70	39,600
1986	5.70	5.70	11.40	42,000	1.45	1.45	2.90	42,000
1987	5.70	5.70	11.40	43,800	1.45	1.45	2.90	43,800
1988	6.06	6.06	12.12	45,000	1.45	1.45	2.90	45,000
1989	6.06	6.06	12.12	48,000	1.45	1.45	2.90	48,000
1990	6.20	6.20	12.40	51,300	1.45	1.45	2.90	51,300
1991	6.20	6.20	12.40	53,400	1.45	1.45	2.90	53,400
1992	6.20	6.20	12.40	55,500	1.45	1.45	2.90	125,000
1993	6.20	6.20	12.40	57,600	1.45	1.45	2.90	130,200
1994	6.20	6.20	12.40	60,600	1.45	1.45	2.90	135,000
1995	6.20	6.20	12.40	61,200	1.45	1.45	2.90	No limit
1996	6.20	6.20	12.40	62,700	1.45	1.45	2.90	"

Year						
1997	6.20	12.40	65,400	1.45	1.45	2.90	"
1998	6.20	12.40	68,400	1.45	1.45	2.90	"
1999	6.20	12.40	72,600	1.45	1.45	2.90	"
2000	6.20	12.40	76,200	1.45	1.45	2.90	"
2001	6.20	12.40	80,400	1.45	1.45	2.90	"
2002	6.20	12.40	84,900	1.45	1.45	2.90	"
2003	6.20	12.40	87,000	1.45	1.45	2.90	"
2004	6.20	12.40	87,900	1.45	1.45	2.90	"
2005	6.20	12.40	90,000	1.45	1.45	2.90	"

Source: *The 2004 Annual Report of the Board of Trustees of the Federal Old Age and Survivors Insurance and Disability Insurance Trust Funds*, pp. 125–26.

TABLE 7 Breakout of Medicaid Payments (millions of dollars)

Year	Amount	Year	Amount	Year	Amount
1961	23	1976	2,229	1991	52,533
1962	103	1977	9,875	1992	67,827
1963	157	1978	10,680	1993	75,774
1964	210	1979	12,407	1994	82,034
1965	272	1980	13,957	1995	89,070
1966	770	1981	16,833	1996	91,990
1967	1,173	1982	17,391	1997	95,552
1968	1,806	1983	18,985	1998	101,234
1969	2,285	1984	20,061	1999	108,041
1970	2,727	1985	22,655	2000	117,921
1971	3,362	1986	24,995	2001	129,434
1972	4,601	1987	27,435	2002	147,650
1973	4,600	1988	30,462	2003	160,693
1974	5,818	1989	34,604	2004	176,231
1975	6,840	1990	41,103	2005	

Source: *Historical Tables, Budget of the United States Government, Fiscal Year 2006,*
Table 8.5, pp. 129–134.

TABLE 8 Performance of COLA Price Index Alternatives Third Quarter-to-Third Quarter Annual Increases–%

Year	Consumer Price Index	Personal Consumption Expenditures	Proposal: PCE plus 0.5% with 2.0% minimum increase	Average Wage Indexing Series
1975	8.7	7.8	8.3	7.5
1976	5.6	5.3	5.8	6.9
1977	6.6	6.7	7.2	6.0
1978	8.0	7.1	7.6	7.9
1979	11.7	9.2	9.7	8.8
1980	12.9	10.5	11.0	9.0
1981	10.9	9.7	10.2	10.1
1982	5.8	5.4	5.9	5.5
1983	2.5	4.3	4.8	4.9
1984	4.3	3.5	4.0	5.9
1985	3.3	3.1	3.6	4.3
1986	1.7	2.3	2.8	3.0
1987	4.2	3.8	4.2	6.4
1988	4.1	4.1	4.6	4.9
1989	4.7	4.2	4.7	4.0
1990	5.6	4.7	5.2	4.6
1991	3.9	3.3	3.8	3.7
1992	3.1	2.9	3.4	5.2
1993	2.8	2.2	2.7	0.9
1994	2.9	2.4	2.9	2.7
1995	2.7	1.9	2.4	4.0
1996	2.9	2.1	2.6	4.9
1997	2.2	1.6	2.1	5.8
1998	1.6	0.9	2.0	5.2
1999	2.3	1.8	2.3	5.6
2000	3.5	2.4	2.9	5.5
2001	2.7	2.0	2.5	2.4
2002	1.6	1.6	2.1	1.0
2003	2.2	1.7	2.2	2.4
2004	2.7	2.2	2.7	n/a
Social Security Trustees Forecasts—Calendar Year				
2005	1.5			4.1
2006	2.0			3.8
2007	2.4			3.9
2008	2.8			4.1

TABLE 8 (continued)

Year	Consumer Price Index	Personal Consumption Expenditures	Proposal: PCE plus 0.5% with 2.0% minimum increase	Average Wage Indexing Series
2009	2.8			4.0
2010	2.8			4.0
2011	2.8			4.0
2012	2.8			4.0
2013	2.8			4.0

Sources: U.S. Department of Labor, Bureau of Labor Statistics, www.bls.gov, CPI Index, All Urban Consumers, seasonally adjusted. Bureau of Economic Analysis, *National Economic Accounts,* Table 2.3.4. Price Indexes for Personal Consumption Expenditures by Major Type of Product. *The 2004 Annual Report of the Federal Old Age and Survivors Insurance and Disability Insurance Trust Funds*, pp. 88–89. Social Security Online, Average Wage Indexing (AWI) Series.

TABLE 9 How PCE plus* Performed on an Annual Basis Against the CPI, the Basic PCE, and the Average Wage Index. Third Quarter-to-Third Quarter Annual Increases–%

Year	Consumer Price Index	Personal Consumption Expenditures	Wage Index
1975	−0.4	+0.5	+0.8
1976	+0.2	+0.5	−1.1
1977	+0.6	+0.5	+1.2
1978	−0.4	+0.5	−0.3
1979	−2.0	+0.5	+0.9
1980	−1.9	+0.5	+2.0
1981	−0.7	+0.5	+0.1
1982	+0.1	+0.5	+0.4
1983	+2.3	+0.5	−0.1
1984	−0.3	+0.5	−1.9
1985	+0.3	+0.5	−0.7
1986	+1.1	+0.5	−0.2
1987	+0.1	+0.5	−2.1
1988	+0.5	+0.5	−0.3
1989	0.0	+0.5	+0.7
1990	−0.4	+0.5	+0.6
1991	−0.1	+0.5	+0.1
1992	+0.3	+0.5	−1.8
1993	−0.1	+0.5	+1.8
1994	0.0	+0.5	+0.2
1995	−0.3	+0.5	−1.6
1996	−0.3	+0.5	−2.3
1997	−0.1	+0.5	−3.7
1998	+0.4	+1.1	−3.2
1999	0.0	+0.5	−3.3
2000	−0.6	+0.5	−2.6
2001	−0.2	+0.5	+0.1
2002	+0.5	+0.5	+1.1
2003	0.0	+0.5	−0.2
2004	0.0	+0.5	n/a

*PCE plus 0.5 percent plus 2.0 percent minimum increase
Sources: U.S. Department of Labor, Bureau of Labor Statistics, www.bls.gov, CPI Index, All Urban Consumers, seasonally adjusted. Bureau of Labor Statistics, *National Economic Accounts*, Table 2.3.4. Price Indexes for Personal Consumption Expenditures by Major Type of Product. *The 2004 Annual Report of the Board of Trustees of the Federal Old Age and Survivors Insurance and Disability Insurance Trust Funds*, pp. 88–89. Social Security Online, Average Wage Indexing (AWI) Series.

TABLE 10 Estimated Ownership of U.S. Treasury Securities (billions of dollars)

End of Month	Foreign and International	Federal Reserve	Government Accounts*	Private Domestic Accounts	Total
Sep 2001	1,006	534	2,469	1,799	5,808
Dec 2001	1,051	552	2,550	1,790	5,943
Mar 2002	1,067	575	2,562	1,802	6,006
Jun 2002	1,135	591	2,663	1,738	6,127
Sep 2002	1,201	604	2,676	1,747	6,228
Dec 2002	1,247	629	2,758	1,772	6,406
Mar 2003	1,287	641	2,750	1,783	6,461
Jun 2003	1,383	652	2,854	1,781	6,670
Sep 2003	1,456	656	2,859	1,812	6,783
Dec 2003	1,538	667	2,954	1,839	6,998
Mar 2004	1,705	674	2,954	1,798	7,131
Jun 2004	1,800	687	3,056	1,731	7,274
Sep 2004	1,862	699	3,075	1,743	7,379
Sep 2001–04**	+856	+165	+606	−56	+1,571

*These are government IOUs, and did not finance the budget deficits.
**Three fiscal years. Federal Reserve Bulletins, Table 1.18; Treasury Bulletins Table FD-1 and Table OFS-2

TABLE 11 1997 Trustees' Receipts Forecasts versus Actual Data (billions of dollars)

Year	1997 Estimates		Actuals		Differentials	
	OASI	DI	OASI	DI	OASI	DI
1997	392	60	397	60	+5	-0-
1998	409	62	425	64	+16	+2
1999	430	65	457	70	+27	+5
2000	450	72	491	78	+41	+6
2001	476	77	518	84	+42	+7
2002	503	81	540	87	+37	+6
2003	532	85	544	88	+12	+3
2004	562	90				
2005	595	95				
2006	629	99				

TABLE 12 1997 Trustees' Expenditure Forecasts versus Actual Data (billions of dollars)

Year	1997 Estimates		Actuals		Differentials	
	OASI	DI	OASI	DI	OASI	DI
1997	322	49	322	47	–	−2
1998	337	52	332	50	−5	−2
1999	353	56	340	53	−13	−3
2000	370	60	358	57	−12	−3
2001	389	65	378	61	−11	−4
2002	410	70	394	68	−16	−2
2003	430	76	406	73	−24	−3
2004	453	83				
2005	476	90				
2006	501	98				

TABLE 13 1997 Trustees' Surplus Forecasts versus Actual Data (billions of dollars)

Year	Actual Receipts Versus Estimates		Actual Expenditures Versus Estimates		Net Actuals Versus Estimates	
	OASI	DI	OASI	DI	OASI	DI
1997	+5	-0-	-0-	−2	+5	+2
1998	+16	+2	−5	−2	+21	+4
1999	+27	+5	−13	−3	+40	+8
2000	+41	+6	−12	−3	+53	+9
2001	+42	+7	−11	−4	+53	+11
2002	+37	+6	−16	−2	+53	+8
2003	+12	+3	−24	−3	+36	+6

Source: *Annual Reports of the Board of Trustees of the Federal Old-Age and Survivors Insurance and Disability Insurance Trust Funds*; 2004, p. 85; 2004, pp. 129–32.

TABLE 14 Productivity and Real GDP Growth

| Year | Productivity–% | | Real GDP Growth–% | |
	1997 Trustee Estimates	Actuals	1997 Trustees Estimates	Actuals
1998	+1.3	+2.6	+2.5	+4.2
1999	+1.3	+2.9	+2.0	+4.5
2000	+1.3	+2.9	+2.0	+3.7
2001	+1.3	+2.2	+2.0	+0.5
2002	+1.3	+4.9	+1.9	+2.2
2003	+1.3	+4.5	+1.9	+3.1
Average	+1.3	+3.3	+2.0	+3.1

Sources: *Economic Indicators*, April 2004, United States Government Printing Office, pp. 3 and 16; *Annual Report of the Board of Trustees of the Federal Old-Age and Survivors Insurance and Disability Insurance Trust Fund*, 1998, p. 57.

TABLE 15 2004 Official Receipts Estimates Excluding Imputed Interest (billions of dollars)

Year	OASI	DI	HI*	SMI Premium Income*	Total
2004**	465	79	156	32	732
2005	500	85	169	37	791
2006	523	89	178	52	842
2007	549	93	187	56	885
2008	575	98	197	60	930
2009	602	102	207	65	976
2010	634	108	217	69	1,028
2011	665	113	228	74	1,080
2012	693	118	239	80	1,130
2013	723	123	250	87	1,183
2015	973		303		
2020	1,214		381		
2025	1,501		474		
2030	1,852		589		
2035	2,285		729		
2040	2,818		900		

*In 2004, the average monthly premium paid per beneficiary for Part B is $66.60. By 2013, it is estimated to be $104.70. In 2006, Part D premiums begin. In 2006, the average is estimated to be $37.23. By 2013, it is estimated to be $60.78.

Sources: *The 2004 Annual Report of the Board of Trustees of the Federal Old-Age and Survivors Insurance and Disability Insurance Trust Funds*, pp. 144, 145, 181, 183. *2004 Annual Report of the Boards of Trustees of the Federal Hospital Insurance and Federal Supplementary Medical Insurance Trust Funds*, pp. 42, 71, 164. *Budget of the United States Government, Fiscal Year 2005*, Summary Table 5-12, p. 386.

**Actuals for 2004 were OASI $457 billion; DI $78 billion; HI $151 billion; SMI $30 billion, for a total of $716 billion. Source: *Final Monthly Treasury Statement of Receipts and Outlays of the United States Government*, September 2004.

TABLE 16 2004 Official Expenditures Estimates (billions of dollars)

Year	OASI	DI	Medicare HI	Medicare SMI	Medicaid	Total
2004**	418	77	174	138	183	990
2005	431	83	188	150	188	1,040
2006	445	88	201	242	198	1,174
2007	464	93	213	259	213	1,242
2008	486	100	225	278	232	1,321
2009	514	108	239	297	251	1,409
2010	546	115	253	317	270*	1,501
2011	581	121	269	339	289*	1,599
2012	620	128	286	367	308*	1,709
2013	663	136	305	400	327*	1,831
2015	917		343			
2020	1,299		483			
2025	1,782		691			
2030	2,364		988			
2035	3,032		1,394			
2040	3,778		1,915			

*Not official estimates

Sources: *The 2004 Annual Report of the Board of Trustees of the Federal Old-Age and Survivors Insurance and Disability Insurance Trust Funds*, pp. 144, 145, 181, 183. *2004 Annual Report of the Boards of Trustees of the Federal Hospital Insurance and Federal Supplementary Medical Insurance Trust Funds*, pp. 42, 71, 164. *Budget of the United States Government, Fiscal Year 2005*, Summary Table 5-12, p. 386.

**Actuals for 2004 were OASI $417 billion; DI $79 billion; HI $166 billion; SMI $134 billion; Medicaid $176 billion, for a total of $972 billion. Source: *Final Monthly Treasury Statement of Receipts and Outlays of the United States Government*, September 2004.

TABLE 17 2004 Official Receipts Estimates Minus Official Expenditure Estimates (billions of dollars)

2004*	−258
2005	−249
2006	−328
2007	−357
2008	−391
2009	−433
2010	−473
2011	−519
2012	−579
2013	−648

*Actual for 2004 turned out to be −$244 billion.

TABLE 18 Summary: Net Cash Inflows and Outflows for OASI, DI, HI, SMI and Medicaid (*Billions of dollars*)

Year	OASI	DI	HI	SMI	Medicaid	Total
1937	+265					+265
1938	+382					+382
1939	+489					+ 489
1940	+534					+534
1941	+624					+624
1942	+786					+786
1943	+981					+981
1944	+1,107					+1,107
1945	+1,070					+1,070
1946	+917					+917
1947	+1,033					+1,033
1948	+1,104					+1,104
1949	+1,083					+1,083
1950	+1,379					+1,379
1951	+1,622					+1,622
1952	+1,612					+1,612
1953	+1,470					+1,470
1954	+1,313					+1,313
1955	+748					+748
1956	+1,064					+1,064
1957	−58	+332				+274
1958	−737	+743				+6
1959	−1,631	+539				−1,092
1960	−599	+442				−157
1961	−81	+301			−23	+197
1962	−1,391	−7			−103	−1,501
1963	−728	−113			−157	−998
1964	+663	−127			−210	+326
1965	+341	−236			−272	−167
1966	−515	−191	+893		−770	−583
1967	+3,311	+343	+137	−17	−1,173	+2,601
1968	+1,528	+563	−243	−692	−1,806	−650
1969	+1,752	+1,026	−256	−742	−2,285	−505
1970	−2,871	+1,285	−49	−1,043	−2,727	−5,405
1971	+253	+1,109	−568	−782	−3,362	−3,350
1972	+591	+729	−903	−915	−4,601	−5,099
1973	−1,467	+219	+955	−964	−4,600	−5,857
1974	−71	−12	+2,745	−1,170	−5,818	−4,326
1975	+368	−380	+899	−1,864	−6,840	−7,817
1976	−3,437	−1,536	−280	−2,734	−8,568	−16,555

TABLE 18 (continued)

Year	OASI	DI	HI	SMI	Medicaid	Total
Transition						
Quarter>	−990	−425	+143	−730	−2,229	−4,231
1977	−3,239	−2,349	−1,432	−3,672	−9,875	−20,567
1978	−5,383	+36	−747	−4,421	−10,680	−21,195
1979	−4,182	+1,156	−24	−5,623	−12,407	−21,080
1980	−4,034	+1,729	−576	−7,216	−13,957	−24,054
1981	−1,656	−4,435	+1,431	−9,026	−16,833	−30,519
1982	−11,815	+3,227	−43	−10,975	−17,391	−36,997
1983	−19,340	+760	−2,461	−13,260	−18,985	−53,286
1984	−5,534	−1,972	−1,199	−14,568	−20,061	−43,334
1985	+4,400	−2,306	−2,839	−16,284	−22,655	−39,684
1986	+8,154	−1,815	+2,468	−19,467	−24,995	−35,655
1987	+12,486	−1,560	+6,188	−23,452	−27,435	−33,773
1988	+27,796	−241	+7,997	−24,921	−30,462	−19,831
1989	+35,947	+555	+8,079	−25,306	−34,604	−15,329
1990	+36,074	+2,319	+1,834	−29,956	−41,103	−30,832
1991	+29,383	+1,511	+4,356	−33,651	−52,533	−50,934
1992	+21,820	−1,071	−1,476	−35,847	−67,827	−84,401
1993	+17,153	−3,389	−9,311	−37,715	−75,774	−109,036
1994	+26,316	−4,404	−11,288	−41,102	−82,034	−112,512
1995	−4,526	+26,787	−17,378	−44,239	−89,070	−128,426
1996	+11,884	+12,392	−18,911	−48,236	−91,990	−134,861
1997	+23,849	+9,894	−25,300	−51,973	−95,552	−139,082
1998	+34,510	+9,335	−15,436	−55,381	−101,234	−128,206
1999	+51,176	+10,485	+2,982	−58,812	−108,041	−102,210
2000	+63,783	+14,697	+7,831	−66,654	−117,921	−98,264
2001	+66,355	+15,303	+10,569	−75,163	−129,434	−112,370
2002	+56,597	+10,578	+3,741	−82,474	−147,650	−159,208
2003	+51,209	+6,247	−4,781	−94,905	−160,693	−202,923
2004	+45,963	+1,413	−13,176	−101,254	−176,231	−243,285

TABLE 19 Social Security Programs for Selected Countries

| Country | Old age, disability, survivors | Sickness and maternity | | Work injury | Unemployment | Family allowances |
		Cash benefits for both	Cash benefits +medical care			
Argentina	x	x	x	x	x	x
Austria	x	x	x	x	x	x
Australia	x	x	x	x	x	x
Belgium	x	x	x	x	x	x
Brazil	x	x	x	x	x	x
Canada	x	x	x	x	x	x
Chile	x	x	x	x	x	x
Czech Republic	x	x	x	x	x	x
Denmark	x	x	x	x	x	x
Finland	x	x	x	x	x	x
France	x	x	x	x	x	x
Germany	x	x	x	x	x	x
Greece	x	x	x	x	x	x
Hungary	x	x	x	x	x	x
India	x	x	x	x	x	*
Ireland	x	x	x	x	x	x
Italy	x	x	x	x	x	x
Japan	x	x	x	x	x	x
Mexico	x	x	x	x	x	x
Netherlands	x	x	x	***	x	x
Norway	x	x	x	x	x	x

Poland	x	x	x	x	x
Portugal	x	x	x	x	x
Romania	x	x	x	x	x
Russia	x	x	x	x	x
Serbia	x	x	x	x	x
Slovak Republic	x	x	x	x	x
South Africa				x	x
South Korea	*	**	x	x	x
Spain	x	x	x	x	x
Sweden	x	x	x	x	x
Switzerland	x	x	x	x	x
Ukraine	x	x	x	x	x
United Kingdom	x	x	x	x	x
United States	x	x	x	x	x

*Has no program or information is not available

**Medical care only

***Coverage is provided under other programs or through social assistance.

Sources: *Social Security Programs Throughout the World: Europe*, 2002, pp. 16 and 17; *Social Security Programs Throughout the World: Asia and the Pacific*, 2002, pp. 16 and 17; *Social Security Programs Throughout the World, the Americas*, 2003, pp. 16 and 17.

TABLE 20 Types of Mandatory Systems for Retirement Income

Country	Flat-rate	Earnings related	Means-tested	Flat-rate universal	Provident funds	Occupational retirement schemes	Individual retirement schemes
Argentina		x	x				x
Austria		x	x				
Australia							
Belgium		x	x				
Brazil		x	x				
Canada		x	x				
Chile		x					x
Czech Republic	x	x					
Denmark		x		x			x
Finland		x	x				
France		x	x			x	
Germany		x					
Greece		x					
Hungary		x					x
India		x			x		
Ireland	x		x				
Italy		x	x				
Japan	x	x					
Mexico		x					x
Netherlands	x		x				
Norway		x	x				

Poland	x				x
Portugal	x	x			
Romania	x				
Russia	x		x		x
Serbia	x		x		
Slovak Republic	x				
South Africa		x			
South Korea	x				
Spain	x				
Sweden	x	x			
Switzerland	x	x		x	x
Ukraine	x	x			
United Kingdom	x	x			
United States	x	x			

Sources: *Social Security Programs Throughout the World: Europe, 2002*, pp. 16 and 17; *Social Security Programs Throughout the World: Asia and the Pacific, 2002*, pp. 16 and 17; *Social Security Programs Throughout the World, the Americas, 2003*, pp. 16 and 17.

TABLE 21 Demographics and Other Statistics Related to Social Security—2003

Country	Total population (millions)	Percentage 65 or older	Dependency Ratio(a)	Life expectancy at birth (yrs)		Statutory pensionable age		Early pensionable age (b)		GDP per capita (US$)
				Men	Wom.	Men	Wom.	Men	Wom.	
Argentina	37	9.7	59.8	70.6	77.7	65	60	*	*	12,377
Austria	8	15.6	47.4	75.4	81.5	65	60	61.5	56.5	26,730
Australia	19.1	12.3	48.8	76.4	82.0	65	62.5	*	*	25,693
Belgium	10.2	17	52.2	75.7	81.9	65	63	60	60	25,520
Brazil	170.4	5.1	51.4	64.7	72.6	65**	60**	*	*	7,625
Canada	30.7	12.6	46.5	76.2	81.8	65	65	*	*	27,840
Chile	15.2	7.2	55.3	73	79	65	60	*	*	9,417
Czech Rep.	10.2	13.8	43.4	72.1	78.7	61.5	56	58.5	53	14,720
Denmark	5.3	15	49.8	74.2	79.1	65(c)	65(c)	60	60	29,000
Finland	5.1	14.9	49.2	74.4	81.5	65	65	60	60	24,430
France	59.2	16	53.2	75.2	82.8	60	60	*	*	23,990
Germany	82	16.4	46.9	75	81.1	65	65	60	60	23,350
Greece	10.6	17.6	48.4	75.9	81.2	65	65	60	55	17,440
Hungary	9.9	14.6	46.2	67.8	76.1	62	59	60	57	12,340
India	1,008	5	62.5	63.6	64.9	55	55	*	*	2,358
Ireland	3.8	11.3	49	74.4	79.6	66	66	*	*	32,410
Italy	57.5	18.1	47.8	75.5	81.9	65	60	*	*	24,670
Japan	127	17.2	46.8	77.8	85.0	65	65	60	60	26,755
Mexico	98.8	4.7	60.9	70.4	76.4	65	65	*	*	9,023

Netherl.	15.8	13.6	46.9	75.6	81	65	65	*	*	27,190
Norway	4.5	15.4	54.2	76	81.9	67	67	*	*	29,620
Poland	38.6	12.1	45.5	69.8	78	65	60	*	*	9,450
Portugal	10	15.6	47.7	72.6	79.6	65	65	55	55	18,150
Romania	22.4	13.3	46.1	66.5	73.3	65	60	55	55	5,830
Russia	145.5	12.5	43.8	60	72.5	60	44	*	*	7,100
Serbia	10.6	15.3	52.9	71	77.1	63	58	53	53	2,200
Slovak Rep.	5.4	11.4	44.7	69.8	77.6	62	62	*	*	11,960
So. Africa	39.9	17	46.4	75.4	82.3	65	65	*	*	20,150
So. Korea	46.7	7.1	38.7	71.8	79.1	60	60	55	55	17,380
Spain	39.9	17	46.4	75.4	82.3	65	65	*	*	20,150
Sweden	8.8	17.4	55.3	77.6	82.6	65	65	61	61	24,180
Switzerl.	7.1	16	48.5	75.9	82.3	65	63	*	*	28,100
Ukraine	49.5	13.8	46.3	62.7	73.5	60	55	*	*	4,350
U.K.	59.4	15.8	53.2	75.7	80.7	65	60	*	*	24,160
U.S.	283.2	12.3	51.5	74.6	80.4	65	65	*	*	34,142

(a) Population aged 14 and under plus population 65 or older, divided by population aged 15–64.
(b) General early pensionable age only; excludes early pensionable ages for specific groups of employees.
(c) From July 1, 2004.

*The country has no early pensionable age, has one only for specific groups, or information is not available.
**Urban employees

Sources: *Social Security Programs Throughout the World: Europe, 2002*, pp. 16 and 17; *Social Security Programs Throughout the World: Asia and the Pacific, 2002*, pp. 16 and 17; *Social Security Programs Throughout the World, the Americas, 2003*, pp. 16 and 17.

TABLE 22 Percentage of Contribution Rates for Social Security Programs—2003

Country	Old age, disability, survivors			All social security programs		
	Insured person	Employer	Total	Insured person	Employer	Total
Argentina	7	0	7	13	13.4	26.4
Austria	10.25	12.55	22.8	17.5	24.95	42.1
Australia	0	9	9	0	9	9
Belgium	7.5	8.86	16.36	13.07	17.92	30.99
Brazil	7.65	20	27.65	7.65	20	27.65
Canada	4.95	4.95	9.9	7.05	8.89	15.94
Chile	10	0	10	17.6	2.4	20
Czech Republic	6.5	21.5	28	12.5	37	49.5
Denmark	*	*	*	*	*	*
Finland	4.6	22.75	27.35	6.1	25.364	31.464
France	6.65	9.8	16.45	15.45	33.86	49.31
Germany	9.75	9.75	19.5	20	21.33	41.33
Greece	6.67	13.33	20	11.55	24.1	35.65
Hungary	8.5	18	26.5	13.5	32	45.5
India	12	9.28	21.28	13.75	14.03	27.78
Ireland	8	10.75	18.75	8	10.75	18.75
Italy	8.89	23.81	32.7	8.89	30.9	39.79
Japan	8.675	8.675	17.35	13	15.07	28.07
Mexico	1.75	4.9	6.65	2	6.6	8.6
Netherlands	19.15	22.96	29.11	6.15	22.96	29.11
Norway	7.8	14.1	21.9	7.8	14.1	21.9
Poland	16.26	16.26	32.52	29.96	19.68	46.64
Portugal	11	23.75	34.75	11	23.75	34.75
Romania	11.66	23.34	35	19.66	35.34	55
Russia	0	28	28	0	28.2	28.2
Serbia	16	16	32	26.6	26.6	53.2
Slovak Republic	7	19	26	9.4	25.6	35
South Africa	0	0	0	1	1	2
South Korea	4.5	4.5	9	6.81	8.7	15.51
Spain	4.7	23.6	28.3	6.25	31.58	37.83
Sweden	7	11.91	18.91	7	25.87	32.87
Switzerland	11.9	11.9	23.8	12.9	13	25.9
Ukraine	3	32	35	3.25	35	38.25
United Kingdom	11	12.8	23.8	11	12.8	23.8
United States	1.93	4.82	6.75	4.22	9.98	14.2

*Portion of set amount for Old Age, Disability, and Survivors. Central and local government and other types of contributions for the other programs.

TABLE 23 Social Security Beneficiaries with Benefits in Current-Payment Status at the end of Calendar Years, 1945–2080 (in thousands)

Calender Year	Retired Workers and Auxiliaries			Survivors				Total
	Worker	Spouse	Child	Widow-Widower	Mother-Father	Child	Parent	
Historical Data								
1945	518	159	13	94	121	377	6	1,288
1950	1,771	508	46	314	169	653	15	3,477
1955	4,474	1,192	122	701	292	1,154	25	7,961
1960	8,061	2,269	268	1,544	401	1,577	36	14,157
1965	11,101	2,614	461	2,371	572	2,074	35	19,128
1970	13,349	2,668	546	3,227	523	2,688	29	23,030
1975	16,589	2,867	643	3,888	582	2,919	21	27,509
1980	19,564	3,018	639	4,415	563	2,610	15	30,823
1985	22,435	3,069	456	4,863	372	1,918	10	33,123
1986	22,985	3,088	450	4,931	350	1,878	9	33,691
1987	23,444	3,090	439	4,984	329	1,837	8	34,130
1988	23,862	3,086	432	5,029	318	1,809	7	34,543
1989	24,331	3,093	422	5,071	312	1,782	6	35,017
1990	24,841	3,101	421	5,111	304	1,777	6	35,562
1991	25,293	3,104	425	5,158	301	1,792	5	36,078
1992	25,762	3,112	431	5,205	294	1,808	5	36,618
1993	26,109	3,094	436	5,224	289	1,837	5	36,994
1994	26,412	3,066	440	5,232	283	1,865	4	37,303
1995	26,679	3,026	441	5,226	275	1,884	4	37,534

TABLE 23 (continued)

Calendar Year	Retired Workers and Auxiliaries			Survivors				Total
	Worker	Spouse	Child	Widow-Widower	Mother-Father	Child	Parent	
				Historical Data				
1996	26,905	2,970	442	5,210	242	1,898	4	37,671
1997	27,282	2,922	441	5,053	230	1,893	3	37,825
1998	27,518	2,864	439	4,990	221	1,884	3	37,918
1999	27,784	2,811	442	4,944	212	1,885	3	38,081
2000	28,505	2,798	459	4,901	203	1,878	3	38,748
2001	28,843	2,742	467	4,828	197	1,890	3	38,969
2002	29,195	2,681	477	4,770	194	1,908	2	39,226
2003	29,537	2,622	480	4,705	190	1,910	2	39,446
				Estimates				
2005	30,369	2,578	490	4,642	183	1,916	2	40,179
2010	34,090	2,530	496	4,661	170	1,882	1	43,831
2015	40,428	2,478	538	4,714	164	1,891	2	50,215
2020	48,296	2,461	610	4,742	160	1,861	2	58,131
2025	55,483	2,507	687	4,843	162	1,860	2	65,544
2030	61,900	2,444	754	4,914	161	1,860	2	72,034
2035	66,231	2,377	787	4,950	158	1,854	2	76,359
2040	68,429	2,349	800	4,974	154	1,831	2	78,538
2045	69,911	2,382	810	4,995	148	1,799	2	80,047
2050	71,467	2,460	812	5,002	144	1,768	2	81,654
2055	73,633	2,582	827	5,015	139	1,735	2	83,933

Year							
2060	76,096	2,668	838	5,031	135	1,704	2	86,474
2065	78,564	2,745	855	5,082	131	1,675	2	89,054
2070	80,882	2,788	868	5,146	127	1,647	2	91,459
2075	82,960	2,823	879	5,215	123	1,620	2	93,623
2080	85,078	2,877	892	5,259	120	1,597	2	95,825

Source: The 2004 Annual Report of the Board of Trustees of the Federal Old-Age and Survivors Insurance and Disability Insurance Trust Funds, p. 112.

TABLE 24 Disability Insurance Beneficiaries with Benefits in Current-Payment Status at the end of Calendar Years 1960–2080

Calendar Year	Disabled Worker	Auxiliaries		Total
		Spouse	Child	
Historical Data				
1960	455	77	155	687
1965	988	193	558	1,739
1970	1,493	283	889	2,665
1975	2,488	453	1,411	4,351
1980	2,856	462	1,359	4,677
1985	2,653	306	945	3,904
1986	2,725	301	965	3,991
1987	2,782	291	968	4,041
1988	2,826	281	963	4,070
1989	2,891	271	962	4,124
1990	3,007	266	989	4,261
1991	3,191	266	1,052	4,509
1992	3,464	271	1,151	4,886
1993	3,721	273	1,255	5,249
1994	3,958	271	1,350	5,579
1995	4,179	264	1,409	5,852
1996	4,378	224	1,463	6,065
1997	4,501	207	1,438	6,146
1998	4,691	190	1,446	6,327
1999	4,870	176	1,468	6,514
2000	5,036	165	1,466	6,667
2001	5,268	157	1,482	6,907
2002	5,539	152	1,526	7,217
2003	5,869	151	1,571	7,590
Estimates				
2005	6,389	144	1,615	8,147
2010	7,452	146	1,787	9,385
2015	8,069	149	1,891	10,110
2020	8,621	158	1,973	10,752
2025	9,537	189	2,188	11,914
2030	9,802	194	2,383	12,379
2035	10,051	200	2,526	12,777
2040	10,387	206	2,619	13,212
2045	10,967	218	2,677	13,862
2050	11,340	226	2,720	14,286

TABLE 24 (continued)

Calendar Year	Disabled Worker	Auxiliaries		Total
		Spouse	Child	
Estimates				
2055	11,653	234	2,765	14,652
2060	11,728	235	2,809	14,772
2065	11,918	2239	2,853	15,010
2070	12,062	240	2,889	15,912
2075	12,313	244	2,922	15,479
2080	12,528	249	2,956	15,734

Source: *The 2004 Annual Report of the Board of Trustees of the Federal Old-Age and Survivors Insurance and Disability Trust Funds*, p. 119.

TABLE 25 Medicare Enrollment (in thousands)

Calendar year	HI Part A	SMI Part B	SMI Part D	Part C	Total
		Historical Data			
1970	20,104	19,496	-	-	20,398
1975	24,481	23,744	-	-	24,864
1980	28,002	27,278	-	-	28,433
1985	30,621	29,869	-	842	31,081
1990	33,747	32,567	-	1,181	34,251
1995	37,175	35,641	-	2,714	37,594
1996	37,701	36,104	-	3,672	38,122
1997	38,099	36,445	-	4,735	38,514
1998	38,472	36,756	-	5,732	38,889
1999	38,765	37,022	-	6,191	39,187
2000	39,257	37,335	-	6,233	39,688
2001	39,669	37,667	-	5,608	40,102
2002	40,100	38,049	-	5,005	40,523
2003	40,589	38,465	-	4,655	41,004
		Intermediate Estimates			
2004	41,399	39,041	4,651	*	41,805
2005	42,006	39,547	4,726		42,404
2006	42,680	40,083	40,736		43,069
2007	43,463	40,713	41,468		43,843
2008	44,347	41,447	42,296		44,718
2009	45,268	42,216	43,158		45,629
2010	46,241	43,009	44,069		46,592
2011	47,359	43,923	45,117		47,700
2012	48,697	45,055	46,374		49,029
2013	50,173	46,332	47,761		50,496
2015	53,198	48,967	50,607		53,505
2020	61,608	56,349	58,800		61,886
2025	70,917	64,673	67,606		71,185
2030	78,794	72,060	75,063		79,063
2035	83,806	76,530	79,818		84,078
2040	86,792	79,247	82,659		87,064
2045	88,992	81,273	84,758		89,265
2050	91,230	83,449	86,884		91,504
2055	93,878	85,992	89,393		94,153
2060	97,084	88,951	92,432		97,361
2065	100,040	91,591	95,237		100,317

TABLE 25 (continued)

Calendar year	HI Part A	SMI Part B	SMI Part D	Part C	Total
		Intermediate Estimates			
2070	102,924	94,240	97,971		103,200
2075	105,325	96,466	100,244		105,597
2080	107,770	98,746	102,184		108,037

*Enrollment in Medicare Advantage plans is not explicitly projected beyond 2015.

Source: *2004 Annual Report of the Boards of Trustees of the Federal Hospital Insurance and Federal Supplementary Medical Insurance Trust Funds*, p. 27.

TABLE 26 Medicaid Recipients (millions)

Year	Managed care	Other	Total Medicaid population	Percent of total on managed care
1991	2.7	25.6	28.3	9.5
1992	3.6	27.3	30.9	11.8
1993	4.8	28.6	33.4	14.4
1994	7.8	25.8	33.6	23.2
1995	9.8	23.6	33.4	29.4
1996	13.3	19.9	33.2	40.1
1997	15.3	16.7	32.1	47.8
1998	16.6	14.3	30.9	53.6
1999	17.8	14.2	31.9	55.6
2000	18.8	14.9	33.7	55.8
2001	20.8	15.8	36.6	56.8
2002	23.1	17.0	40.1	57.6
2003	25.3	17.5	42.7	59.1

Source: *Centers for Medicare and Medicaid Services*, National Penetration Rates, 2003.

TABLE 27 Number of States and DC That Have Taken Action or Have Planned Medicaid Cost Containment Strategies, FY 2002 and FY 2003

Cost Containment Actions	FY 2002	FY 2003				
	States that implemented in FY 2002	States with new plans at start of 2003	States with new plans midway through FY 2003	States with new plans at start and midway through FY 2003	States with new plans only midway through FY 2003	Total states with new plans at sometime in FY 2003
Provider payment rate freezes or decreases	22	29	21	13	8	37
Pharmacy related	32	40	24	19	5	45
Benefit reductions	9	15	16	6	10	25
Eligibility reductions	8	17	15	5	10	27
Implementation or Increase in nonpharmacy co-pays	4	15	4	2	2	17
Expansion of managed care	10	12	0	1	0	12
Implementation of disease case/management	11	21	6	3	3	24
Enhanced fraud and abuse	16	18	6	4	2	20
Long-term care	7	13	9	3	6	19
Any cost-containment action	45	45	37	32	5	50

Source: KCMU survey of Medicaid officials in 50 states and DC conducted by Health Management Associates, June and December 2002; The *Kaiser Commission on Medicaid and the Uninsured*, Appendix B.

NOTES

Chapter 1

1. Joseph Singer, *The Edges of the Field* (Beacon Press, 2000), p. 2; Jedediah Purdy, *For Common Things: Irony, Trust and Commitment in America Today* (Vintage Books, 2000), p. 180; Roberto Unger, *Democracy Realized* (Verso, 2000), p. 44; Richard Sennett, *The Corrosion of Character: the Personal Consequences of Work in the New Capitalism* (W.W. Norton, 2000), p. 146.

2. On the politics of the "radical middle," see Mark Satin, *Radical Middle: The Politics We Need Now* (2004); Paul DiMaggio, Alan Wolfe et al., *Culture War? The Myth of a Polarized America* (2004); Michael Lind and Ted Halstead, *The Radical Center: The Future of American Politics* (2002). The New America Foundation (http://www.newamerica.net), a think tank created in 2000, seeks to develop this perspective politically, institutionally, and intellectually.

Chapter 2

1. Robert Reich, "Back of the Hand To the Safety Net," *American Prospect* (June 2001).

2. Eric Foner, *The Story of American Freedom* (W.W. Norton, 1998), p. 153; E. J. Dionne, *They Only Look Dead*, p. 291.

3. Cass Sunstein, *The Second Bill of Rights* (2004), p. 80; pp. 1–2.

4. Sunstein, *The Second Bill of Rights* (2004), p. 71, p. 75, p. 90.

5. Sunstein, *The Second Bill of Rights* (2004), pp. 61–63.

6. According to historian Michael Katz, the American state is a mix of public and private. The public is comprised of three sectors: public assistance (welfare and its associated programs), social insurance (Social Security, Medicare), and the tax code (the Earned Income Tax Credit, tax breaks for employer-provided pensions). The private state is divided between the independent sector (charities, social services) and employee benefits. In terms of annual costs, the private state is substantially larger than the public one. Michael Katz, *The Price of Citizenship: Redefining the American Welfare State* (Owl Books, 2002).

7. Olivier Zunz, "Introduction: Social Contracts under Stress," *Social Contracts under Stress: The Middle Classes of America, Europe, and Japan at the Turn of the Century* (2002).

8. On the Serviceman's Readjustment Act (the G.I. Bill), see Mark Santow, "The G.I. Bill," *Work in America* (2003); Michael Bennett, *When Dreams Came True: The G.I. Bill and the Making of Modern America* (1999); Michael Sherry, *In the Shadow of War: The United States Since the 1930s* (1995); Lewis Milford and Richard Severo, *The Wages of War: When America's Soldiers Came Home—From Valley Forge to Vietnam* (1990); Keith Olson, *The G.I. Bill, the Veterans, and the Colleges* (1974); Davis Ross, *Preparing for Ulysses: Politics and Veterans during World War II* (1969).

9. Union membership grew from 3 million to 15 million from 1932 to 1947; in just one generation after 1940, blue-collar income doubled. Meg Jacobs, "Inflation: The 'Permanent Dilemma' of the American Middle Class," *Social Contracts under Stress* (2002).

10. Deborah Tannen, "We the Government: Repairing the Rift between Citizen and State," *American Prospect* (August 2004).

11. Sunstein, *The Second Bill of Rights* (2004), p. 77.

12. Jack Beatty, "Who Speaks for the Middle Class," *Atlantic Monthly* (May 1994).

13. Michael Lind, "Are We Still a Middle-Class Nation?" *Atlantic Monthly* (January–February 2004).

14. Jacob Hacker, "Bigger and Better," *American Prospect* (May 6, 2005).

15. Nancy-Ann Min DeParle, "Celebrating 35 Years of Medicare and Medicaid," *Health Care Financing Review* (fall 2000); Marilyn Moon, "Medicare Matters: Building on a Record of Accomplishments," *Health Care Financing Review* (fall 2000); Michael Katz, *The Price of Citizenship: Redefining the American Welfare State*; Marilyn Moon, *Medicare Now and in the Future* (1993); Paul Starr, *The Social Transformation of American Medicine* (1984); The Century Foundation, "What's Right with Social Security" (1998).

Chapter 3

1. Jacob Hacker, "False Positive: The So-Called 'Good' Economy," *New Republic*, August 16 and 23, 2004.

2. David Cay Johnston, *Perfectly Legal: The Covert Campaign to Rig Our Tax System to Benefit the Super Rich–and Cheat Everybody Else* (Portfolio Hardcover, 2003), pp. 25–26.

3. David Wessel, "Workers Wages Trail Growth in Economy," *Wall Street Journal* (April 21, 2005).

4. Steven Greenhouse, "As Demands on Workers Grow, Groups Push for Paid Family and Sick Leave," *New York Times* (March 6, 2005).

5. Henry Farber, "Job Loss in the U.S., 1981–2001," *National Bureau of Economic Research* (2003).

6. Peter Gosselin, "The New Deal: If America is Richer, Why Are Its Families So Much Less Secure?" *Los Angeles Times* (October 10, 2004); Drum Major Institute, *The Middle-Class Squeeze: An Overview*" (2005).

7. Nicholas Riccardi, "Long-Term Jobless Find a Degree Just Isn't Working," *Los Angeles Times*, March 11, 2005.

8. Peter Gosselin, "The New Deal: The Poor Have More Things Today—Including Wild Income Swings," *Los Angeles Times* (December 12, 2004).

9. Jacob Hacker, "False Positive," p. 16.

10. Christopher Swann, "Real Wages Fall at Fastest Rate in 14 Years," *Financial Times* (May 10, 2005).

11. Jacob Hacker, "Privatizing Risk without Privatizing the Welfare State: The Hidden Politics of Social Policy Retrenchment in the U.S.," forthcoming in *American Political Science Review*.

12. The Census Bureau defines a middle-class income as between 200 percent of the federal poverty threshold and the nation's top 5 percent of income earners—roughly \$25,000 to \$100,000 a year.

13. See "Out of Reach 2003," *National Low Income Housing Coalition*, September 2003, and *Millennial Housing Commission*, "Meeting Our Nation's Housing Challenges," May 2002.

14. Drum Major Institute, "The Middle-Class Squeeze: An Overview," 2005.

15. Jacob Hacker, "Privatizing Risk without Privatizing the Welfare State: The Hidden Politics of Social Policy Retrenchment in the U.S.," p. 17.

16. David Callahan, "Bush's Ownership Society: Great Idea, If Low-Income Families Benefit," *Christian Science Monitor*, September 21, 2004.

17. Edward Wolff, "Recent Trends in Wealth Ownership, 1983–1998," *Assets for the Poor* (2001), Russell Sage Foundation, p. 38; Gar Alperovitz, *America Beyond Capitalism: Reclaiming Our Wealth, Our Liberty, and Our Democracy* (John Wiley and Sons, NJ 2005), p. 300.

18. Peter Gosselin, "The New Deal: If America is Richer, Why Are Its Families So Much Less Secure?" *Los Angeles Times* (October 10, 2004).

19. Elizabeth Warren and Amelia Warren Tyagi, *The Two-Income Trap: Why Middle-Class Mothers and Fathers Are Going Broke*; Elizabeth Warren, "Middle-Class and Broke," *American Prospect* (May 2004).

20. Michael Powell, "A Bane Amid the Housing Boom," *Washington Post*, May 30, 2005.

21. Michael Powell, *Washington Post*, May 30, 2005; Lee Walczak et al., "I Want my Safety Net," *Business Week*, May 16, 2005.

22. Editorial, "Morally Bankrupt," *The Washington Post*, February 24, 2005.

23. Frank Furstenberg et al., "Growing Up Is Harder To Do," *Contexts* (summer 2004).

24. Tamara Draut and Javier Silva, "Generation Broke: The Growth of Debt Among Young Americans," Briefing Paper, Demos Foundation (2004), p. 6.

25. *Families USA 2003*.

26. Gosselin, *Los Angeles Times*, October 10, 2004.

27. Gosselin, *Los Angeles Times*, December 12, 2004.

28. Gosselin, *Los Angeles Times*, October 10, 2004.

29. Timothy Smeeding and Katherine Ross Phillips, "Cross-National Differences in Employment and Economic Sufficiency," *Annals of the American Academy of Political and Social Science* 580 (2002).

30. The College Board, *Trends in College Pricing, 2003*; Drum Major Institute, "The Middle-Class Squeeze: An Overview," 2005.

31. Tamara Draut and Javier Silva, "Generation Broke: The Growth of Debt among Young Americas," Briefing Paper, Demos Foundation, 2004, p. 7; Drum Major Institute, "The Middle-Class Squeeze: An Overview," 2005.

32. Draut and Silva, p. 11; see also Melvin Oliver and Thomas Shapiro, *Black Wealth/White Wealth: A New Perspective on Racial Inequality* (Routledge, 1995).

33. Draut and Silva, p. 12.

34. Robert Schoeni and Karen Ross, "Material Assistance Received from Families during the Transition To Adulthood," *On the Frontier of Adulthood: Theory, Research, and Public Policy* (2004); David Hage, "Purgatory of the Working Poor," *American Prospect* (September 2004).

35. For a survey of the research of early childhood education, see W. S. Barnett, "Early Childhood Education," *School Reform Proposals: The Research Evidence* (2002).

36. Suzanne Helburn and Barbara Bermann, *America's Child Care Problem: The Way Out* (St. Martin's Press, 2002), p. 21.

37. Karen Schulman, *Issue Brief: The High Cost of Child Care Puts Quality Care Out of Reach for Many Families,* CDF 2000.

38. Pew Research Center for the People and the Press, "Economic Inequality Seen as Rising, Boom Bypasses Poor," June 2001; Everett C. Ladd and Karlyn Bowman, *Attitudes Toward Economic Inequality* (AEI Press, 1998).

39. Congressional Budget Office, "Effective Federal Tax Rates, 1979–2000," August 2003.

40. Lester Thurow, *The Future of Capitalism* (1996), p. 42; Congressional Budget Office, Historical Effective Federal Tax Rates: 1979 to 2002, March 2005; Thomas Pickety and Emmanuel Saez, "Income Inequality in the United States, 1913–1998," *Quarterly Journal of Economics* 118, 2003.

41. David Wessel, "As Rich-Poor Gap Widens in U.S., Class Mobility Stalls," *Wall Street Journal*, May 13, 2005; see also Miles Corak, *Generational Income*

Mobility in North America and Europe (Cambridge University Press, 2004); Samuel Bowles and Herbert Gintis, *Unequal Chances: Family Background and Economic Success* (Princeton University Press, 2005).

42. Bruce Ackerman and Anne Alstott, "$80,000 and a Dream," *American Prospect* (July 2000).

43. "Meritocracy in America: Ever Higher Society, Ever Harder to Ascend," *The Economist,* December 29, 2004.

44. Robert Putnam, *Making Democracy Work* (1993), p. 3.

45. Thomas Jefferson, letter to John Adams, "The Natural Aristocracy," October 28, 1813, in *The Portable Jefferson,* edited by Merrill Peterson (New York: Penguin Books, 1977), p. 538.

46. Center on Budget and Policy Priorities, "Recent Tax and Income Trends among High-Income Taxpayers," April 2005.

47. Johnston, p. 94; p. 22.

48. Johnston, pp. 120–22.

49. Congressional Budget Office, "Effective Federal Tax Rates, 1997–2000," Government Printing Office, August 2003.

50. Economic Policy Institute, *State of Working America 2004–2005*, pp. 83–84.

51. Center on Budget and Policy Priorities, April 2005.

52. Gosselin, *Los Angeles Times*, December 12, 2004.

53. Gosselin, *Los Angeles Times*, October 10, 2004.

54. Jacob Hacker, "Privatizing Risk without Privatizing the Welfare State: The Hidden Politics of Social Policy Retrenchment in the U.S.," p. 14.

55. Jacob Hacker, "Privatizing Risk without Privatizing the Welfare State: The Hidden Politics of Social Policy Retrenchment in the U.S.," p. 23; Hacker, "False Positive: The So-Called 'Good' Economy," pp. 7–8.

56. William Greider, "Riding into the Sunset," *The Nation,* June 27, 2005.

57. Alperovitz, pp. 188–189.

58. William Greider, "Riding into the Sunset," *The Nation,* June 27, 2005.

59. Gar Alperovitz, *America Beyond Capitalism*, p. 190.

60. Seth Sandronsky, "Over 55 in U.S.? Get Back to Work," www.commondreams.org, March 14, 2005.

61. Thomas Frank, "The Trillion-Dollar Hustle: Hello Wall Street, Goodbye Social Security," *Harper's* (January 2002).

62. Ellen Dannin, "Private Pensions: The Real Retirement Crisis," http://people link5.inch.com/pipermail/portside/Week-of-Mon-20050214/014835.html; Government Accounting Office, http://www.gao.gov/cgi-bin/getrpt?GAO-05-207.

63. Michele Landis Dauber, "The Hazards and Vicissitudes of Social Security Privatization," Center for American Progress, September 2004.

Chapter 4

1. Denise Levy and Sonya Michel, "More Can Be Less: Child Care and Welfare Reform in the U.S.," *Child Care Policy at the Crossroads: Gender and*

Welfare State Restructuring (2002); Suzanne Mettler and Andrew Milstein, "A Sense of the State: Tracking the Role of the American Administrative State in Citizens Lives over Time," paper presented to the Annual Meeting of the Midwestern Political Science Association, Chicago, 2003.

2. For a summary of existing state programs, go to http://www.nccic.org/poptopics/univprek.pdf. New Jersey initiated its program as part of an order issued by the State Supreme Court in *Abbott v. Burke* (1998), a landmark case first brought in the 1970s questioning the constitutionality of the state's school funding system. Technically, New Jersey's program is only universal within the poor and largely urban school districts covered by Abbott. Georgia and Oklahoma, among other states, are working toward broader provision of public preschool. See Education Law Center, "The Abbott Preschool Program: Fifth Year Report on Enrollment and Budget" (August 2003); E. Frede, "Closing the Gap at the Starting Gate: Why the New Jersey Supreme Court Ordered Preschool," presented at "African-American Education Achievement: Progress Made, Challenges Ahead," Educational Testing Service, Princeton, NJ, 2003; Debra Williams, "Universal Preschool," *Catalyst* (April 2003).

3. Anne Mitchell, "How States Finance Pre-Kindergarten Programs and Estimate Costs," remarks to Florida Universal Pre-Kindergarten Council (August 20, 2003), http://www.upkcouncil.org/docs/products_08202003amitchell.pdf.

4. Linda Jacobson, "Study: Early Head Start Children Outpace Peers," *Education Week*, http://www.edweek.org/ew/ew_printstory.cfm?slug=40headstart.h21 (June 12, 2002).

5. Bruce Ackerman and Anne Alstott, *The Stakeholder Society*, p. 32.

6. See David Shipler, *The Working Poor: Invisible in America* (2004), Economic Policy Institute, *State of Working America, 2004–2005* (2004); Barbara Ehrenreich, *Nickel and Dimed* (2002).

7. Tamara Draut and Javier Silva, "Generation Broke: The Growth of Debt among Young Americas," Briefing Paper, Demos Foundation, 2004, p. 11.

8. David Hage, "Purgatory of the Working Poor," *American Prospect* (September 2004).

9. On the Pew poll, see http://people-press.org/reports/pdf/235.pdf.

10. Amy Chasanov, *No Longer Getting By: An Increase in the Minimum Wage Is Long Overdue* (2004), Washington, D.C.: Economic Policy Institute; Fiscal Policy Institute, *State Minimum Wages and Employment in Small Business* (2004), available at http://www.fiscalpolicy.org.

11. David Cay Johnston, *Perfectly Legal*, p. 95.

12. Ibid., p. 113.

13. Ibid., pp. 96–97, p. 99, pp. 110–11.

14. Thomas Geoghegan, "Real Simple," www.Salon.com (July 2004).

15. 2003 Social Security Trustees Annual Report, p. 110.

16. Dean Baker and David Rosnick, "Basic Facts on Social Security and Proposed Benefit Cuts/Privatization," Center for Economic and Policy Research, November 2004, p. 8.

17. Johnston, *Perfectly Legal*, p. 120, p. 40.

Chapter 5

1. *Prescription Drug Coverage for Medicare Beneficiaries: An Overview of the Medicare Prescription Drug, Improvement, and Modernization Act of 2004* (Public Law 108–173), Henry J. Kaiser Family Foundation, January 14, 2004.

Chapter 6

1. Benjamin Page and James Simmons, *What Government Can Do: Dealing with Poverty and Inequality* (University of Chicago Press, 2002), pp. 86–87.

2. Paul Krugman, "Confusions about Social Security," *Economist's Voice* 2, issue 1 (2005), pp. 2–4.

3. Robert Dreyfuss, "Bush's House of Cards," *American Prospect*, September 10, 2001.

4. International Monetary Fund, "Staff Report for the 2001 Article IV Consultation," IMF 2001.

5. Eduardo Porter, "Maybe We're Not Robbing the Cradle," *New York Times* (April 10, 2005); Roger Lowenstein, "A Question of Numbers," *New York Times Magazine* (January 16, 2005); Paul Krugman, "America' Senior Moment," *New York Review of Books* (March 10, 2005).

6. Dean Baker, "The Assumptions Are Too Pessimistic," *Challenge* (November–December 1996), pp. 31–32.

7. Krugman, "America's Senior Moment."

Chapter 7

1. Goldman Sachs, US Economics Analyst, "Social Security Reform: No Free Lunch," December 17, 2004; "Economic Snapshot: Private Accounts," Economic Policy Institute, December 22 2004.

2. Jonathan Weisman, "Retirement Accounts Questioned," *Washington Post*, March 19, 2005.

3. Nancy Cauthen, "Whose Security? What Social Security Means To Children and Families," National Center for Children in Poverty, Columbia University Mailman School of Public Health, February 2005, p. 1.

4. Ibid., pp. 5–6.

5. Ibid., p. 3.

6. Ibid., p. 3, 8.

7. Benjamin Page and James Simmons, *What Government Can Do: Dealing with Poverty and Inequality* (University of Chicago Press, 2002), p. 92.

8. Jason Furman, "An Analysis of Using 'Progressive Price Indexing' to Set Social Security Benefits," Center on Budget and Policy Priorities, April 29, 2005; Edmund Andrews and Eduardo Porter, "Social Security: Help for the Poor or

Help for All?" *New York Times*, May 1, 2005; Richard Stevenson, "President's Big Social Security Gamble," *New York Times,* April 30, 2005.

9. Ibid., p. 6.

10. Geoffrey Nunberg, "Privatization and the English Language," *American Prospect*, February 2005.

11. Gene Sperling, "No Pain, No Savings," *New York Times*, January 5, 2005.

12. Michael Sherraden, "Assets and the Poor" (1991); Mark Schreiner et al., "Final Report: Saving Performance in the American Dream Demonstration," Center for Social Development, 2002; Ray Boshara, "Assets for Independent Act Overview," Center for Social Development 1998; and Ray Boshara, "Assets for Independence Demonstration," Corporation for Enterprise Development, April 2003.

13. Gar Alperovitz, *America Beyond Capitalism*, pp. 21–22, pp. 110–111; Ray Boshara, "The $6000 Solution," *Atlantic Monthly* (January–February 2003); J. Larry Brown and Larry Beeferman, "From New Deal To New Opportunity," *American Prospect* (February 12, 2001).

14. Bruce Ackerman and Anne Alstott, *The Stakeholder Society*; Leon Friedman, "A Better Kind of Wealth Tax," *American Prospect*, November 2000; Edward Wolff, *Top Heavy* (2002), pp. 53–61.

Chapter 9

1. Pew Research Center for the People and the Press, "Disapproval of GOP Congressional Leaders, But Dems Fare No Better," Survey Report, March 24, 2005.

2. Lee Walczak et al., "I Want My Safety Net," *Business Week*, May 16, 2005.

3. An explanation of how the annual COLA adjustments are made is in a paper called *United States Wage Growth and Social Security* by William Larson. We quote: "Social Security . . . uses the United States average wage growth as an index to adjust OASI wages of previous years. . . . After your OASI wages have been identified for each year you have worked, they are indexed by the change in U.S. wages. . . . Previous wages are indexed to today's equivalent. This means if a spike in U.S. wages occurs, then all previous years' wages are indexed by this spike. If the U.S. average wage increases faster than inflation, then each succeeding retiree cohort will retire with a larger initial OASI benefit." All of this is done before the annual increase in the CPI is applied.

4. Editors, "Insuring America," *New Republic*, February 28, 2005.

5. Stephen Teles, "The Dialectics of Trust: Ideas, Finance, and Pension Privatization in the U.S. and U.K.," paper presented at the 1998 Annual Meeting of the Association for Public Policy Analysis and Management, pp. 14–15.

6. Butler and Germanis, "Achieving a 'Leninist' Strategy," *Cato Journal* (fall 1983).

7. Thomas Frank, "The Trillion-Dollar Hustle: Hello Wall Street, Goodbye Social Security," *Harper's Magazine* (January 2002).

8. William Galston, "Taking Liberty: Liberals Ignore and Conservatives Misunderstand America's Guiding Value, Freedom," *Washington Monthly*, April 2005.

9. Galston, "Taking Liberty."

10. Benjamin Barber, "Privatizing Social Security: 'Me' over 'We,'" *Los Angeles Times*, January 27, 2005.

INDEX

ABOUT THE AUTHORS

*D*r. *Leonard Santow* is Managing Director of Griggs & Santow, an economic consulting firm. He graduated from the University of Illinois, where he earned his B.S., M.S., and Ph.D. degrees. He has taught at his alma mater, New York University, and at the Air Force Academy, and has been a guest lecturer at many universities. He served as Financial Economist for the Federal Reserve Bank of Dallas and has also been associated with Aubrey G. Lanston, Lehman Brothers, and J. Henry Schroder Bank & Trust Company. In 1982 he teamed with Dr. William Griggs to start their own consultant firm. One of their early clients was the Congressional Budget Office.

Dr. Santow was previously a member of the Board of Directors and Investment Committee for closed and open-end funds that were part of Fortis, and now are part of The Hartford. Other past associations include the Board of Directors and Finance Committee of Employers Reinsurance Corporation, the Investment Committee of U.S. Central Credit Union, the Board of Trustees of Geonomics, and Vice Chairman of the Monetary Policy Forum. He currently is on the Board of Advisors of TexStar, an investment organization that serves Texas cities, counties, school districts, and other public entities.

Dr. Santow was industry chairman of the Public Finance Program sponsored by the University of Michigan and the Securities Industry Association and was President of the New York Downtown Economists Club. He is a Colonel in the U.S. Air Force Reserves (retired) and the recipient of the Air Force Meritorious Service Medal. His publications include *The Budget Deficit: The Causes, The Costs, The Outlook* (1988) and *Helping the Federal Reserve Work Smarter* (1994). He also wrote *Social Security: What's Right, What's Wrong, What Needs To Be Done* (1998).

Dr. *Mark Santow* received his B.S. from Vanderbilt University, his M.A. from the University of Massachusetts at Amherst, and his Ph.D. from the University of Pennsylvania. He has taught at the University of Pennsylvania, Fordham University, and Gonzaga University; presently he is Assistant Professor of American History at the University of Massachusetts–Dartmouth. He is also a past recipient of a Mellon Dissertation Fellowship and the Cushwa Fellowship for the study of twentieth-century American Catholicism.

Dr. Santow specializes in twentieth-century American urban history, politics, and social policy, and he has published numerous essays on racial segregation, urban policy, and the War on Poverty. His book *Saul Alinsky and the Dilemmas of Race in the Post-War City* will be published by University of Chicago Press in 2006. Dr. Santow served as Vice Chair of the Spokane Human Rights Commission from 2001 to 2003. He was Academic Director of the Roberto Clemente Course in the Humanities in Spokane, Washington 2002–3, and in New Bedford, Massachusetts 2005–6.

WIDENER UNIVERSITY
WOLFGRAM
LIBRARY
CHESTER, PA